POSTCARD HISTORY SERIES

Astoria

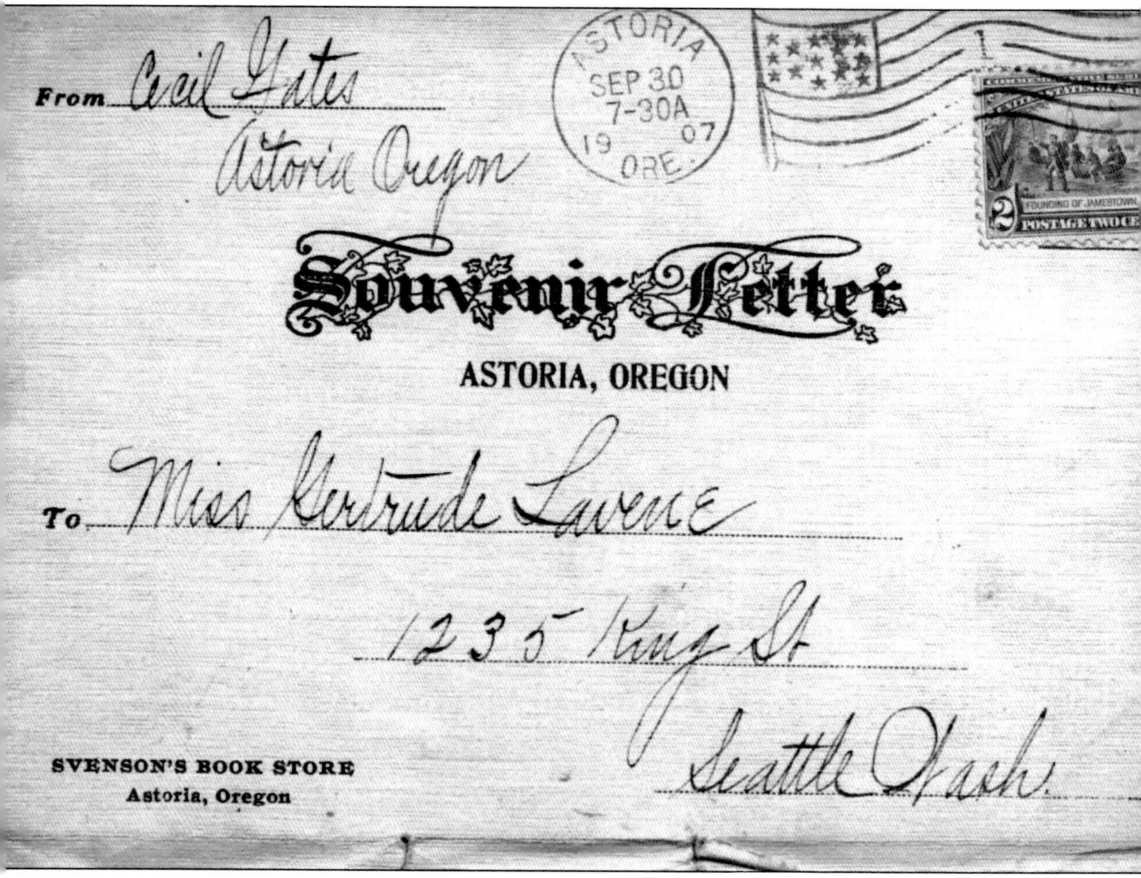

This decorative cover of a vintage postcard booklet from an Astoria retailer, Svenson's Book Store, is postmarked 1907. The accordion-folded contents were popular items in the heyday of postcards. Instead of choosing one card, the sender could share a dozen or more images for the same price as mailing a single card. Svenson's was located at the corner of Fourteenth and Commercial Streets, the present location of the Astor Hotel. (Courtesy of Michael Soderberg.)

On the Front Cover: The centerpiece of the Astoria centennial celebration in 1911 was the mighty salmon, king of the Columbia, as it was depicted on this spectacular float heading down Exchange Street in the parade commemorating the city milestone. (Courtesy of Michael Foster.)

On the Back Cover: This 1930s aerial view of Astoria shows the north-facing hills as they slope down to the banks of the Columbia River, looking east. Astoria is a peninsula. Most of the waterfront buildings and canneries seen here are now gone, and only pilings offshore remain. Note the west mooring basin and the Union Fishermen's Cooperative Cannery at lower right, and the fact that there is no bridge. (Courtesy of Michael Foster.)

POSTCARD HISTORY SERIES

Astoria

Andrea Larson Perez

ARCADIA
PUBLISHING

ISBN 978-1-4671-1647-3

Published by Arcadia Publishing
Charleston, South Carolina

Printed in the United States of America

Library of Congress Control Number: 2015954926

For all general information contact Arcadia Publishing at:
Telephone 843-853-2070
Fax 843-853-0044
E-mail sales@arcadiapublishing.com
For customer service and orders:
Toll-Free 1-888-313-2665

Visit us on the Internet at www.arcadiapublishing.com

Dedicated to everyone who has found inspiration in the spectacular beauty, incredible history, and future prospects of Astoria, Oregon.

Contents

ACKNOWLEDGMENTS

It is with deep appreciation that I would like to acknowledge those who contributed to this book: local collectors Michael Foster, Ray Hakala, Sara Meyer, Michael Soderberg, William "Bill" Young, Sean Fitzpatrick and Ann Carpenter, and Beth and Jeff Newenhoff. Also included are images from the collection of the Clatsop County Historical Society (CCHS). The local collectors generously shared their prized collections, provided personal history and information greatly supplementing the content of the image descriptions, and assisted in fact-checking. Special thanks to Liisa Penner, CCHS archivist, for sharing her infinite knowledge of all things Astoria, and my wonderful editor Sarah Gottlieb at Arcadia. It was my distinct pleasure to work with each of these individuals. Working on this project provided me the opportunity to indulge my lifelong passion for postcards and has taught me so much more about amazing Astoria and made me love it even more!

Introduction

Are you a deltiologist? If you are a postcard collector, the answer is "yes!" That may be the reason you picked up this book: your love of postcards. What is it that you love about them? Is it a certain era you are drawn to? The feel of the card in your hand? The penmanship or content of the message and the accompanying stamp? A style, a particular photographer, or a subject? In this book, the subject is Astoria, Oregon, and the collecting has been done for you. While the hunt is often part of the mystique of postcard collecting, let yourself enjoy the images collected on these pages as they depict many eras of life in Astoria as the types of postcards change over time.

Since their debut in 1893 at the World's Columbian Exposition in Chicago, postcards have played a significant role in our culture and history. Although picture postcards were popular in Europe at the time, the trend was only beginning in America when they were introduced at the World's Fair. Enterprising merchants spotted an opportunity in the enthusiasm of the crowds, returned home, and decided to immortalize practically every aspect of life in their communities by producing and selling postcards. The hobby of postcard collecting took off and was rampant across America during the "Golden Age of Postcards," which lasted from 1901 through 1915. Although several other eras followed, including the Undivided Back Period (1901–1907), the Divided Back Period (1907–1915), the White Border Period (1915–1930), the Linen Period (1930–1945), and the Photochrom Period (1945–present), it was the early part of the 20th century that comprised the true heyday of the craze.

During the decade between 1905 and 1915, postcards were big business. Nearly every Main Street retailer sold postcards, because they took up limited space and produced a good profit. Almost any image available was placed on a postcard: landmarks, homes, businesses, industry, fashion, holidays, oddities, and more were printed, imported, sold, and mailed. People loved them! They preserved them in elaborate albums that they displayed with pride in their homes. They sent out many cards hoping to build their collections when others were sent back to them. They were also a quick way to send a message or keep in touch and share a view. It was estimated by the US Postal Service that through 1913, nearly 900 million postcards were mailed and collected. That may shed some light on why nearly every antique shop will have boxes of vintage postcards for sale.

It was the start of World War I that brought postcard collecting and all associated activities to a near standstill. Citizens had become focused on more serious issues of the time. The hobby rebounded with the advancement of photographic and printing techniques, but never to its former glory. Collectors, however, by their very nature continued to collect. The postcard also remains a wonderful way to keep in touch, just like the early days.

By virtue of the vast numbers of postcards that were produced and preserved in collections during the early part of the 1900s, we have a photographic record of life at the time in nearly every corner and aspect of America. As photography advanced and became more accessible to every person, the images began to be a personal family record, often lacking explanation or interpretation: a young lady in a pretty dress, a group on a front porch, a picnic overlooking a brook printed on postcard stock. Today, that is often part of the fun of postcard collecting: deciphering the story, matching up landmarks, and dating the image.

Covering the period in Astoria from 1901 through the building of the Astoria-Megler Bridge (which celebrates its 50th anniversary in 2016), you will see the early days of plentiful natural resources in fish and timber and the economic growth those industries spurred. The city and aerial views illustrate an expanding business district in the downtown core, a sudden and devastating disaster, and the earnest rebuilding of a beloved city. Families build homes and photograph them with pride. Citizens benefit from civic improvements, and they are celebrated on postcards. Astoria evolves as a destination well before it was described as such. Celebrations and parades occur annually, some of which still exist today. Even more than 100 years ago, the historic significance of Astoria was well recognized and documented. The centennial celebration in 1911 was perfect timing for the peak of the Golden Age of Postcards, and funds from the event provided seed money for the most recognizable landmark in town, the Astoria Column, which has more views on postcards than can be counted.

While the natural beauty of the area garnered much of the attention, the cultural heritage of its citizens greatly informed society. For being one of the first, seemingly remote settlements on the Pacific Coast, the diversity of Astoria is surprising. Native Americans lived here long before anyone else arrived. The Chinook and Clatsop tribes coexisted with Europeans for generations but eventually disappeared. Their contributions and legacy are recognized throughout these images. Next, many Scandinavians settled here, the Finnish being the largest population, with Sweden, Norway, and Denmark amply represented as well. Many of these families remain in the area, and some are specifically identified in some postcards. Chinese immigrants also had a large population in the Lower Columbia, providing labor in the canneries in the early days. Less well known is the history of the Sikhs from India in Astoria. Theirs is an amazing and notable presence in the area. Happily, all of them are represented in these postcards.

Ever-present is the mighty Columbia River. Life on the river, whether for business or pleasure, was the centerpiece of Astoria's existence. Every type of vessel has plied its waters: fishing boats of all kinds, military ships, motorboats, racing boats, and even submarines. Shipbuilding was a key industry for decades, and the Navy housed a mothballed fleet at Tongue Point. Before the bridge, there were ferries. Several images show how the river crossing was handled for many years. Currently, there is an effort to bring back the original *Tourist II* as an attraction on the riverfront.

In the last image in the book, an enthusiastic promoter hails Astoria as "The Future New York of the Pacific." The description continues, "Astoria, the Columbia River gateway seaport, is the nearest and most economic route to the Pacific, the Orient, South America and Europe. The future of Astoria, unless the law of gravity ceases to govern the forces of the earth, and it be cheaper to send commerce uphill than down, the largest city on the Pacific Coast will ultimately be right here at the mouth of this mighty river of the West." Dating from 1929, this grandiose depiction failed to materialize, probably due to the Depression.

However, Astoria continues to inspire grand visions, creative energy, and endless dreaming of the past, present, and future, just as it always has. In many ways, postcards were the precursor to today's social media photo sharing. And Astoria is just as popular a subject as it ever was, maybe even more so. Enjoy the views of yesteryear and revisit the past of the "oldest settlement west of the Mississippi" via picture postcards. Take the book along with you on a stroll around town. Open it up and find many recognizable landmarks on these pages to help you experience the history and charm of Astoria. Evidence of the past remains on every street, and you can jump right in. Enjoy your journey through the photographic history captured on these special postcards.

One

City Views

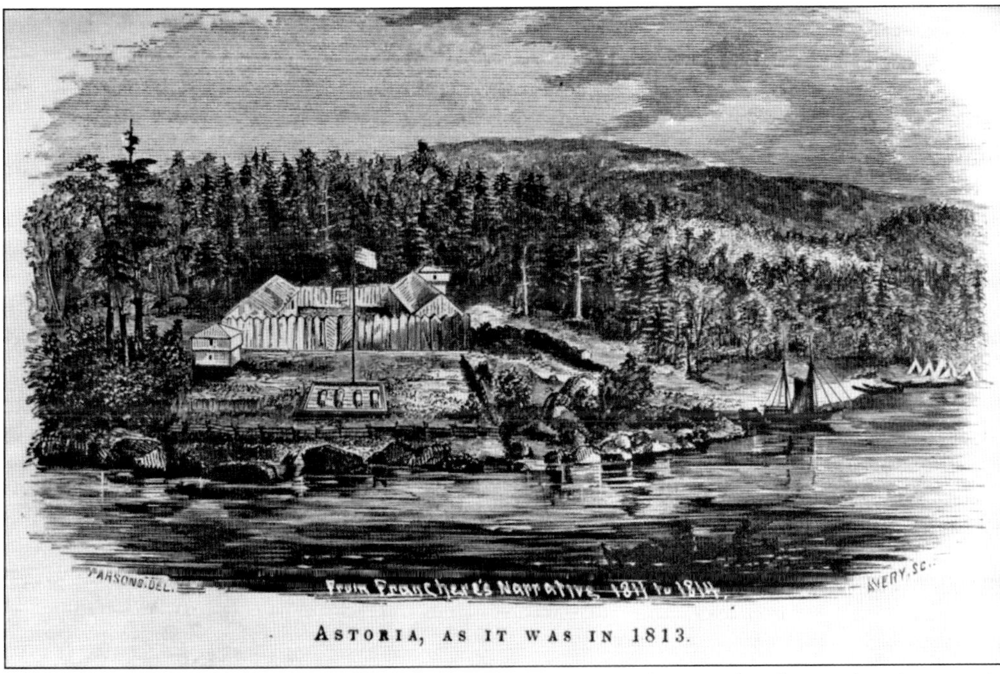

Astoria, as it was in 1813.

The beginnings of Astoria are depicted in this illustration from Gabriel Franchere's *Narrative of a Voyage to the Northwest Coast, 1811–1814.* Early Fort Astoria served as the headquarters for John Jacob Astor's Pacific Fur Company. After arriving on board the *Tonquin*, the party quickly established Fort Astoria, which consisted of several basic structures. Soon after its establishment, the fort fell on hard times and was sold to the British to become Fort George. Eventually, economic interests drew the British north to establish Fort Vancouver, and by the 1840s, Astoria was back in American hands. Soon after, the first houses in Astoria were built on the forested hillside behind the fort. (Courtesy of Michael Foster.)

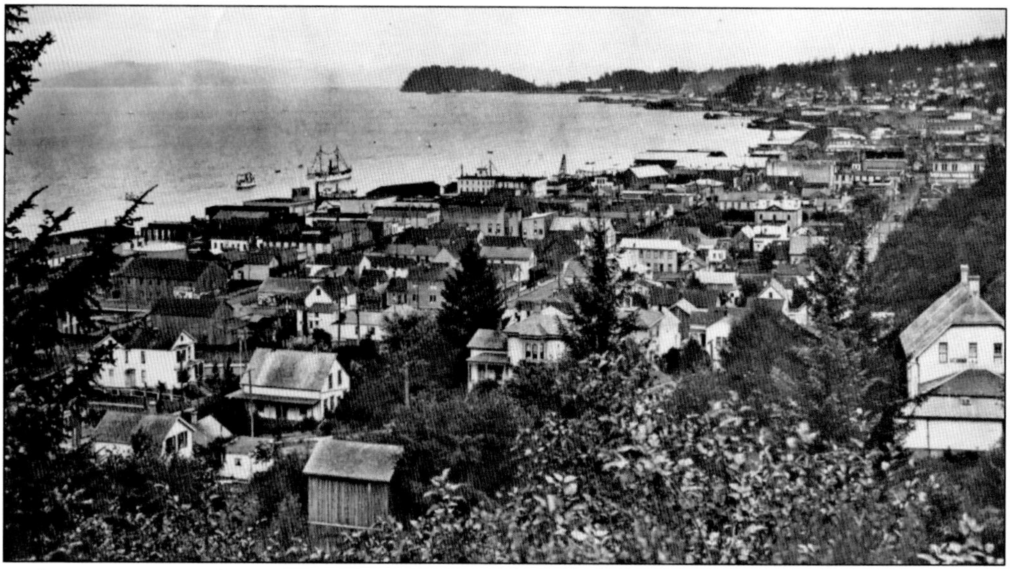

In this c. 1900 view from around the upper Franklin Street area, many long-vanished structures are clearly visible, including August Erickson's Louvre and the Parker House, both near the upper center. An electric trolley can be seen on Commercial Street, just past the old post office, dating this photograph to after 1892. (Author's collection.)

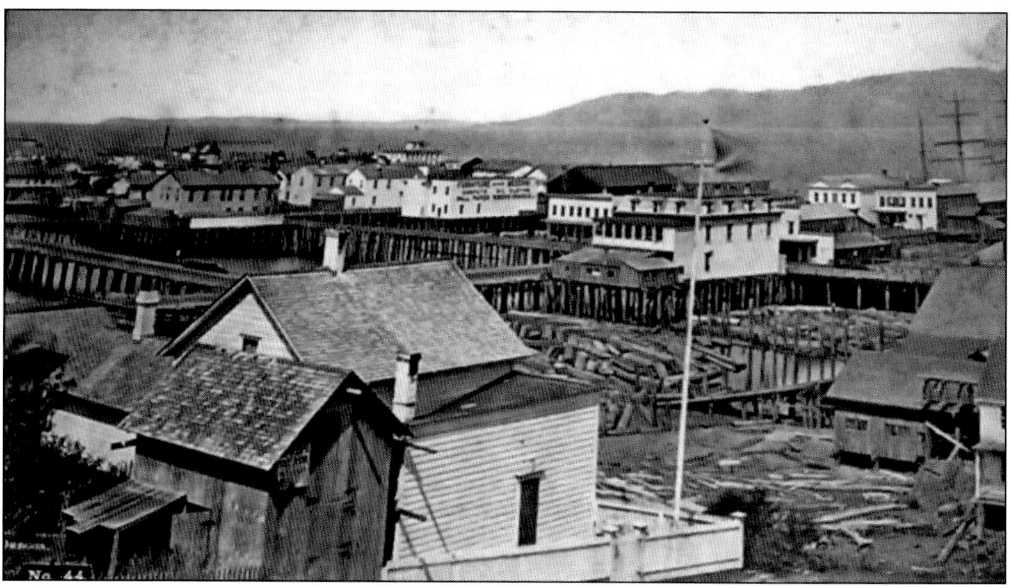

Seen around 1880, this area is near the vicinity of today's Exchange Street (the riverbank) running between Tenth and Fourteenth Streets. The Hume and Ferrell Mill was here and burned in 1883, one of the first major fires to affect Astoria. As is evidenced here, efforts were constantly underway to connect the various parts of town cut off by water with streets on pilings. The new planked streets eventually extended east to the area known as Scow Bay. (Author's collection.)

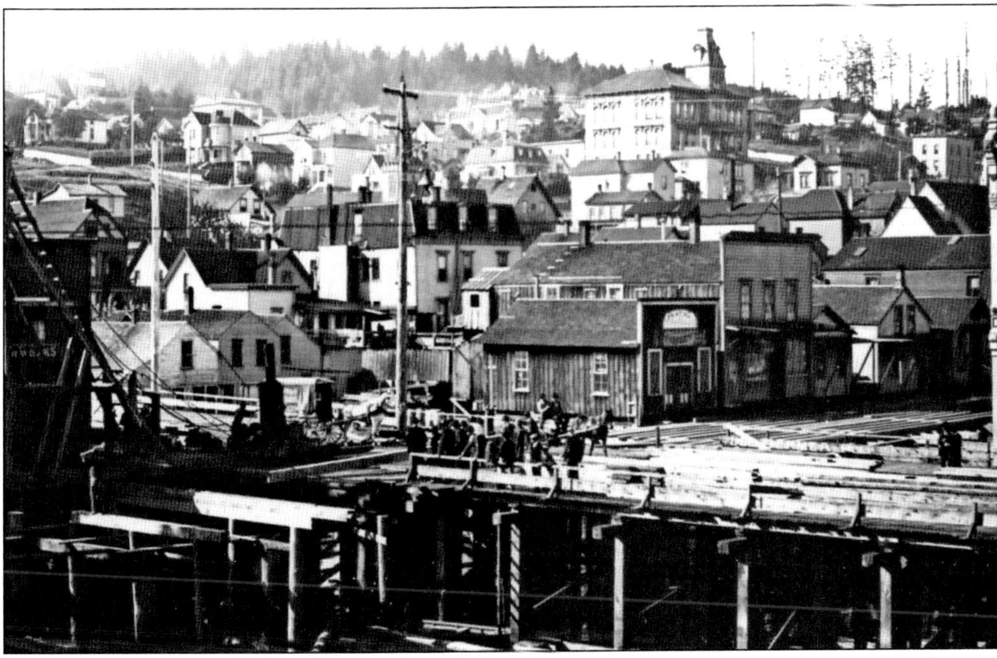

In this image from about 1880, the wood-plank construction of Commercial Street near Eleventh Street above the river's edge is clearly shown. Looking southwest, McClure School is prominent on the hillside at Eighth and Franklin Streets. Many of the homes up on the hill still stand. (Courtesy of Ray Hakala.)

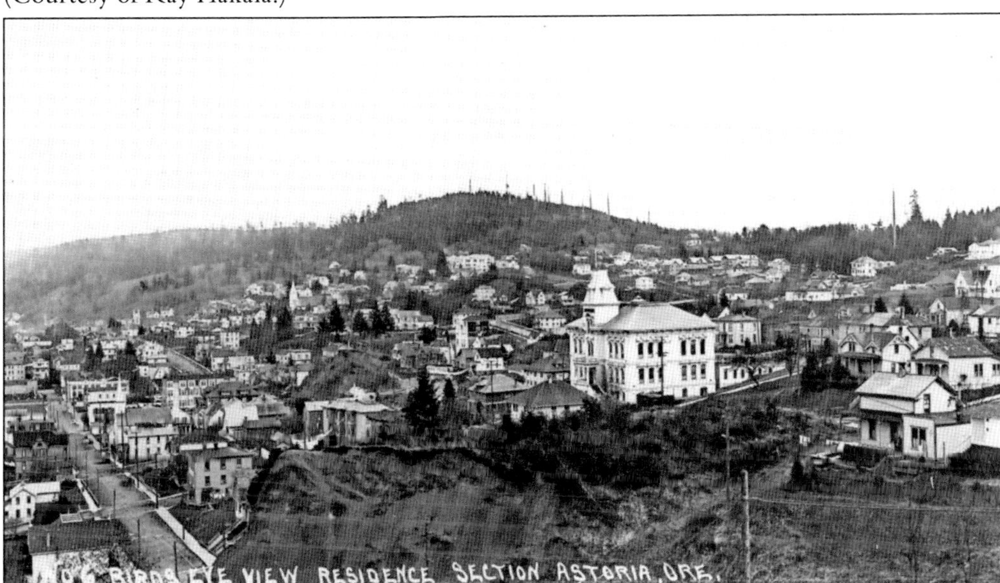

Using the McClure School at the corner of Eighth and Franklin Streets as a point of reference, this view of Astoria looking east reveals a city under development and expansion around 1910. The hillsides are cleared of the old-growth trees that once measured 150 to 200 feet in height and up to 15 feet in diameter, and resulting slides in the area of Franklin Avenue are visible in the foreground. At the lower left, the Flavel carriage house is at the corner of Seventh and Exchange Streets. (Courtesy of Michael Foster.)

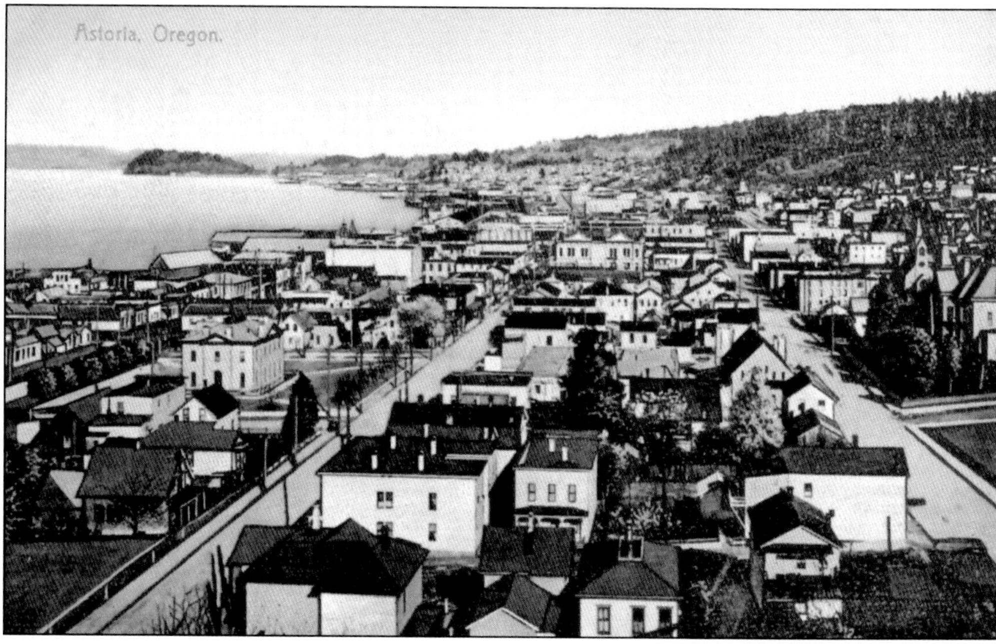

An early view of downtown about 1890 looks east toward Tongue Point. Commercial Street is to the left, and Duane Street is on the right. This is before the courthouse was built (although its foundation appears to be present), and the old post office is seen between Seventh and Eighth Streets. The Flavel House is to the right, and there are no trolley tracks on the streets. In the distance is Tongue Point, at the upper left. It was named in 1792 by the British who explored the area prior to Lewis and Clark. (Courtesy of Michael Foster.)

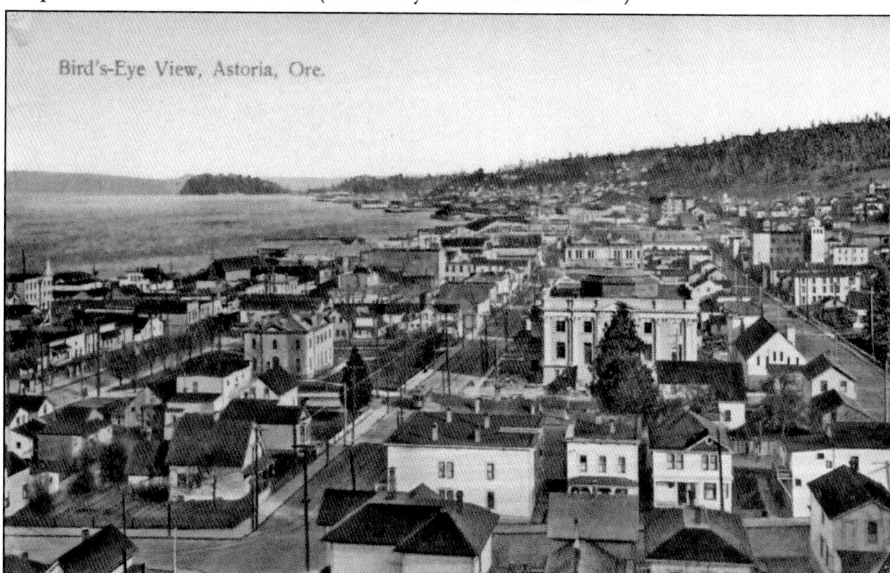

A very similar image to the previous view of downtown has the notable addition of the Clatsop County Courthouse, completed in 1908, across from the old post office. Sixth Street is now visible in the foreground, as are trolley tracks and power lines. On the far left is the Parker House, with its turret and spire added after its 1906 renovation. The jail building is also seen behind the courthouse, to the left. (Courtesy of Michael Foster.)

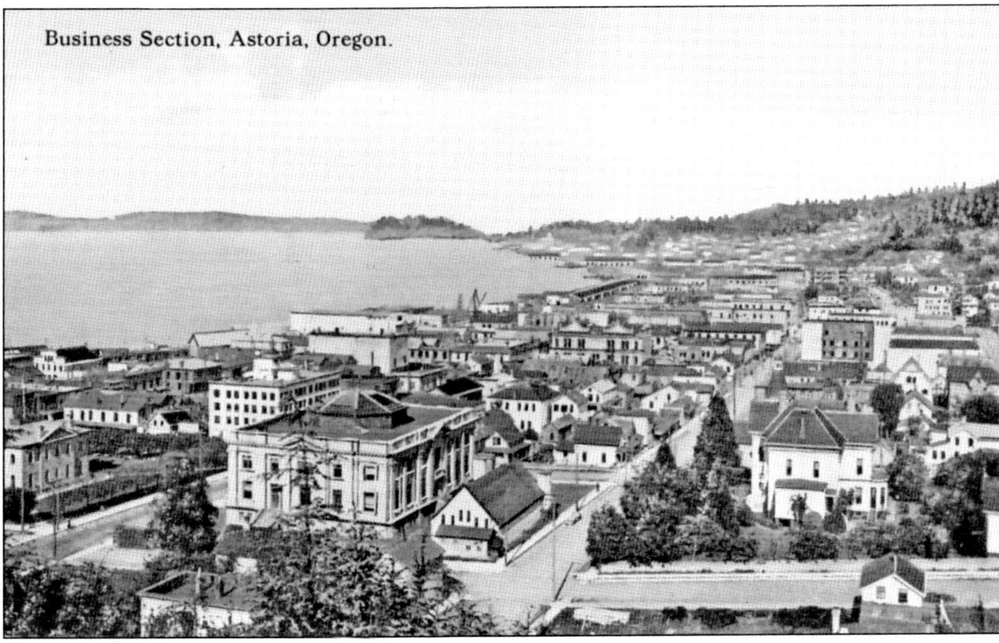

The evolution of downtown Astoria is captured looking east, with Duane Street in the center. The Capt. George Flavel house is seen in the lower right when it was painted white. Most of the trees seen here are still on the property today. The building on the same block as the courthouse, across from the Flavel House, was the second jail, built in 1883. Across from the old post office is the Spexarth Building, completed in 1911. (Courtesy of Michael Foster.)

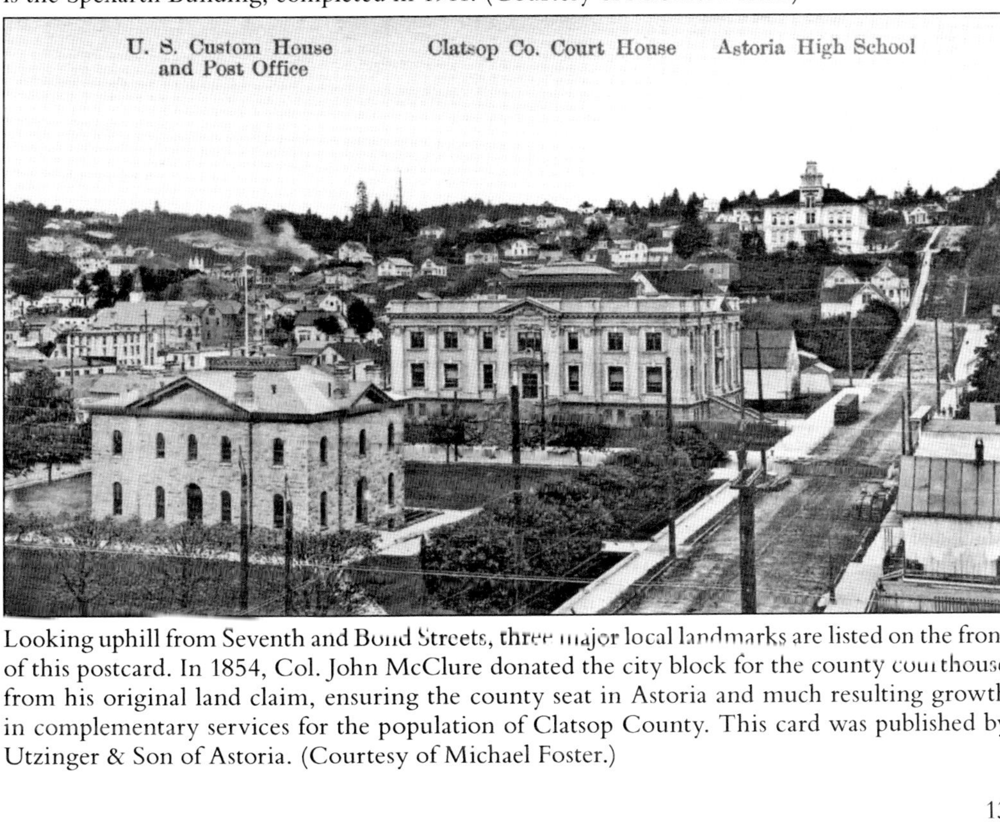

Looking uphill from Seventh and Bond Streets, three major local landmarks are listed on the front of this postcard. In 1854, Col. John McClure donated the city block for the county courthouse from his original land claim, ensuring the county seat in Astoria and much resulting growth in complementary services for the population of Clatsop County. This card was published by Utzinger & Son of Astoria. (Courtesy of Michael Foster.)

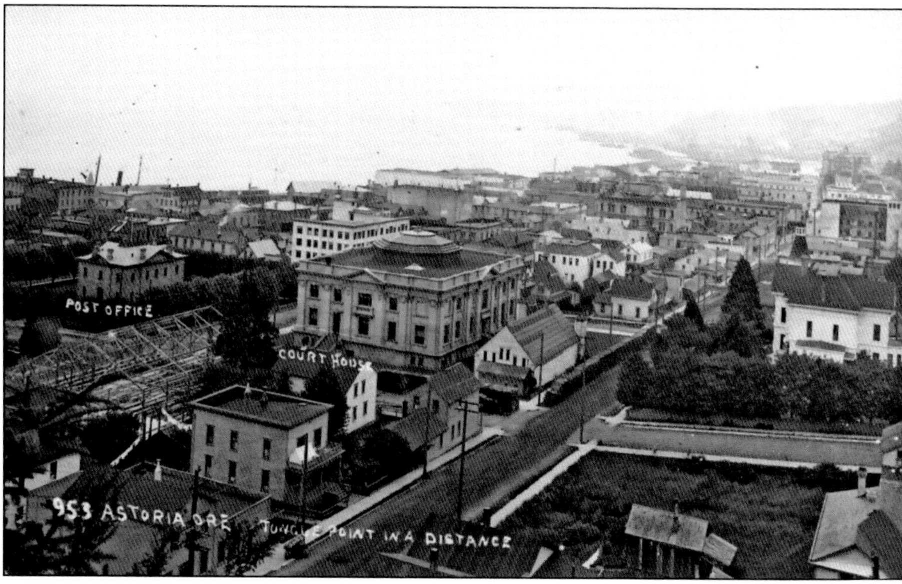

On the site of the First Baptist Church of Astoria, on the left of this real-photo postcard, postmarked 1912, is a wood frame structure used for tent revivals. Today, the sturdy brick building on the same site still holds services and stands next to the present-day jail on Seventh Street between Commercial and Duane Streets. The building at the lower right corner of the courthouse is the jail used from 1883 to 1913, when it was determined a new jail was needed. (Courtesy of Michael Foster.)

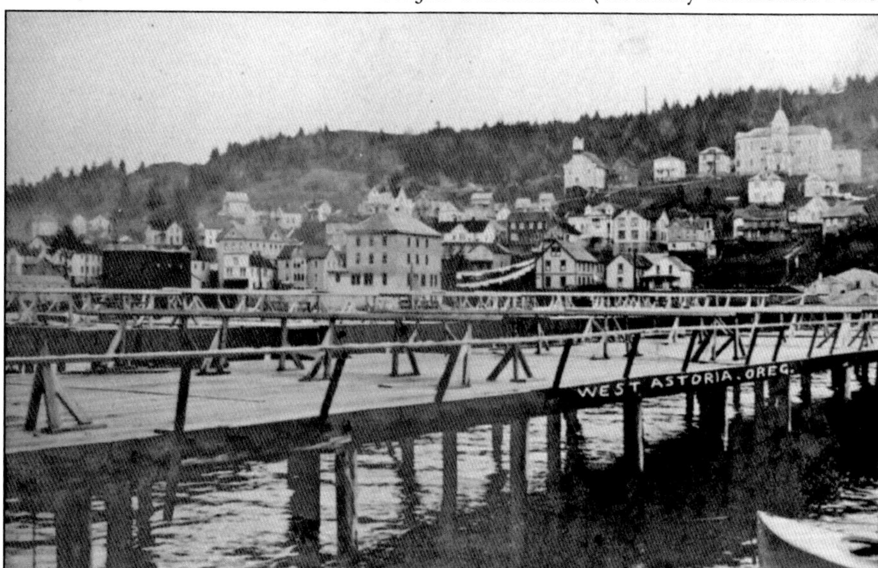

The inscription on the postcard reads "West Astoria," but this area is also referred to as "Uniontown" or "Finn Town," established in the 1880s by Finnish immigrants and known as the "Helsinki of the West." It is near where the Astoria-Megler Bridge connects to Astoria. Looking east, Taylor School is visible on the hillside. According to a local historian, the school was torn down by a minister who ferried the materials across the Columbia to the Naselle area, where he built a home for his family. The Finnish Congregational Church is to the left of Taylor School. Many Finnish-owned businesses were in this area, as well as the Hannula Boarding House at 200 West Marine Drive, visible in the picture, which burned down in 1943. (Author's collection.)

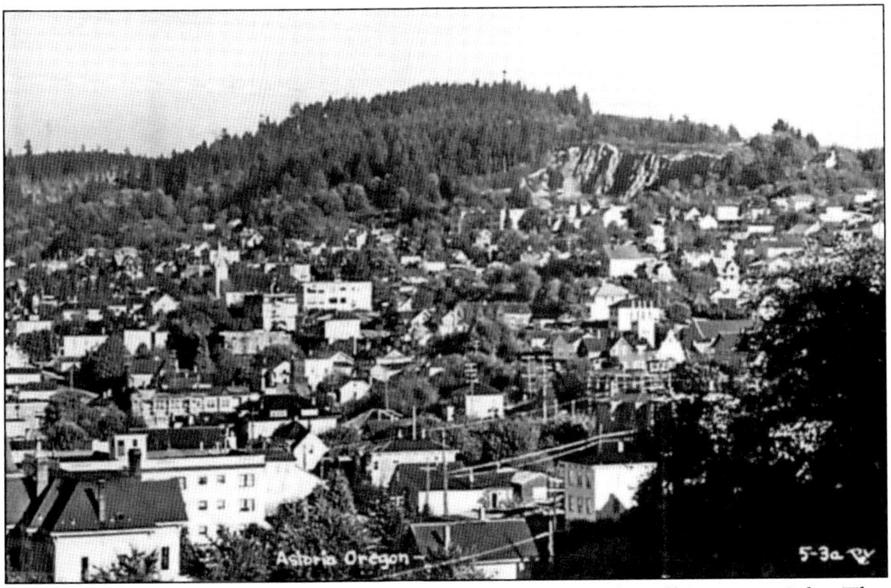

Still looking east, the Flavel House is at lower left and Coxcomb Hill is at top right. The Astor Column has yet to be built, and Hildebrand's Crushed Rock quarry is visible. Rocks from the quarry were used in many local projects including the Astoria Waterworks, Astoria High School, US Post Office and Customhouse (1878), and many residential properties. Directly below this is the new Astoria High School, now Clatsop Community College. The Clatsop County administration building is in front of the Flavel House. (Author's collection.)

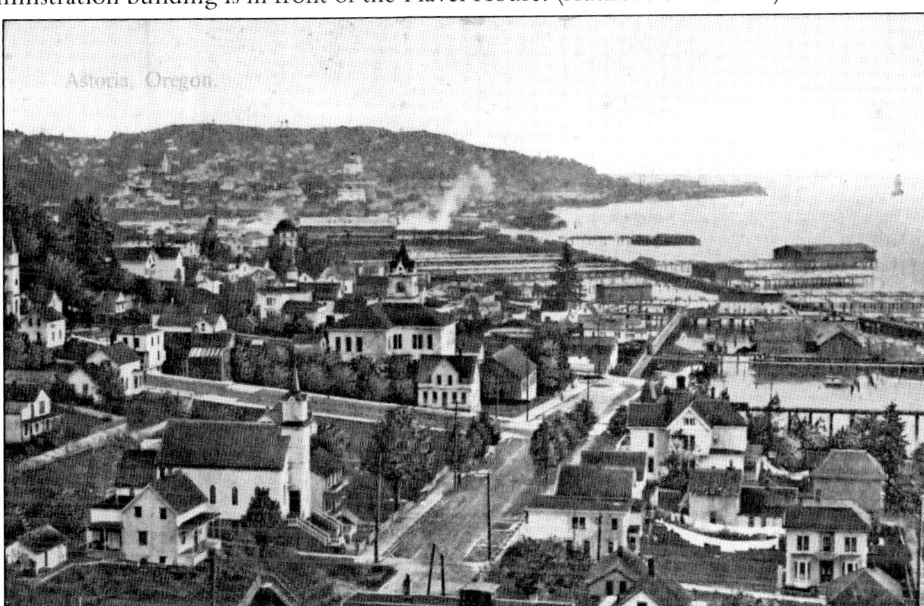

This c. 1900 view of "Uppertown" Astoria looking west is from the area of the Thirty-Ninth Street hillside (possibly near the site of the present-day Goonies House). The Adair School (center) is between Thirty-Fifth and Thirty-Sixth Streets on Duane Street. Built in 1888, the Benjamin Young house (with the carriage house) is at lower right. Across the street is the First Evangelical Lutheran Church, which no longer exists. The waterfront area is near what is now known as the east mooring basin. (Courtesy of Michael Soderberg.)

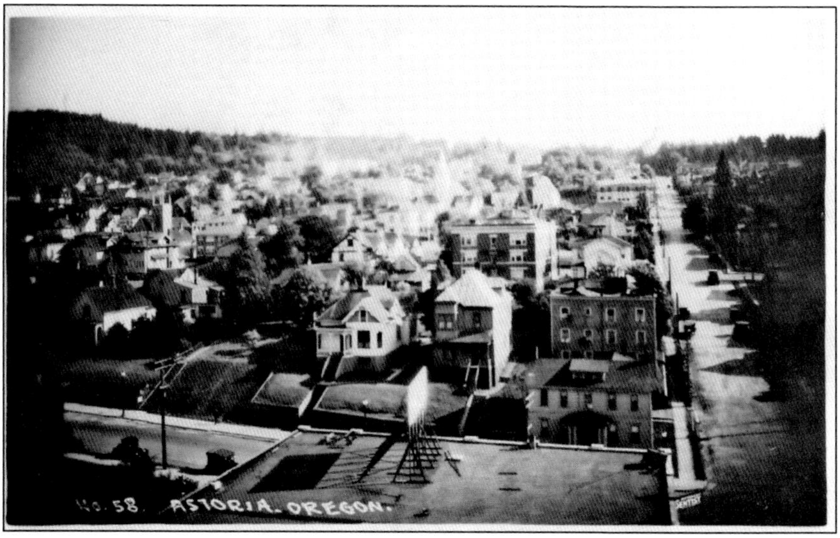

From the corner of Fourteenth and Exchange Streets looking south, the Trullinger House (built in 1892) faces Exchange Street and is the present-day home of KMUN Coast Community Radio. Directly behind it is the landmark Franklin Apartments, with Grace Episcopal Church visible to the left. This postcard shows the density of the downtown residential area. As the population of Astoria tended to double every five years after the Civil War, using the available land efficiently was very important, because the topography does not allow extensive expansion. The permanent population leveled off around 10,000 in the early 1900s. (Courtesy of Michael Foster.)

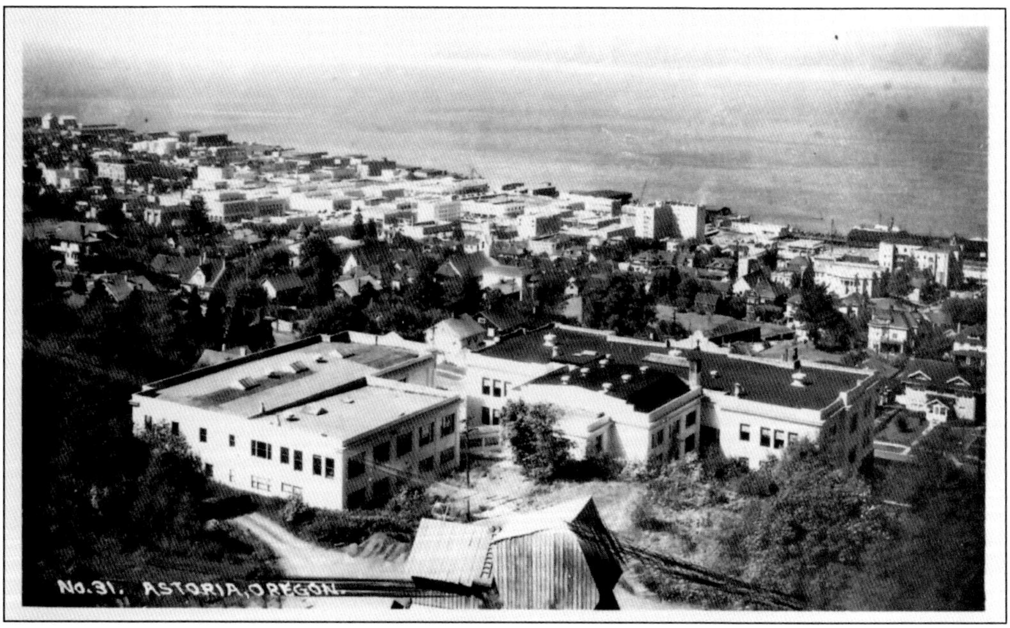

This sweeping view of a gleaming downtown from atop Coxcomb Hill is from about the 1930s. In the foreground are Hildebrand's Crushed Rock quarry and the stately Astoria High School. The main building was constructed in 1911 and the gym added by 1920. It is now Clatsop Community College and is undergoing expansion. Near the Columbia River waterfront, from the right, are St. Mary's Hospital with its brick expansion, the Masonic lodge, and farther down, the John Jacob Astor Hotel (the tallest building). (Courtesy of Michael Foster.)

Two

Fishing

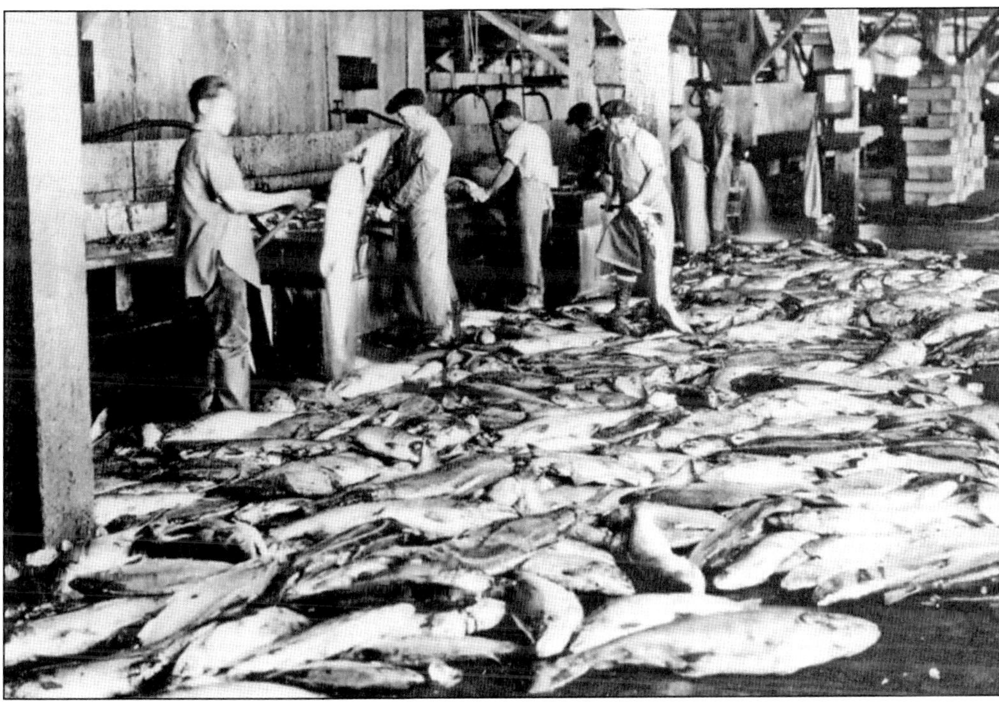

This undated photo postcard of the interior of an Astoria cannery is from the Burlington, Northern & Spokane Portland and Seattle Railroad Collection. This promotional photograph conveys the message that Astoria was a land of abundance, particularly in salmon. Chinese labor (pictured) began around 1870 in Astoria as brokers contracted to bring hundreds from Guangdong Province. By 1880, one third of Astoria's population was Chinese and dominated the workforce in the canneries. Valued for their skill and speed, hard-working Chinese laborers (almost exclusively men) endured long hours in Astoria's fish processing industry. (Courtesy of Ray Hakala.)

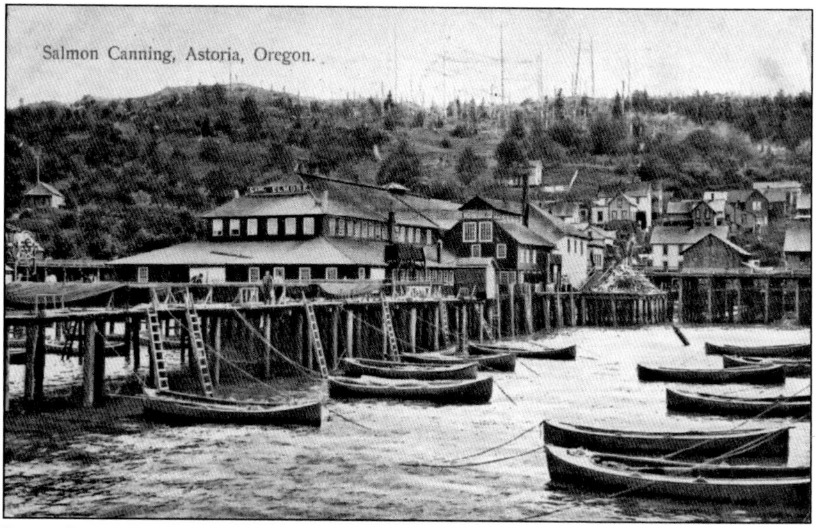

Samuel Elmore's Union Cannery, built in 1889, was the longest continuously operated salmon cannery in the United States until its decommissioning in 1980. The mid-1880s were boom years, and the Elmore Cannery was known as one of the best operations on the Pacific coast. It was also the source of the name "Uniontown." As salmon stocks declined, the cannery diversified into tuna in the late 1930s and Astoria became the home of Bumble Bee brand tuna. This great view from the river is from the foot of Flavel Street at the east edge of Uniontown. Astoria Warehousing is located on this site today. (Courtesy of Michael Soderberg.)

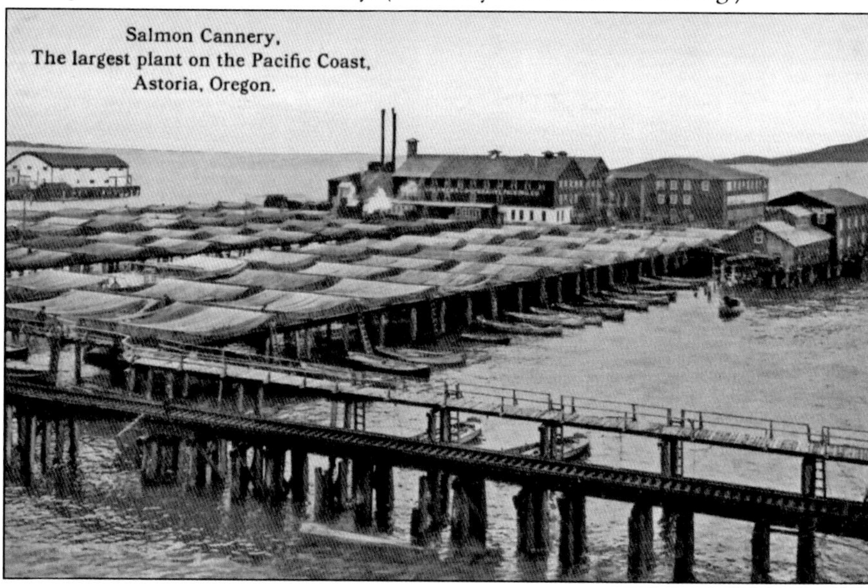

The Union Fishermen's Cooperative Packing Company was formed in 1899 after a tense era between cannery owners and fishermen. After the Oregon National Guard was called in to break a strike in 1896, about 200 mostly Finnish fishermen pooled their resources, opening the cannery that became the largest in Astoria and remained fisherman-owned until the late 1940s. Shown here are fishermen drying and repairing their nets around 1910. Natural fiber nets, which often were made in the fishermen's homes during the winters, needed to be dried between uses. Fishermen could navigate their boats right up under the building, where a hoist would lift the nets to dry. (Courtesy of Michael Foster.)

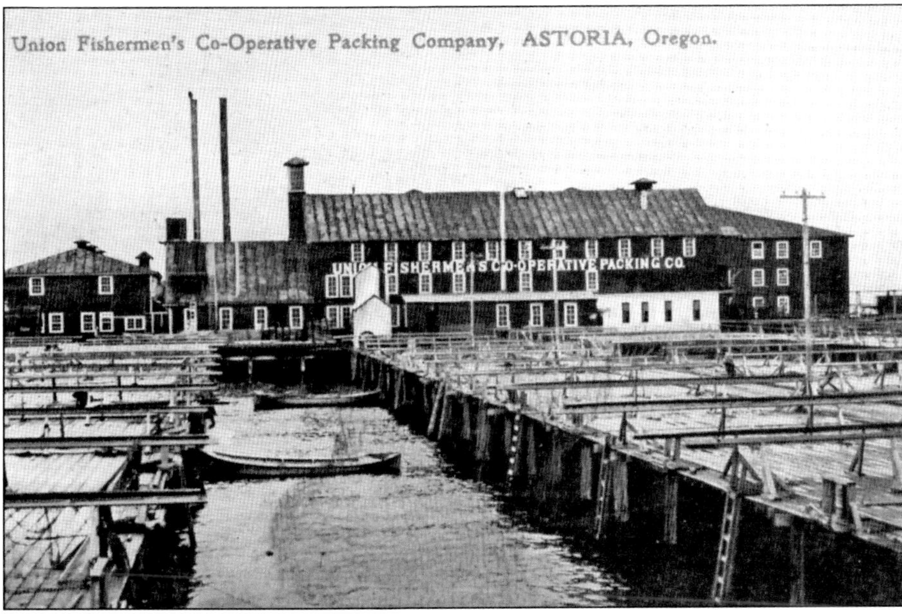

This image of the Union Fishermen's Cooperative Packing Company is from about 1909. Until its sale in 1950 to Peter Pan Seafood, the co-op's label, Gillnetter's Best, was world famous for quality. After it closed, it was destroyed by fire. Today, its historic profile is recognizable as the luxury Cannery Pier Hotel, built in the original location on the remaining pilings next to the Astoria-Megler Bridge. This postcard was one of a series for the 1909 Alaska-Yukon-Pacific Exposition in Seattle. (Courtesy of Michael Foster.)

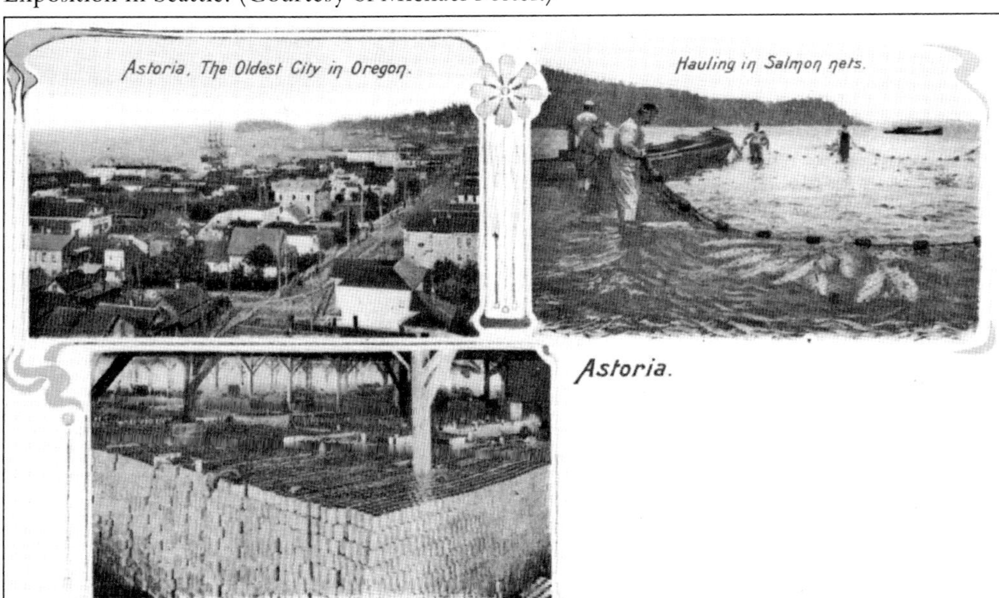

This decorative photo montage postcard celebrates the modern city of Astoria and the industry that made it famous. One shows "2,000,000 Cans of Salmon" and fishermen pulling in their nets at low tide. The soldering and canning was the specialty of Chinese labor. In the early days of canning, tremendous explosions occasionally occurred due to improper seals and spoilage. As always, every industry is continually refining its methods. (Courtesy of Michael Foster.)

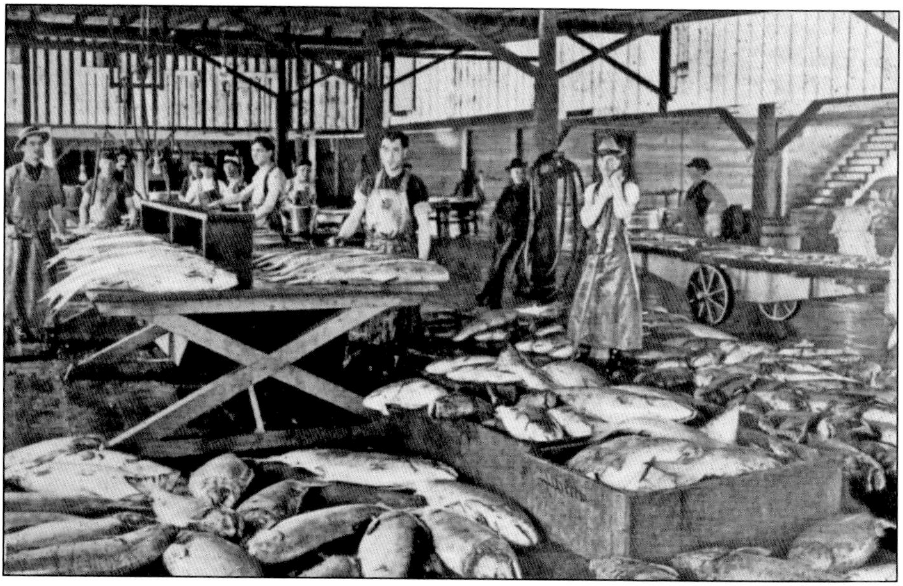

This interior view of a salmon cannery shows men preparing fish for processing. In 1876, Astoria had five canneries. By 1883, it had 24 working around the clock during salmon season. Note the huge fish. This is possibly a salting or pickling operation due to the barrels. A message from a postcard sent in 1911 from Astoria to Jewell read, "Dear Friend, Saw the fisherman the other day, said he could pack fish for me and would cost 6 cents per pound or about $12.00 per barrel. Let me know at once if you want any packed as the season is nearing an end!" (Courtesy of Michael Soderberg.)

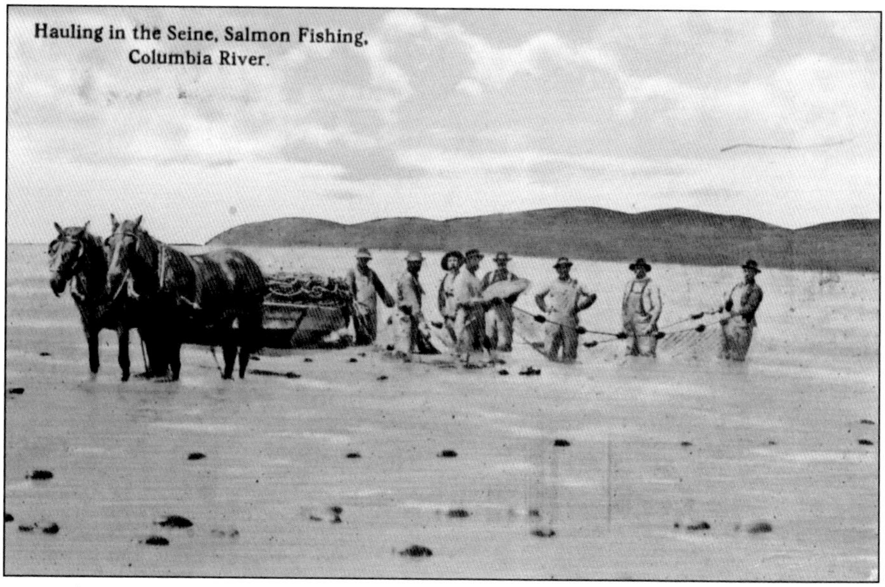

This postcard, postmarked 1914, demonstrates the fishing technique developed in the 1890s by R.D. Hume called "horse seining." After the large nets were laid out for the outbound tide, teams of horses (usually hearty Percherons and Clydesdales) were used to pull overflowing nets from the channel onto the sand. A horse seine crew would range from two to 40 people and use up to seven teams of horses. They worked from sun up to sundown during the salmon run. (Courtesy of Michael Foster.)

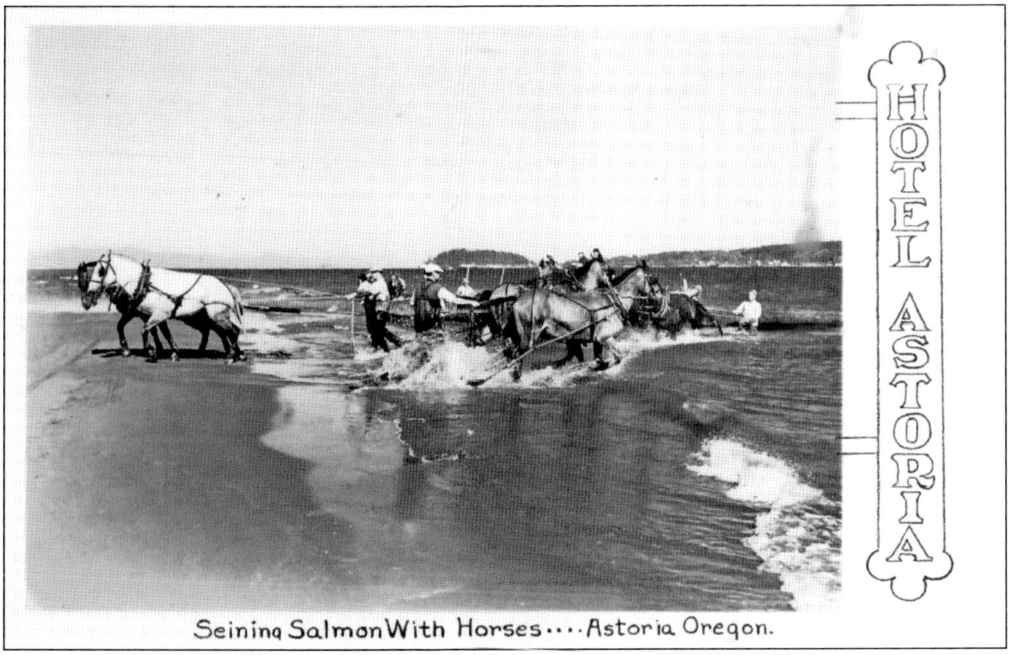

"Plowing for salmon" continued off the Astoria waterfront until the early 1950s, when it was outlawed. It must have been quite a spectacle for visitors to witness—so much so that the Hotel Astoria devoted a postcard to its practice. Crews often worked, ate, and slept on the sands, just like the horses. At low tide today, the pilings that once supported the horse barns and cookhouses can be seen in the middle of the river. (Courtesy of Michael Foster.)

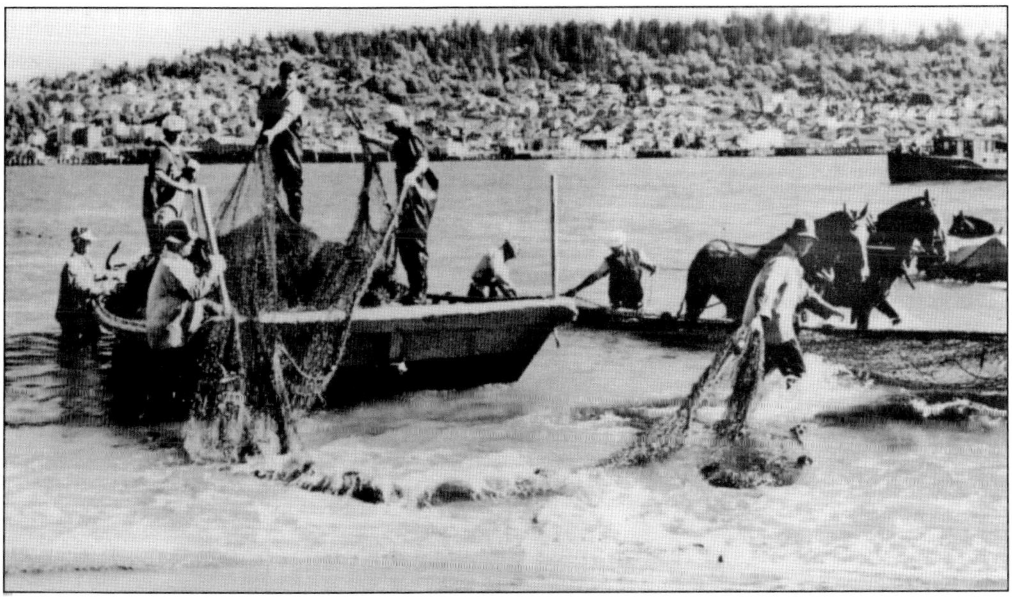

During the peak of horse seining on the Columbia in the 1930s, up to 15 percent of the salmon catch came from this practice. This image shows the crew preparing to deploy the nets for the outgoing tide off Astoria's waterfront on the area known as the Desdemona Sands. The canneries claimed specific areas or territories on the sands they seined. A cannery tender is off to the left, waiting to transfer the catch to the docks. (Courtesy of Sara's Old Photos.)

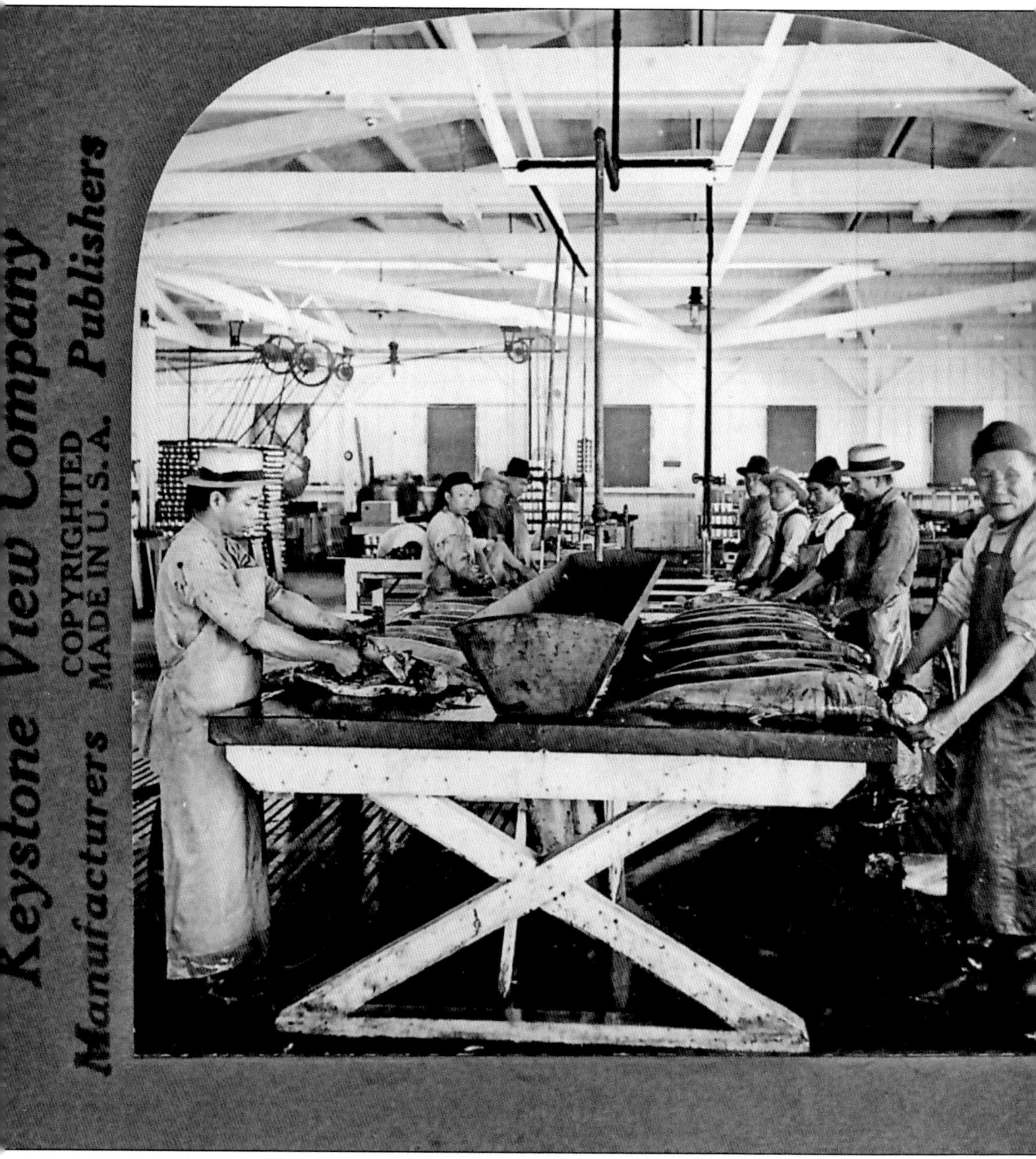

Despite the significant contribution to the fishing industry of the Chinese, prejudice and exploitation led to passage of the 1882 Chinese Exclusion Act. Columbia River cannery owners began replacing Chinese labor with Smith Butchering Machines, sometimes called "Iron Chinks." As employment opportunities disappeared, workers returned to China or moved to other cities. From its peak in 1880, the local Chinese population shrank to 925 in 1890, and by 1900, it was

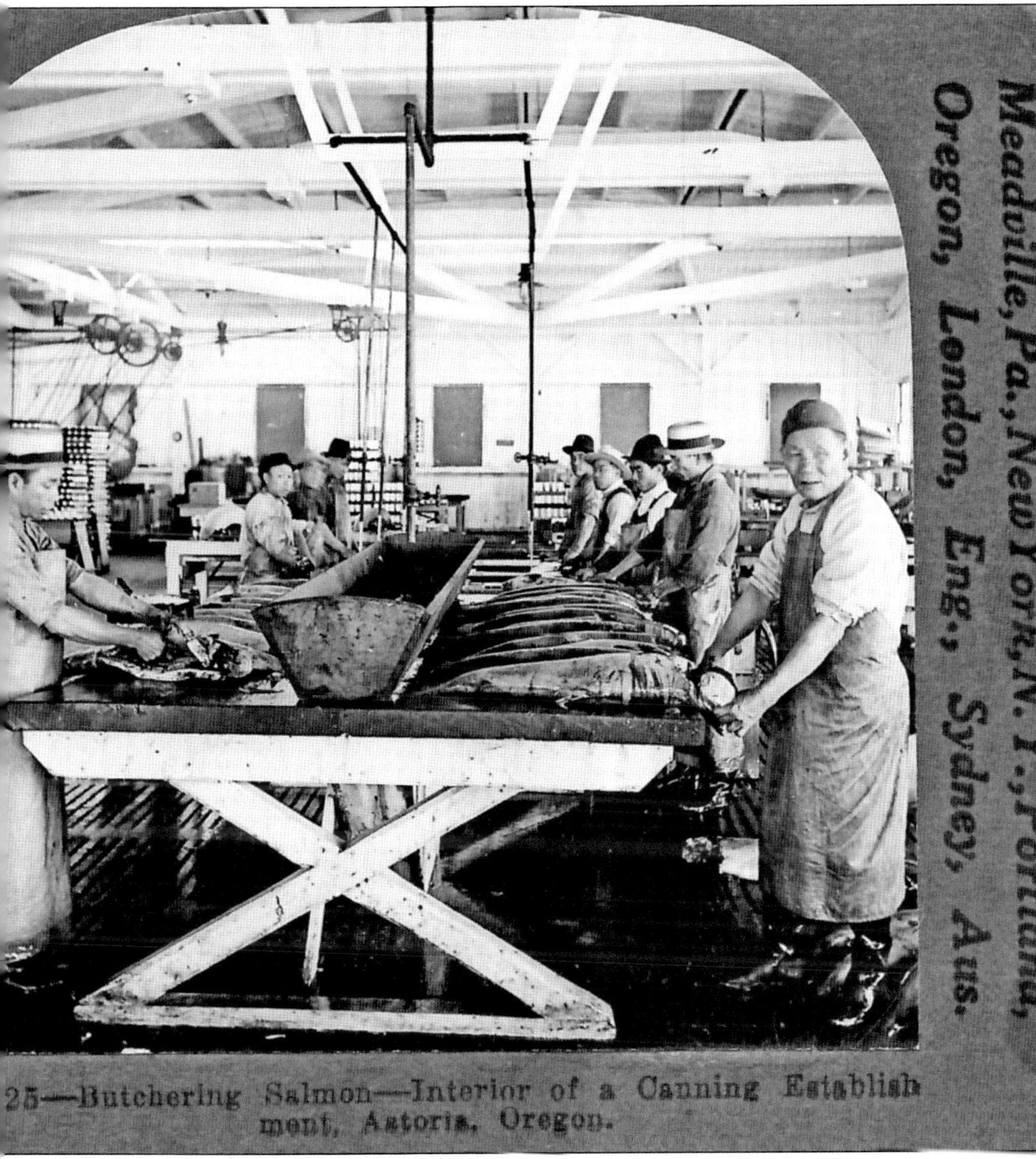

601. By the time the Chinese Exclusion Act was repealed in 1943, Astoria's Chinese numbered just over 100. Although this image is a stereo-view and not a postcard, it was selected for its clear and detailed depiction of a fully operational cannery fueled by Chinese labor. (Courtesy of Ray Hakala.)

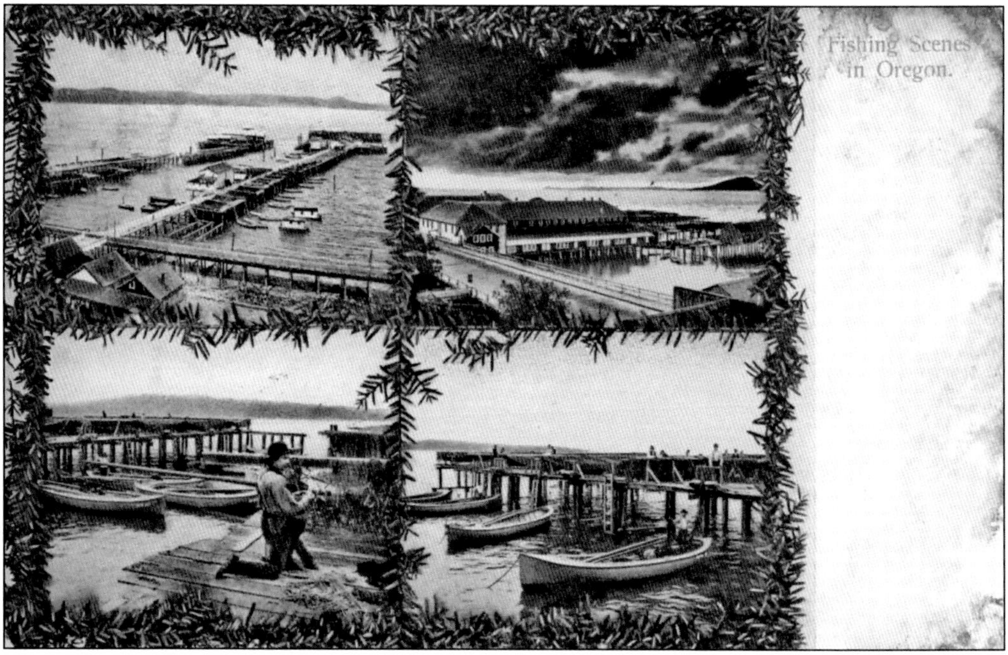

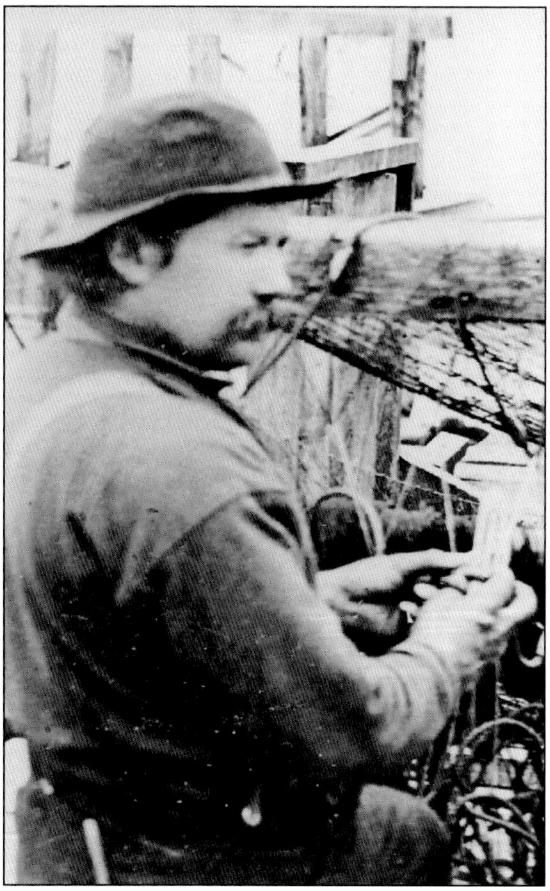

Adapted from the 1895 book *Columbia River Salmon Fishing Photographic Album* by J.H. Bratt, this postcard shows everyday aspects of the salmon fishing life at the Kinney Cannery, which was located at the foot of Fifth Street. The cannery burned in 1894 and was completely rebuilt. It was in operation until the mid-1950s, then used for waterfront storage for years. Scenes include net racks, boats, and a fisherman mending his net. (Courtesy of Michael Soderberg.)

This detail from the previous postcard, shows the fisherman in the lower left corner. In this real-photo postcard is Finnish-Swede immigrant Jacob Baker, great-grandfather of native Astorian Michael Soderberg. He is shown mending his gillnet at the Kinney Cannery dock at the foot of Fifth Street in 1894. (Courtesy of Michael Soderberg.)

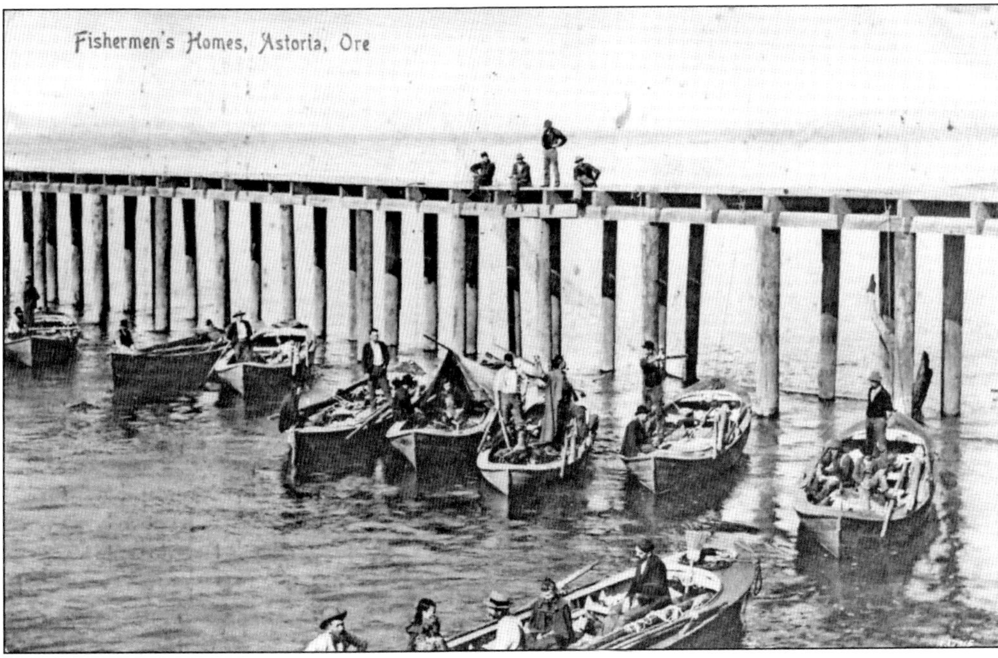

Hard-working Columbia River salmon fishermen prepare their gillnet boats for another day around 1908. The postcard reads "Fishermen's Homes." Some gillnetters did sleep on their boats, protected by tents made from their sails (center), in order to position themselves for the tides. The message on the reverse of this card reads: "In bed again. It is awful six weeks and don't know how much longer." (Courtesy of Michael Soderberg.)

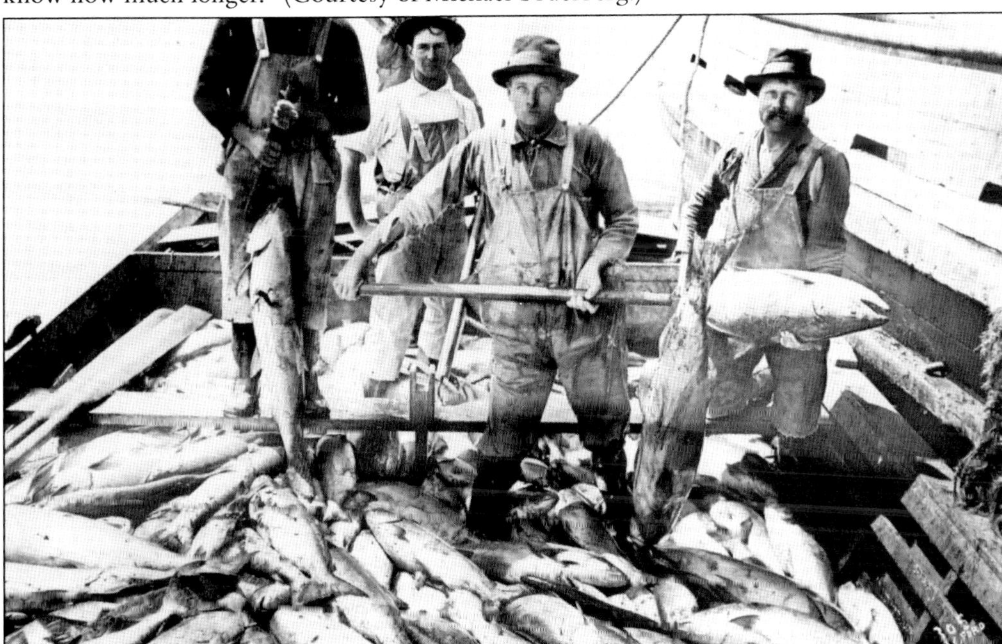

This great photograph possibly shows a seining crew unloading their skiff to a cannery tender just off the sands after one of the many harvests of the day. (Courtesy of Sean Fitzpatrick and Anne Carpenter.)

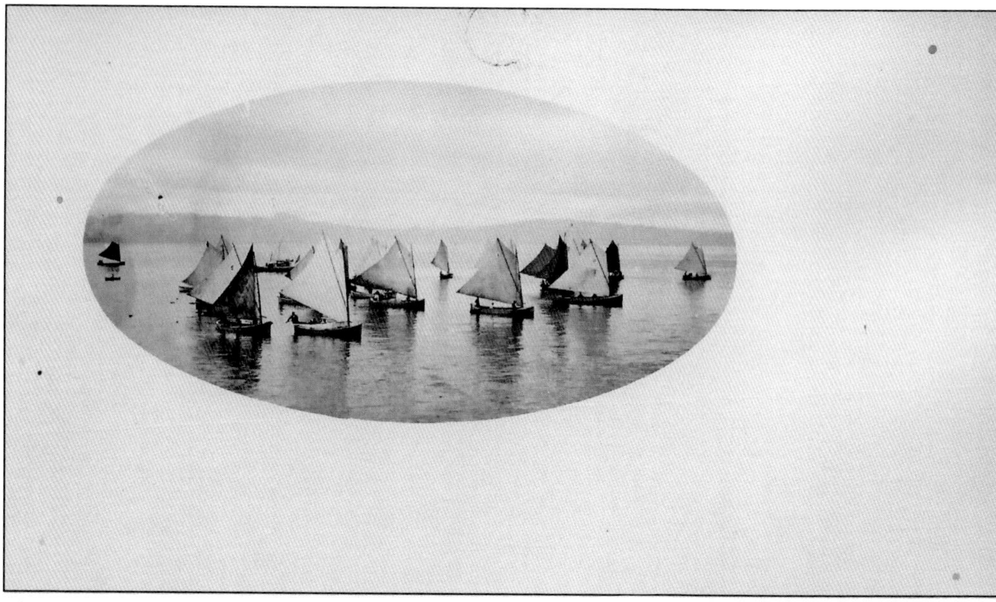

Photographed while the river was amazingly calm (possibly from the Elmore or Union Cannery docks), the "Butterfly Fleet" drifts toward Astoria's waterfront with the Washington hills in the background. The fishermen are sailing gillnet boats, wide-beamed boats developed specifically for Lower Columbia waters, operated from the 1860s to the early 1900s. At its peak, the fleet numbered over 1,600. (Courtesy of Michael Soderberg.)

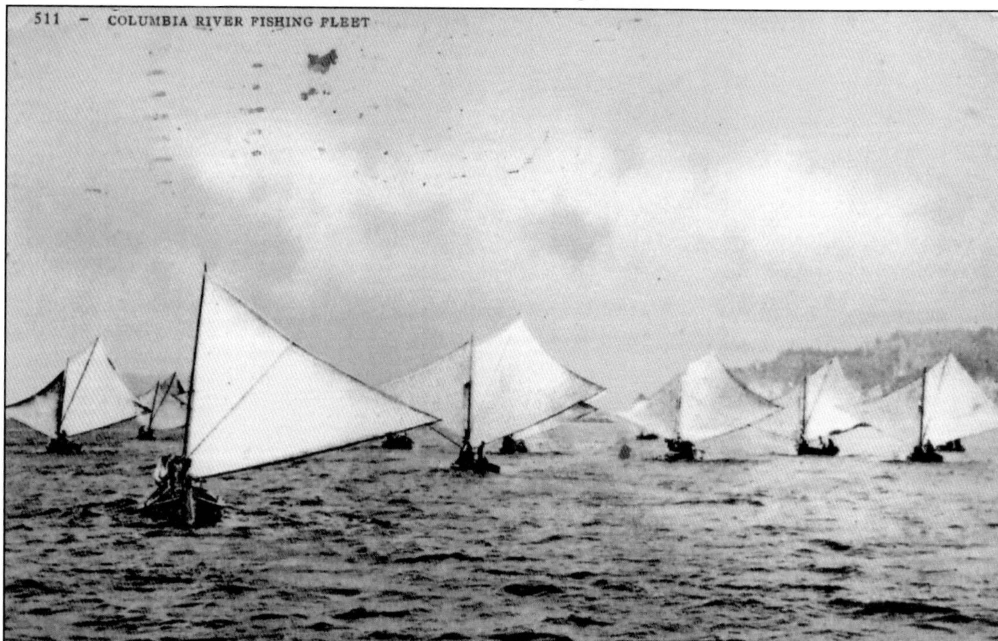

The Butterfly Fleet sails downwind, "wing on wing," along the riverfront. In the background is downtown Astoria to the right, with Uppertown and Tongue Point to the left in the shadows. Engines came on board about 1905–1906, relegating the sailboat to history in salmon fishing. Typically, the boats and nets were owned by the cannery and only rented by the fishermen. (Courtesy of Michael Soderberg.)

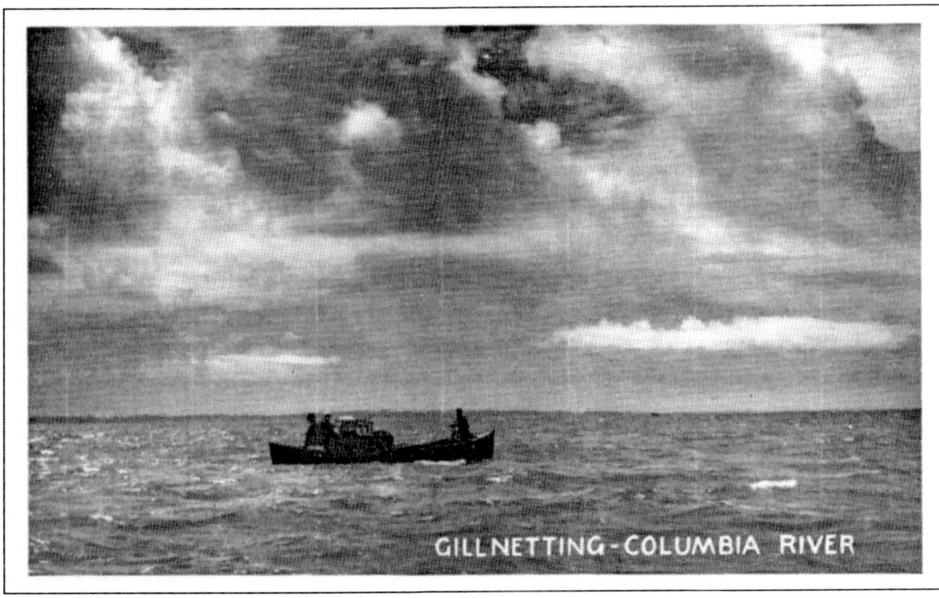

Gillnetters operated small boats in crews of one or two. At the peak, as many as 2,000 gillnetting vessels plied the Columbia. Gillnetting was a dangerous trade. Weather could change quickly, and the sandbars and shallows where some of the best fish could be caught were unpredictable and dangerous. Boats capsized, and drownings were common. Once gillnet boats adopted engines, the design was adapted, and they were called "bowpickers," as shown here. (Courtesy of Michael Soderberg.)

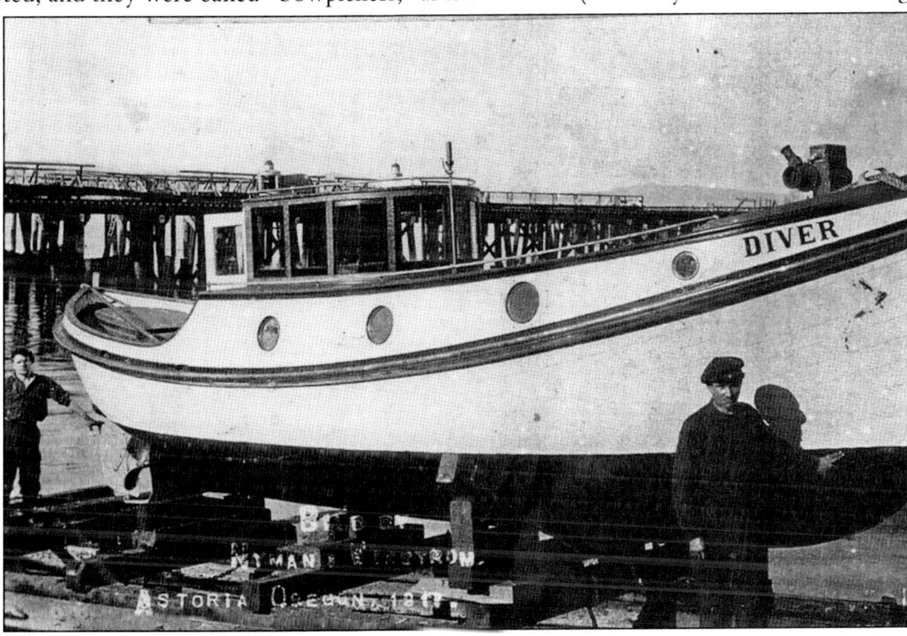

Axel Nyman and John Wickstrom of Astoria Motor Boat Construction Company built gillnet boats (and many other types) for use on the Columbia River and beyond. Their craftsmanship was highly respected. Their shop was located on Young's Bay. It was noted in a June 1922 issue of the *Marine Journal* that "Owing to the unusual demand on the Columbia River for fishing boats this year, the Wickstrom & Nyman yards have been working twenty-four hours a day to turn out all their contracts." The postcard is from around 1912. (Courtesy of Sara's Old Photos.)

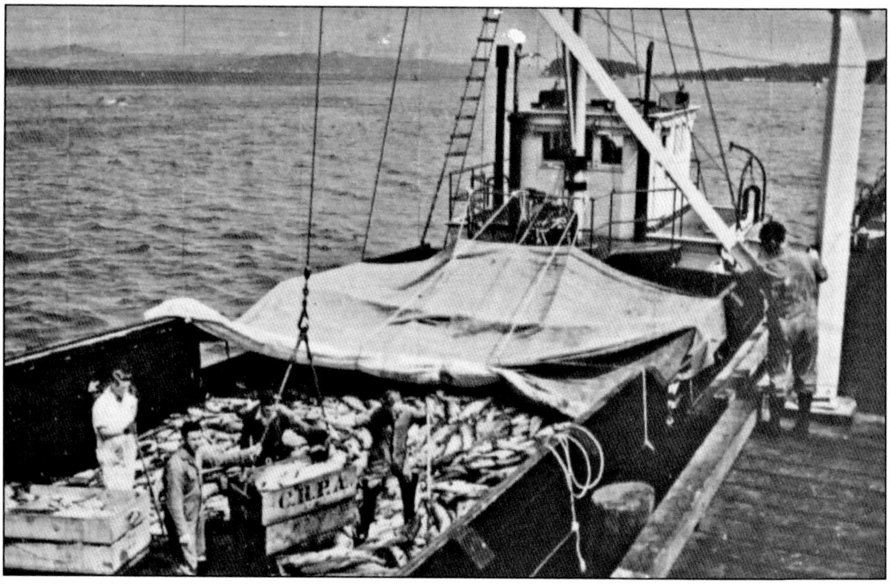

Seen here is a fully loaded scow used to collect fish from fishermen and receiving stations along the river and transport the catch to the main Columbia River Packers Association (CRPA) plant in Astoria. These scows greatly streamlined the process from catch to processor on the Columbia and helped ensure the quality of the catch. This postcard image may be from the J.O. Hanthorn Cannery in the 1930s, but is not identified specifically. Built in 1875, the Hanthorn Cannery building is the last of its kind on Astoria's waterfront, known today as Pier 39 at the east end of town. (Courtesy of Michael Soderberg.)

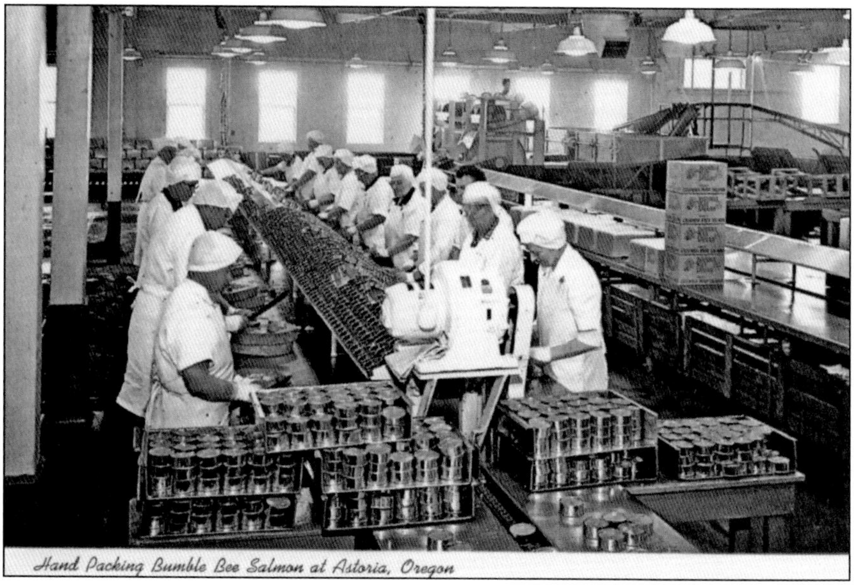

Pictured in the early 1960s at the Bumble Bee Cannery, the hand-packing of tuna employed many workers in Astoria. Typically Scandinavian women, the laborers worked long hours to keep up with both the supply and demand of the prized salmon. The Bumble Bee Cannery was the former Samuel Elmore Packing Company Cannery that was built in the 1890s. In 1899, many independent canneries on the Astoria waterfront formed the CRPA. In 1962, the CRPA was bought out by Bumble Bee, which is owned by Dole. (Courtesy of Michael Soderberg.)

Three

TIMBER

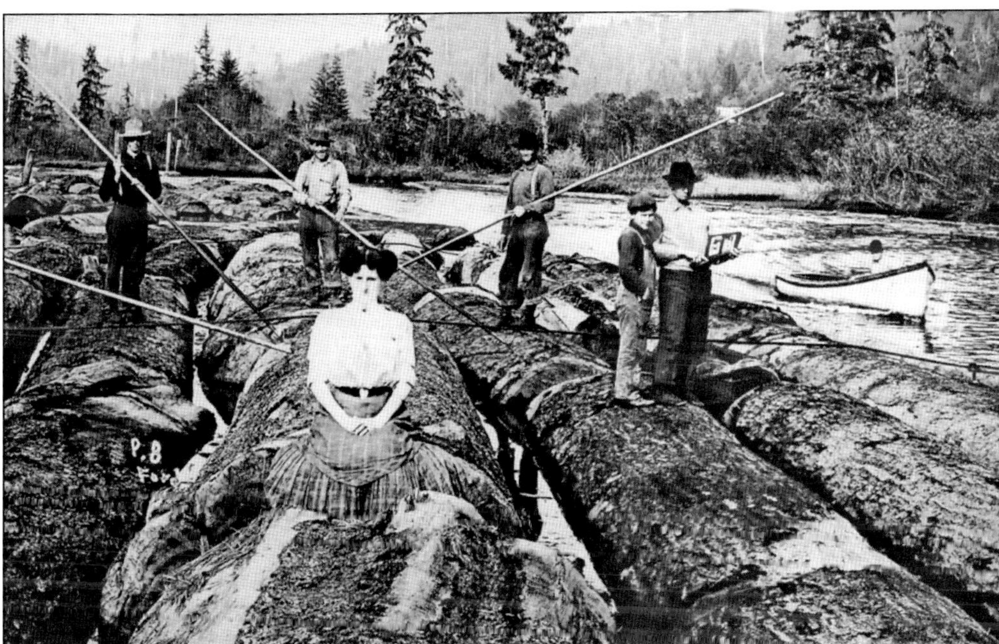

Logging rivaled fishing as the lead industry in the area due to an insatiable demand for wood products and a seemingly unending supply of timber. In the early days, it was called "jack screw" logging. It was a very hands-on job using crosscut saws, wedges, and cable. In this undated postcard, huge logs are being maneuvered with rafters' hooks. Pike poles, usually made of spruce or fir, were used to control floating logs on a river log drive and when constructing log rafts. Considering the cable across the logs, it is possible that a log raft is being assembled. (Courtesy of Sean Fitzpatrick and Anne Carpenter.)

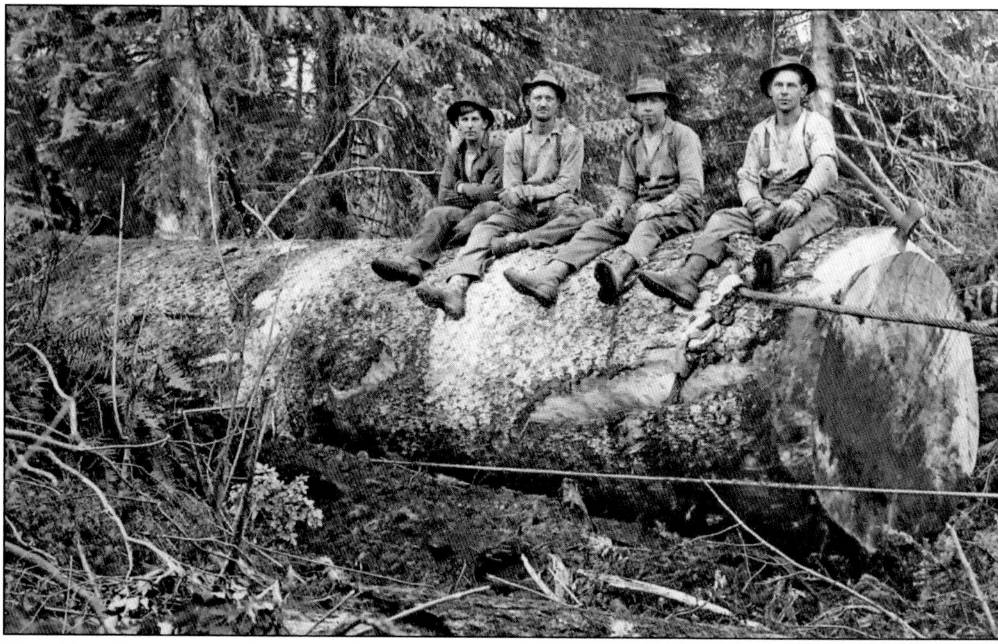

Here lies a huge spruce log around the 1920s. It has been felled and "sniped" with cable, making it easier to move to the skid road and down to the water. The first harvests were focused on hillsides along the edges of waterways. Once those were gone, loggers moved inland. The work got harder, and labor-saving innovations were developed. (Courtesy of Michael Soderberg.)

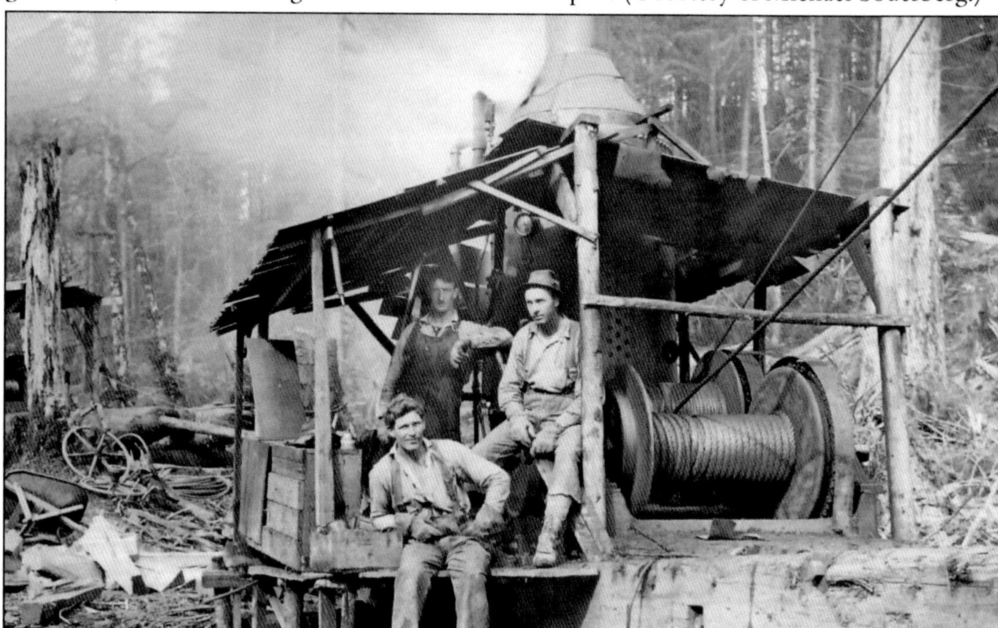

Steam donkeys, pictured here with crew, were introduced around 1900 and made work much easier, although not much safer. They were used in "high lead" logging to haul trees that were further into the woods. Local inventor John Fox built the machines, first used in Clatsop County. After the steam donkey, it wasn't long until tractors and bulldozers completely changed the face of the logging industry. (Courtesy of Michael Foster.)

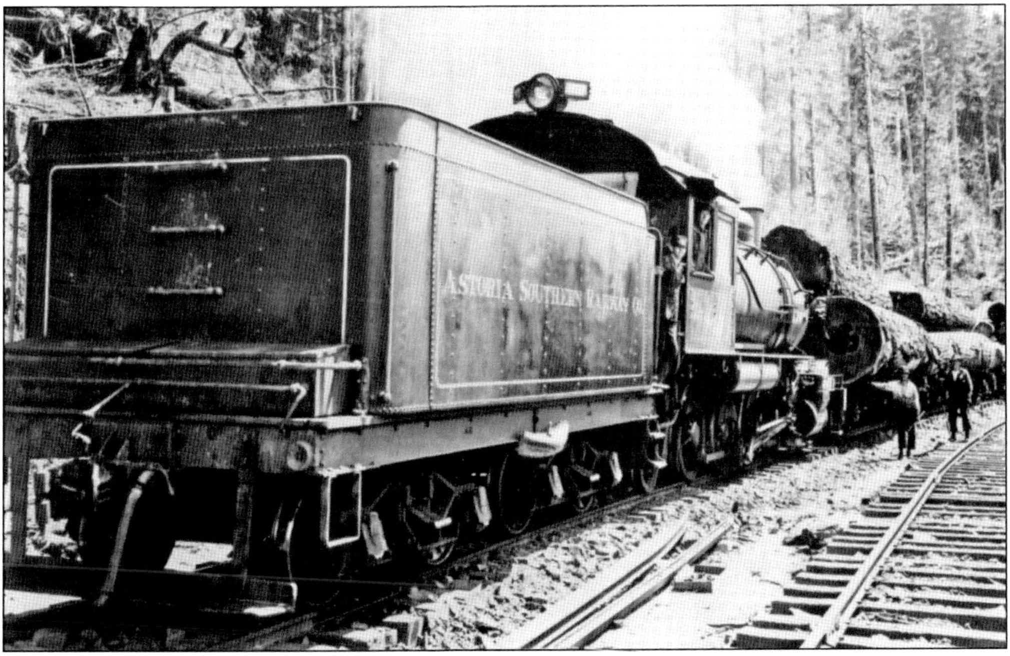

Eventually, railways were built into the forest to reach even more distant stands of timber. They moved logs to a "dumpsite" on the closest river or slough. About 1910, the *Oregonian* reported that the railroad was able to reach areas "shut off by an impenetrable wall of rugged mountains and twisting river valleys." Pictured here is the Astoria Southern Railway line serving the logging operations of Tidewater Timber Co. near Olney. (Courtesy of Bill Young.)

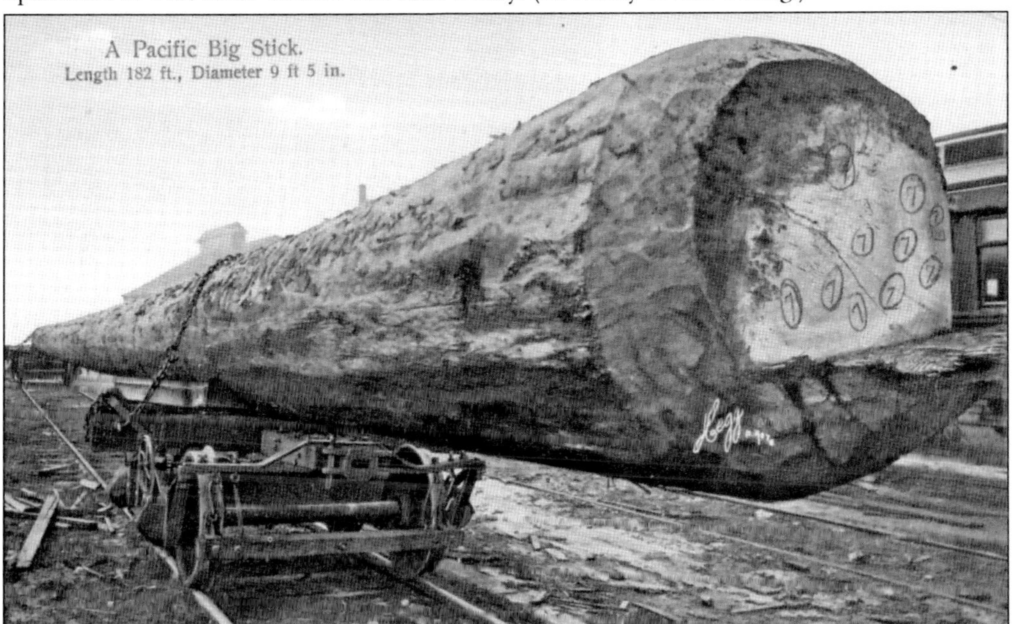

The sender was clearly making an effort to impress the recipient of this postcard by the sheer size of what was called "A Pacific Big Stick." With dimensions like those listed, the disconnected log truck under it is dwarfed by its size. (Courtesy of Bill Young.)

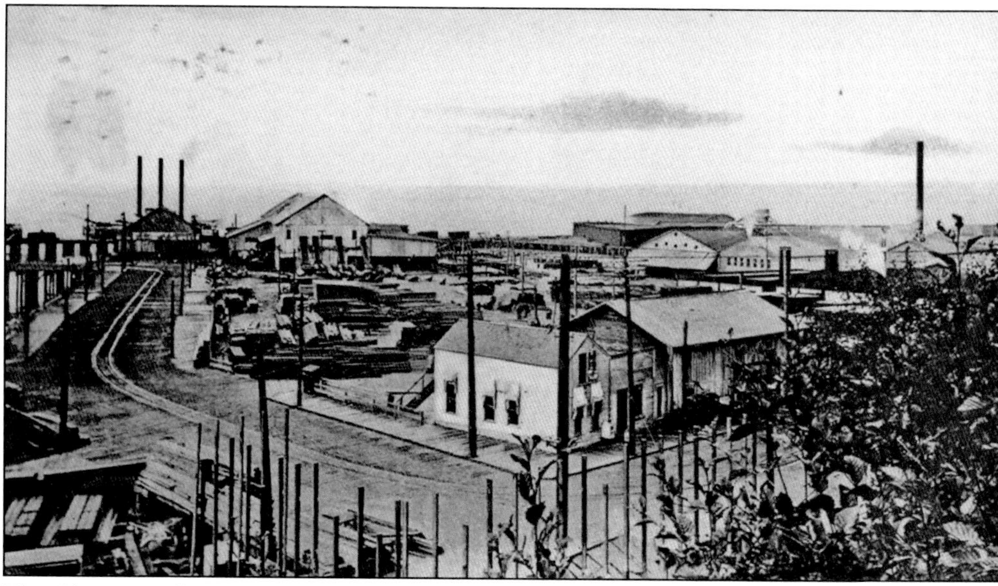

The Clatsop Mill, pictured here in 1909, was built by the Kinney family in 1884 at the site of today's Mill Pond Village. The original mill, at Fourteenth and Exchange Streets, burned down in 1883. It burned at its new location in 1914. It was rebuilt again, ran until the 1930s, and then was closed for many years. In 1951, the Astoria Plywood Mill opened, and it ran until about 1990. Another current local business, City Lumber, was the result of a consolidation of three manufacturing businesses, Clatsop Mill being one. (Courtesy of Michael Foster.)

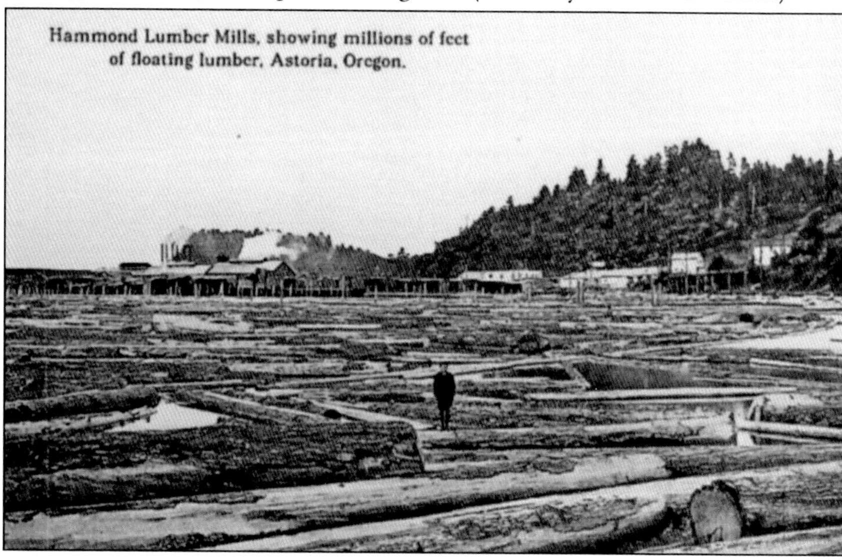

In 1890, Andrew B. Hammond formed the Hammond Lumber Company, expanding upon the first sawmill in the area, built by John Shively. Hammond had already invested in Astoria's railroad, and he recognized the further opportunity in the logging industry. He continued to expand his lumber holdings in the area. By the time of this c. 1910 postcard, Astoria had 15,000 residents, and the lumber mills were running nonstop. Much of this demand was fueled by the reconstruction of San Francisco following its devastating earthquake and fire. During World War I, Hammond was the single largest owner of Sitka spruce timberland in Oregon. Sitka spruce was the only lumber suitable for airplane manufacture. (Courtesy of Sean Fitzpatrick and Anne Carpenter.)

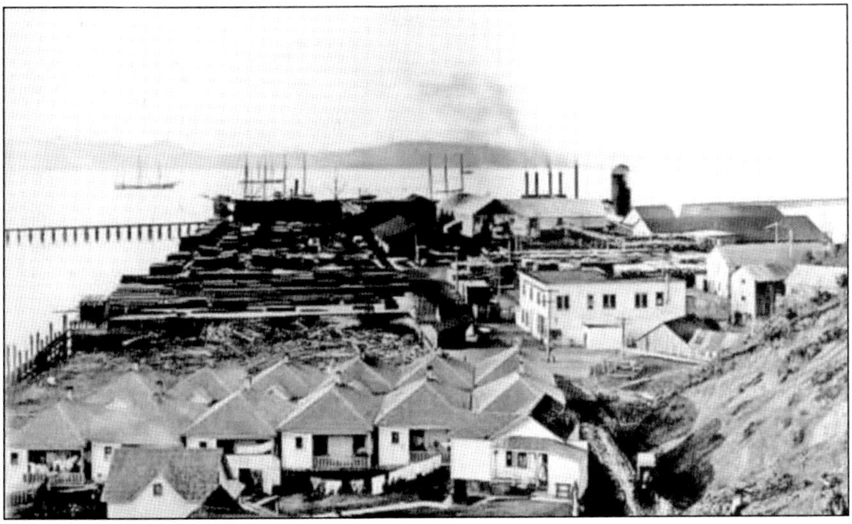

This c. 1915 postcard provides another view of Hammond Lumber Mill. The mill employed Punjabis from India. The housing pictured was referred to as "Hindu Alley," although the men were Sikhs. Hammond Mill in Alderbrook had a generator that sold surplus energy to the Pacific Power and Light Company. Hammond also owned five steamers that serviced his lumber operations up and down the Columbia between Astoria and Portland. In 1919, Hammond milled 120 million board feet of lumber. The mill burned down in 1922 and was not rebuilt. This fire occurred just three months before Astoria's Great Fire of December 1922. (Author's collection.)

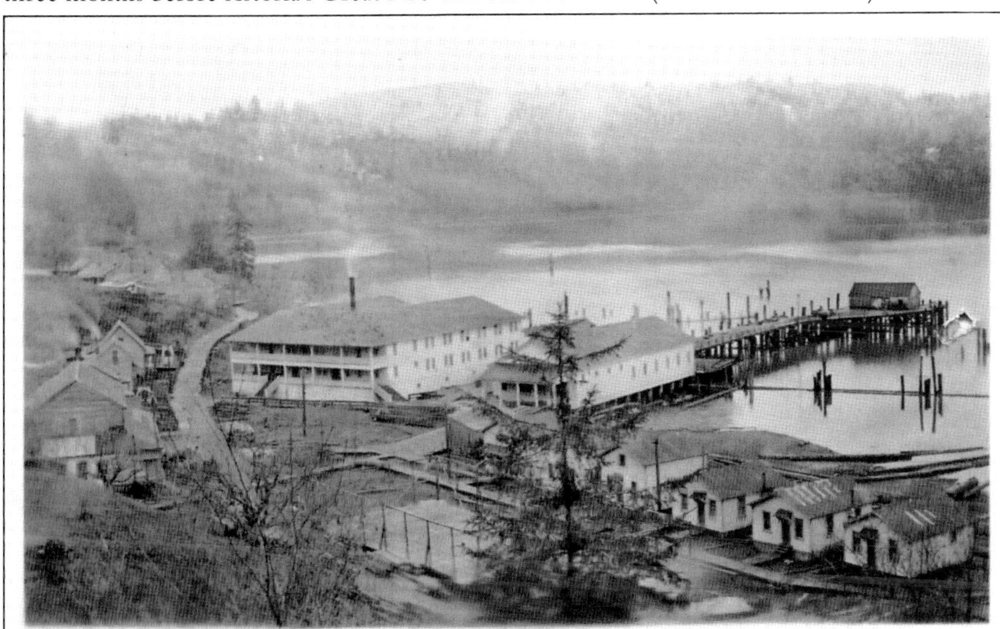

Located in Washington, the Knappton Mill Hotel, pictured around 1915, was owned by the Brix Lumber Company, which operated on the Lower Columbia River from the 1880s until the entire company town burned to the ground. This operation, directly across the river from Astoria, was a typical company town, providing room and board for the workers. A cafeteria staffed by local women served meals daily. Other basic services were also on site, as the mill ran continuously. (Courtesy of Mike Soderberg.)

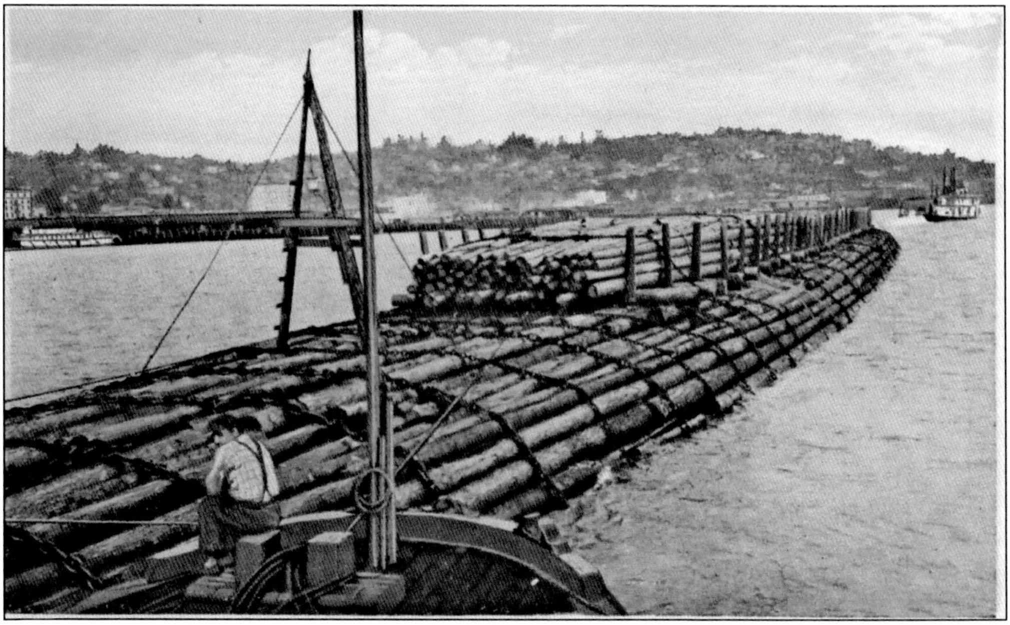

The Benson raft, or "Cigar Raft," was a huge seagoing log raft that reliably transported millions of board feet of lumber long distances through the open ocean. It was first used on the Pacific coast in 1906 by Simon Benson, a Portland lumber baron. The practice continued through World War II. These rafts were held together with giant logging chains. The destinations for these behemoths included San Diego, San Francisco, and other ports along the Pacific Coast. Benson had a lumber mill in San Diego, 1,100 miles away, and it was a cost-cutting practice to move raw timber this way. (Courtesy of Sean Fitzpatrick and Anne Carpenter.)

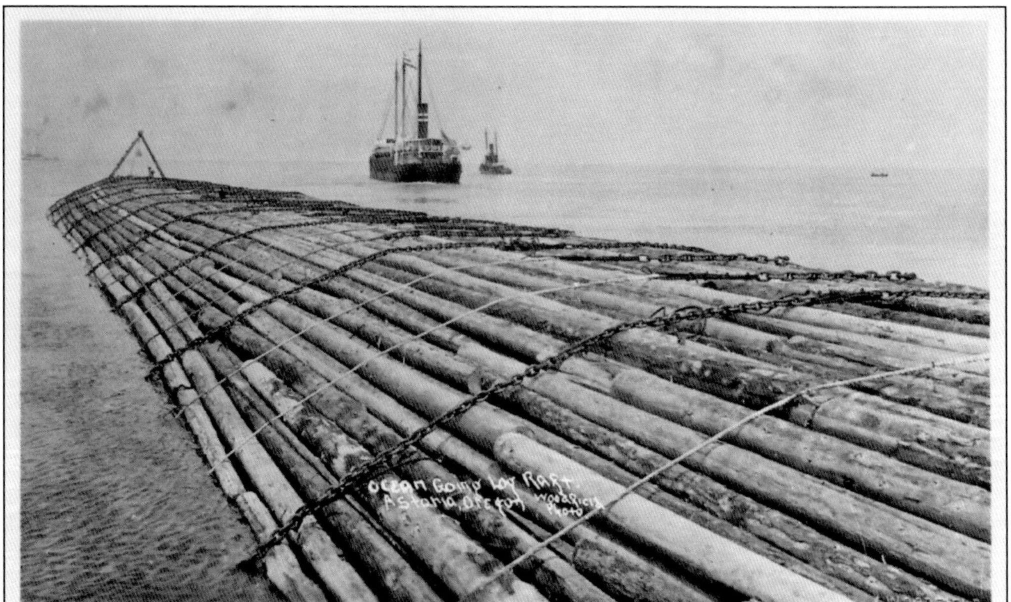

A freighter and tug pass each other near an oceangoing Benson log raft at Astoria. Smaller versions of these rafts were assembled in the sloughs and rivers that flow into the Columbia from the dumpsites of the inland logging camps. (Courtesy of Michael Foster.)

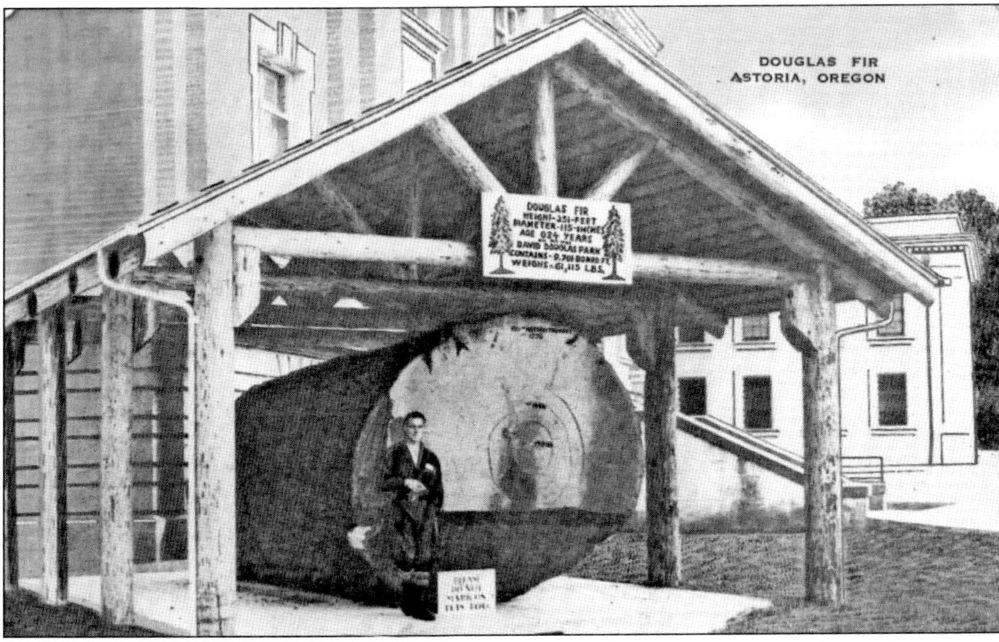

In a fitting homage to the incredible size of the logs and their importance to the local economy, this display was constructed at the corner of the Clatsop County Courthouse. It is still there, although the log has had to be replaced. The log in this postcard is from a tree over six-and-a-half centuries old. (Courtesy of Michael Foster.)

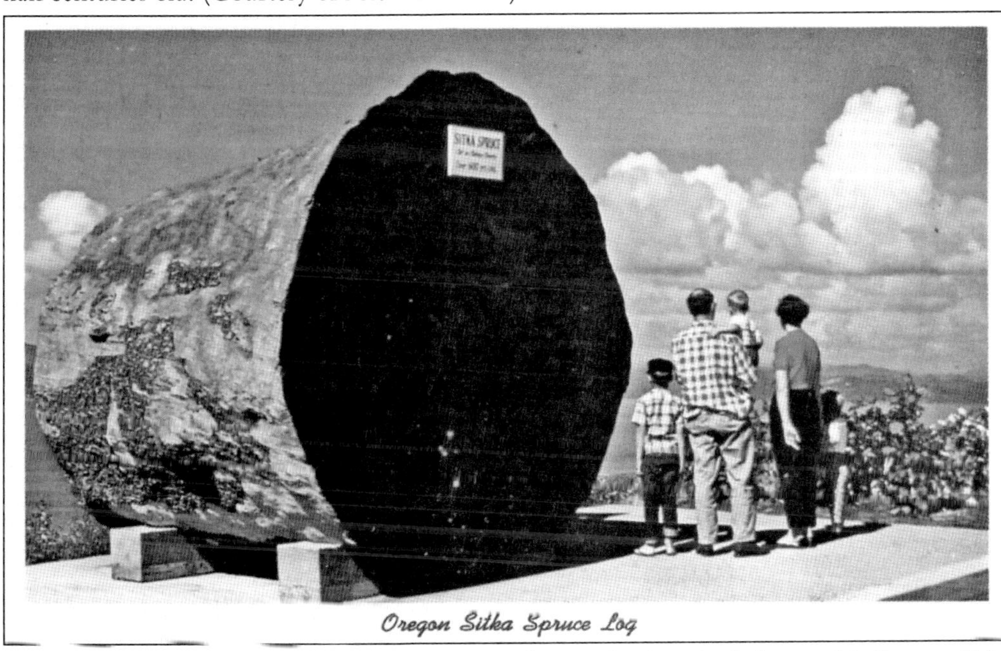

In a more modern image from atop Coxcomb Hill, near the Astoria Column, this Oregon Sitka spruce dwarfs the family standing next to it. Over 10 feet in diameter at the base, it was 257 feet high when the tree was standing. It is between six and seven hundred years old. This was typical of some of the virgin forests of Oregon until the old growth was logged. (Courtesy of Bill Young.)

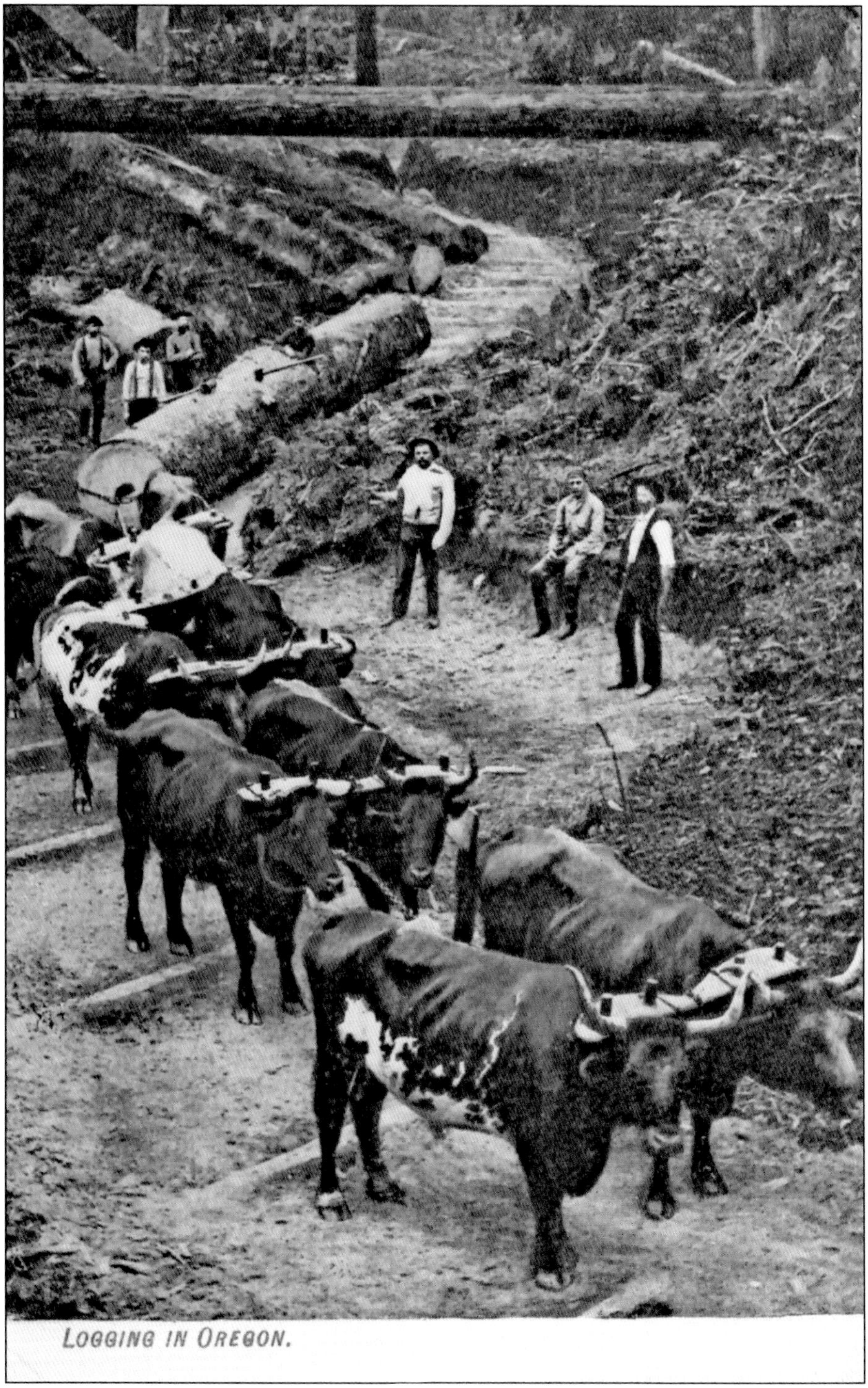

Teams of oxen appeared in logging camps around 1880. As the trees were harder to move and farther away from a water source, oxen were used to pull logs to the skid road and to a chute leading to water. The "bull puncher," the driver of the ox team, was critical to the operation. (Courtesy of Sara's Old Photos.)

Four

River Industry

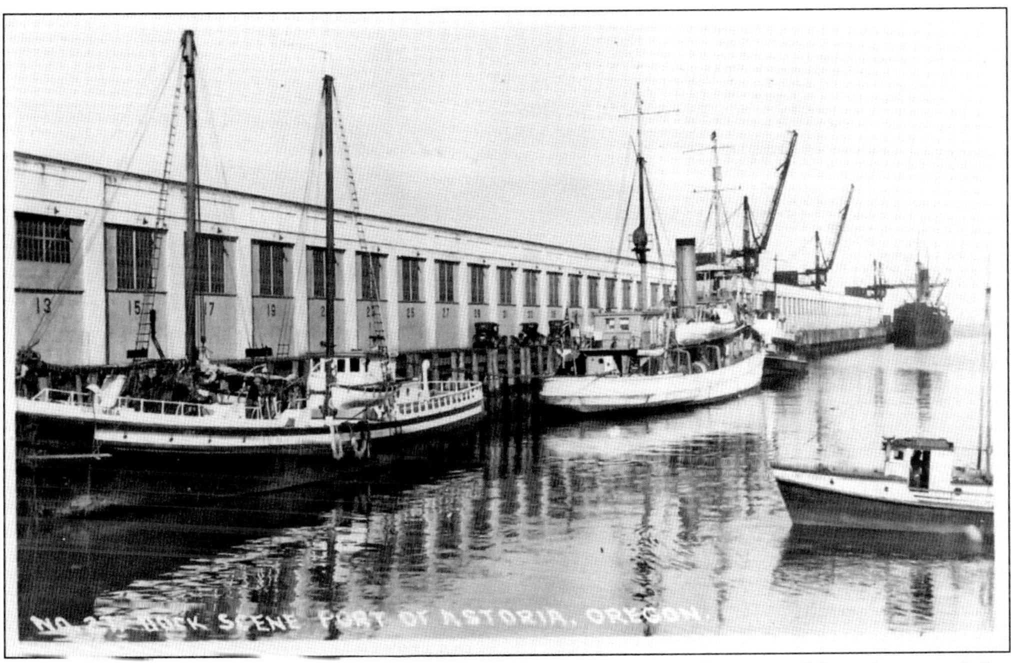

Here is a wonderful collection of working boats at Pier Three at the Port of Astoria around the 1930s. The Columbia River is truly an international superhighway hosting myriad forms of commerce and service. Pictured here, from left to right, are old *Columbia*, a bar pilot's schooner; the Coast Guard cutter *Unadaga*; a commercial tug boat; a freighter at a loading dock; and a fishing trawler entering in the foreground. (Courtesy of Michael Foster.)

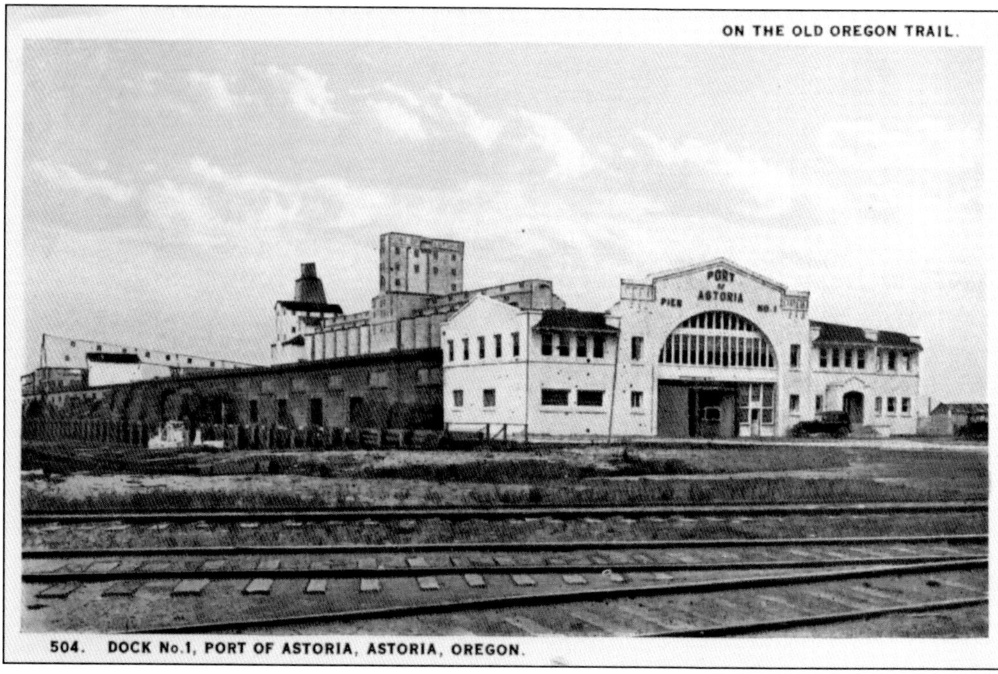

This c. 1927 postcard shows Pier One at the Port of Astoria. The building was constructed in 1919 and was in operation until the 1990s. When it was torn down, much care was taken to reclaim the valuable wood products used in its construction. It was reused in new construction projects regionally. The Pillsbury Flour Mill is in the background. Pier One had a 500,000-bushel capacity for sacked grain. (Courtesy of Michael Foster.)

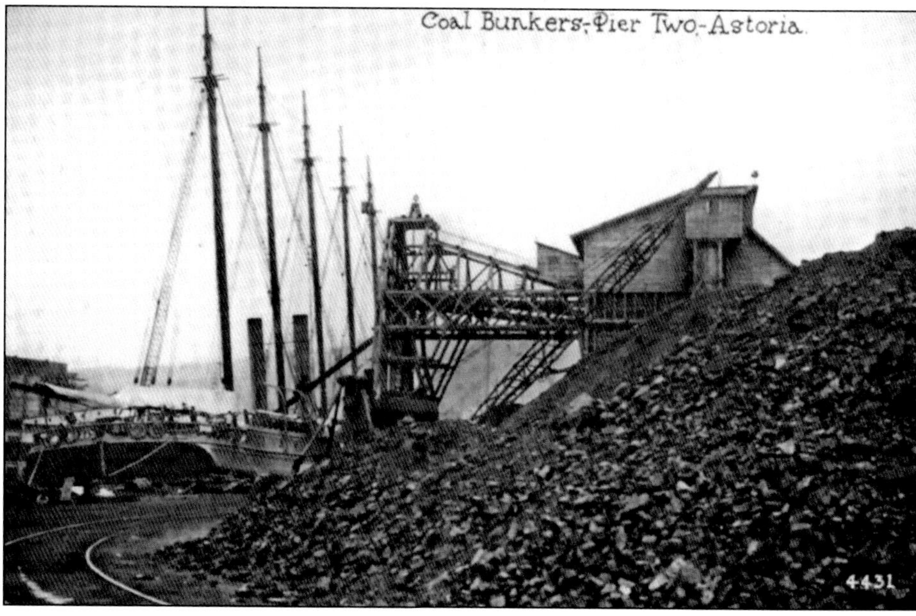

This picture illustrates the massive coal operation that was active for a short time at the Port of Astoria on Pier Two. The bunker had a capacity of 3,000 tons, with adjacent open storage space for an additional 20,000 tons. Ships were supplied directly from the bunker using electric conveyors at a rate of 175 tons per hour. (Courtesy of Sara's Old Photos.)

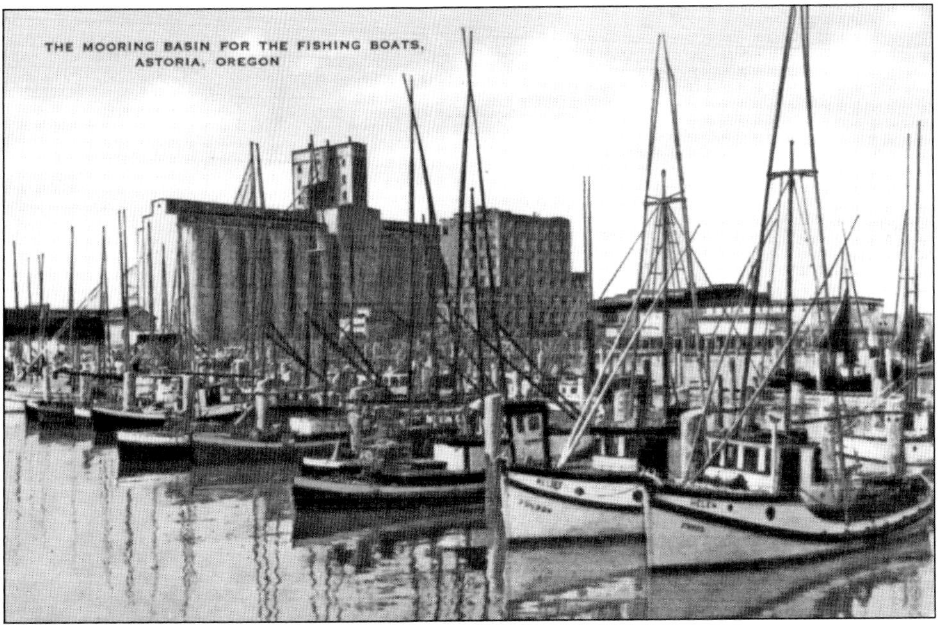

This idyllic image shows salmon trawlers moored at the west mooring basin with the Pillsbury Flour Mill in the background. The mill was built in 1914 and was in operation until 1961, when global economics forced its closure. It provided employment for many Astorians over the years. After sitting empty for 25 years, it was decided to bring down the buildings using dynamite. There are many stories about how many blasts it took to accomplish the task, plus an online video. (Courtesy of Michael Foster.)

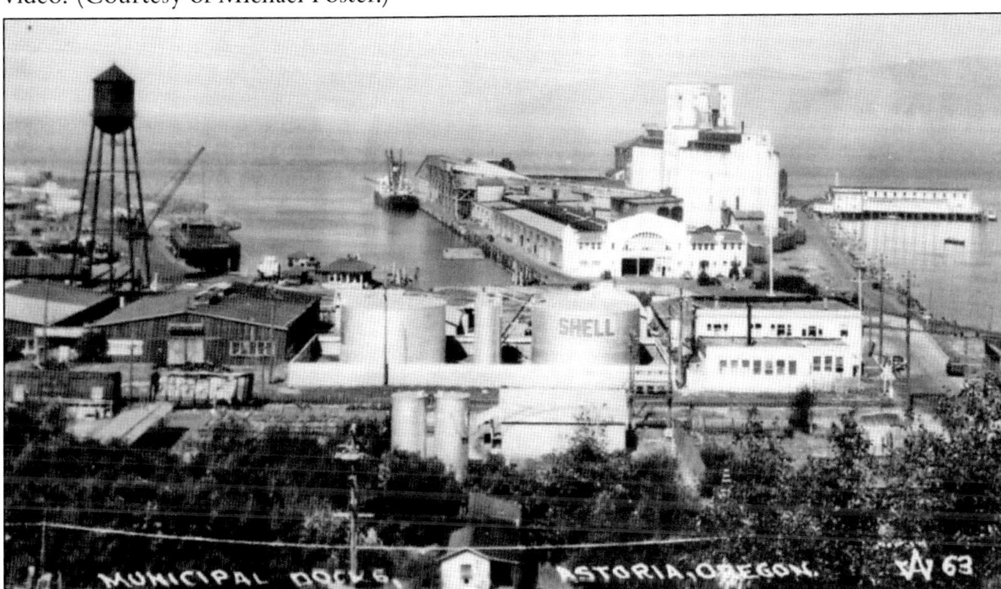

This 1950s real-photo postcard shows a busy industrial scene at the Port of Astoria. Also visible at upper right is the Barbey Packing Plant, built in 1926 on Pier One. The flour mill had a combined capacity of 4,000 barrels per day with a 1,250,000-bushel bulk grain elevator. The water tower to the left stood on port property since 1925, but it developed significant rust damage and was taken down in 2002. (Courtesy of Michael Foster.)

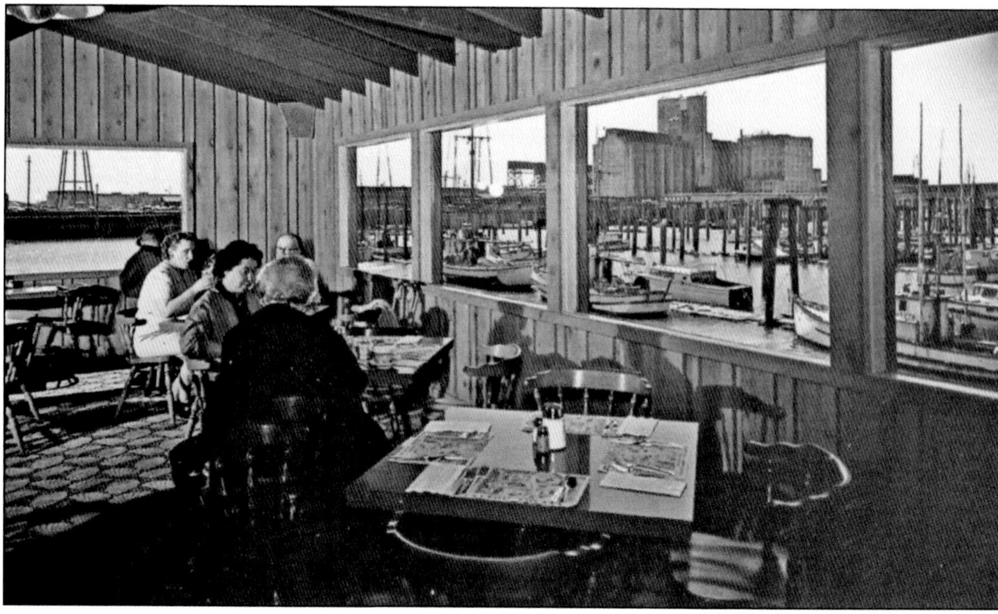

Featuring the interior of the Sea Fare Restaurant, this postcard shows the familiar view of pleasure and commercial fishing boats overlooking the busy Port of Astoria. The Sea Fare was Astoria's finest through the 1970s. It was also featured in scenes from *Kindergarten Cop* with Arnold Schwarzenegger. Several locals were extras in the filming throughout the project. (Courtesy of Michael Foster.)

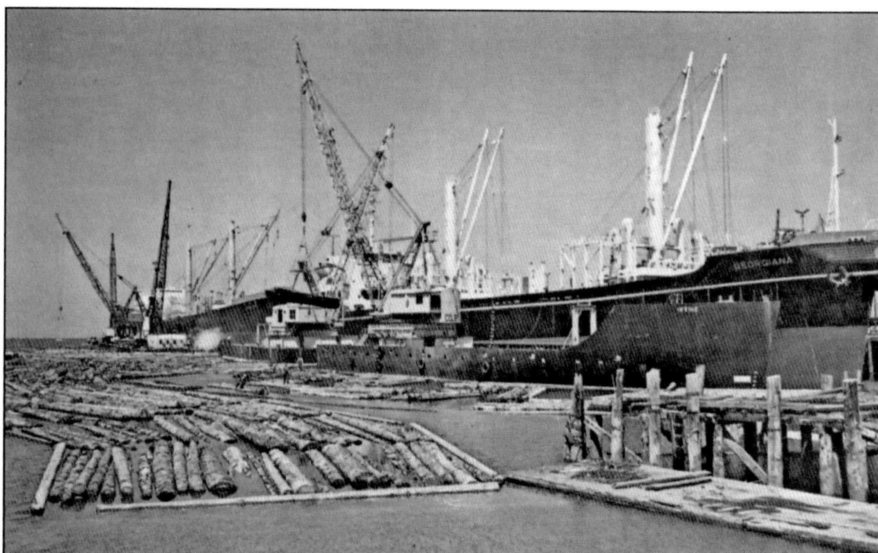

Logs are being loaded for export at Pier Two on the west side of the Port of Astoria. At the time of this 1960s image, the port received log rafts towed in by tugs and then loaded the timber on freighters to be shipped to all parts of the world. Water cranes were used to hoist log cargo before ships' gear was capable of lifting loads of logs into their holds. Log exporting was active through much of the 20th century. In the mid-1990s, market forces caused it to cease. The business returned to the Port of Astoria in 2010 and can be witnessed today. (Courtesy of Michael Soderberg.)

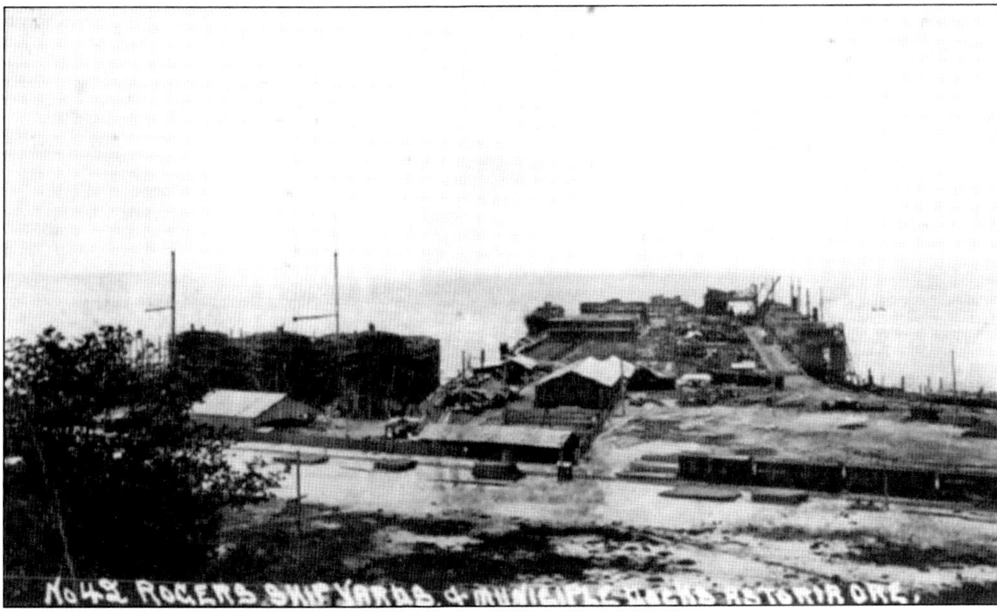

The Rogers Ship Building Yard, shown here about 1916, was located on Pier Two at the Port of Astoria. From the early 1900s through the World War II era, in addition to Rogers, there were three shipbuilders side by side on Young's Bay in the area of Smith Point near the port: Wilson, Columbia, and McEachern. Smith Point is named for Samuel Cole "Ticky" Smith, whose land claim included the area. (Author's collection.)

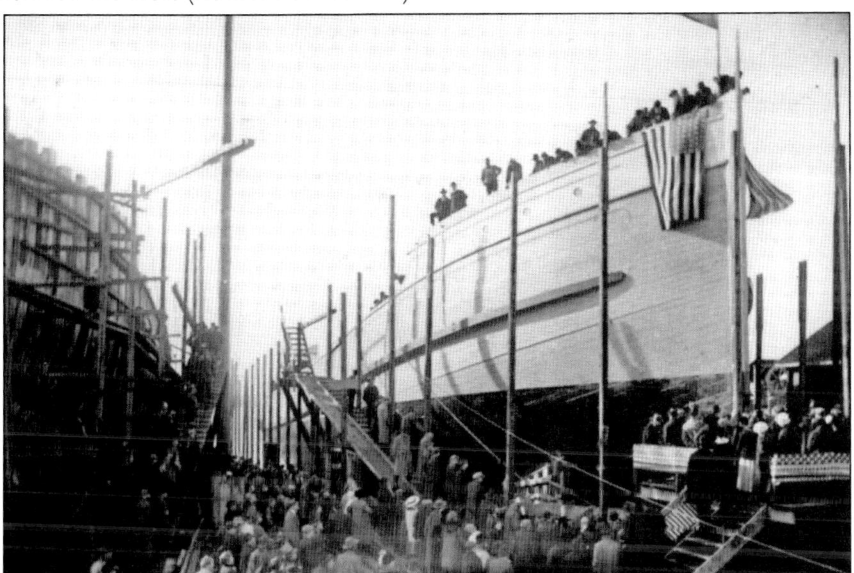

During the decades of operation on Young's Bay, Astoria shipbuilders produced transport and small gunboats for World War I, World War II, and the Korean War. Wilson Shipbuilding worked around the clock producing wooden freighters during World War II. Until 1917, Wilson Shipbuilding specialized in building cannery tenders for use in the local fishing industry. This is the 1916 launch of the *Wahkeena*, a 325-foot Ferris-type wood steamer, at the Wilson Boat Yard at Smith Point. Wilson also had a company band that performed at launchings. (Courtesy of Sara's Old Photos.)

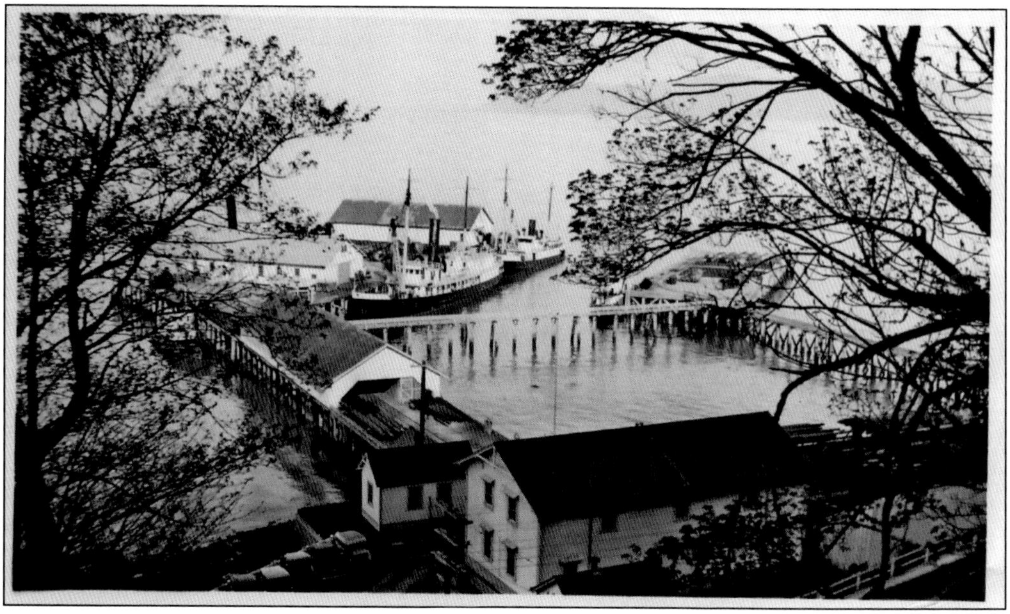

There were also federal operations present on the Columbia River at Tongue Point. This image shows the US Lighthouse Service facility that merged with the Coast Guard in 1939. The lightships *Relief* and *Swiftsure* (pictured) became part of the Coast Guard fleet. (Courtesy of Michael Foster.)

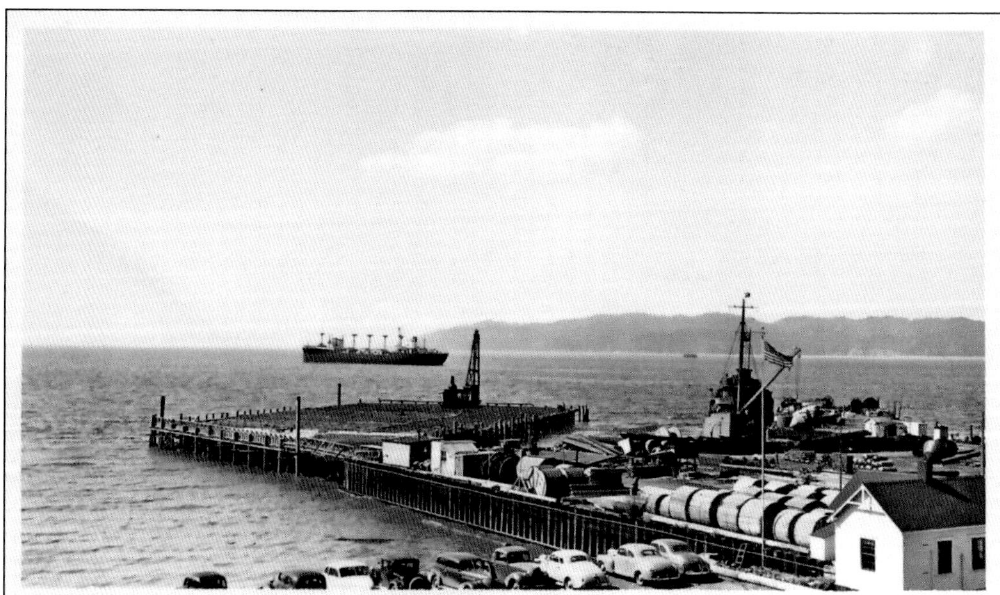

This postcard from the 1930s featuring an image by local photographer Frank Woodfield shows the Buoy Tender Port at Tongue Point. (Courtesy of Michael Foster.)

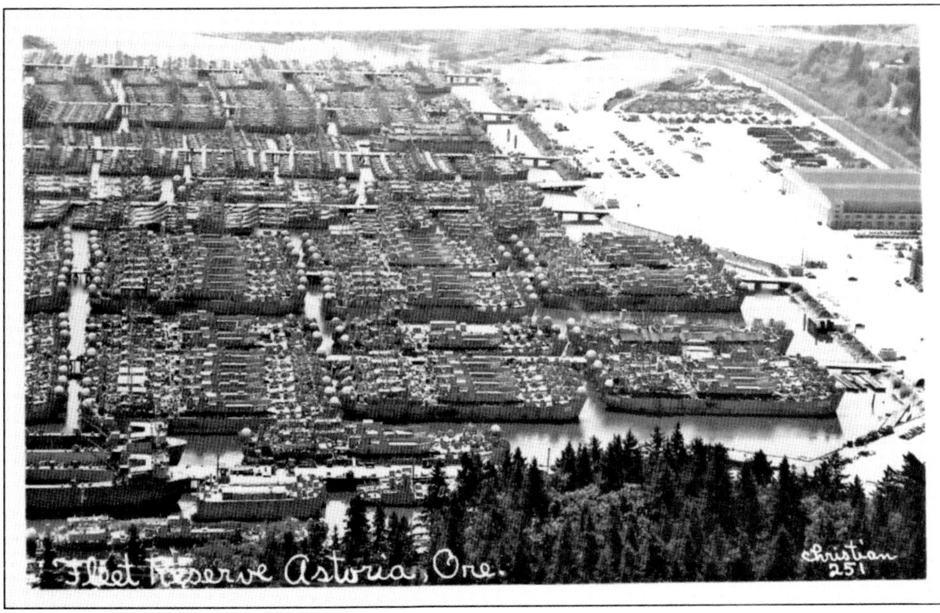

Tongue Point Naval Air Station was built and manned in 1940. After World War II, the US Navy built eight concrete piers to accommodate surplus warships, establishing the National Defense Reserve Fleet. The piers hosted over 900 vessels, including amphibious ships, destroyers, and fleet tugboats. Some were used in the Korean War. Some were redistributed to Suisun Bay and Bremerton, and the operation ceased in 1963. Many ships were converted and used for grain storage, but most were scrapped at Schnitzer Steel in Portland or sent to Japan. (Courtesy of Michael Foster.)

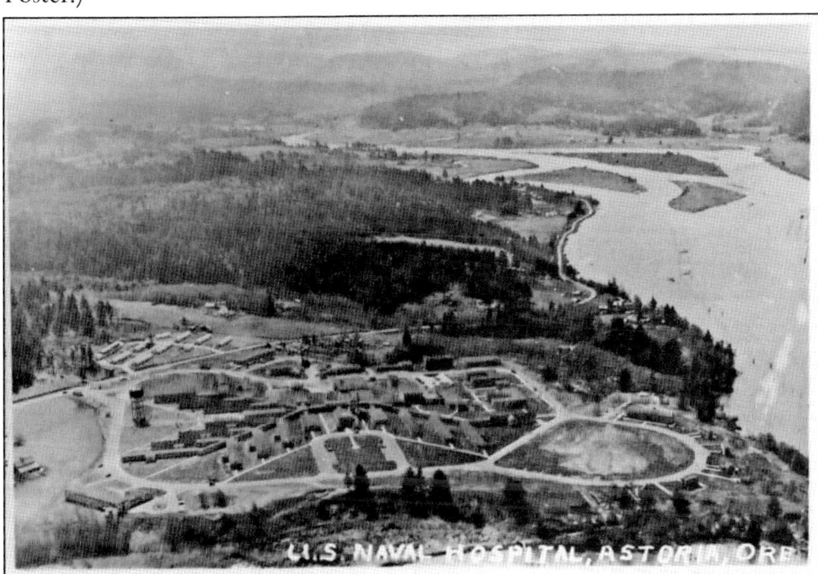

In support of the US Navy operations in the Lower Columbia region, an extensive naval hospital complex was built across Young's Bay off Highway 202. It stood ready for an influx of war casualties that never materialized. The only remnant of this entire facility is the foundation of the water tower and garage. The land is now an upscale housing development called River Point. (Author's collection.)

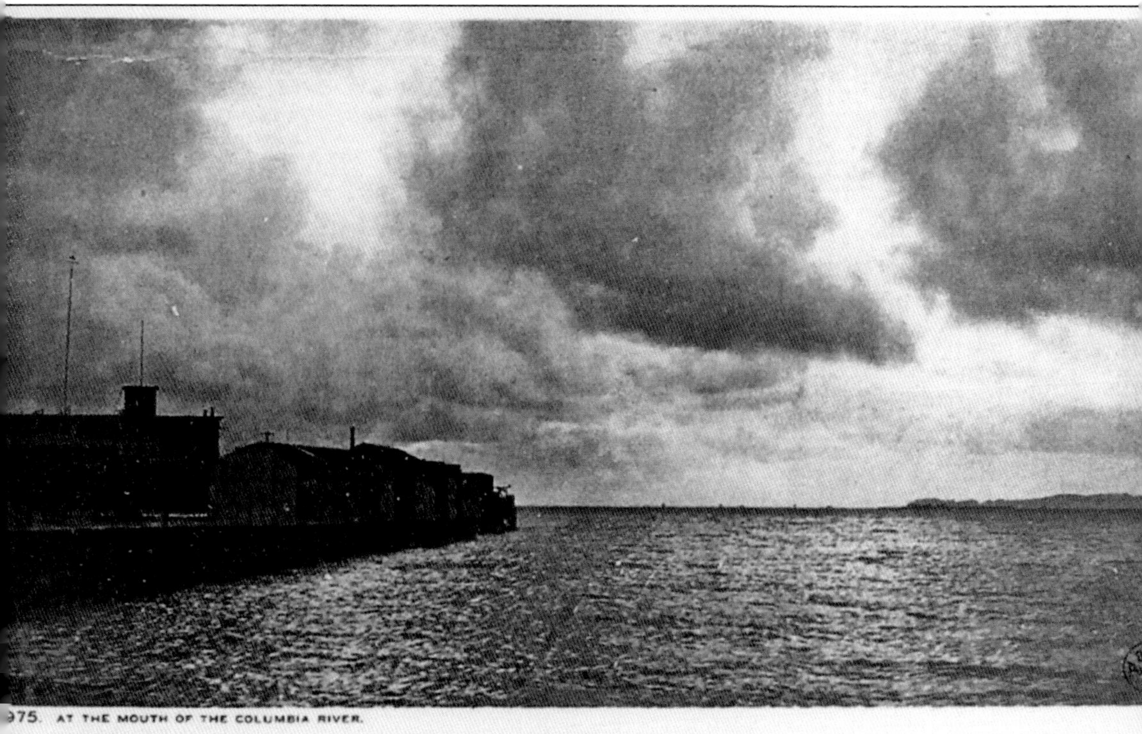

A serene Columbia River scene at dusk is seen around 1900. With all of the important business and activity on the river, this is an unusual image with not a single watercraft. The building on the waterfront was called the "Armory" and was used for military purposes. It also served as the viewing stands during the annual regatta festivities. The Parker House hotel is the structure in the background. It was built in 1883 and was considered one of the finest hotels in Astoria until 1937, when it was torn down. (Author's collection.)

Five

CELEBRATION

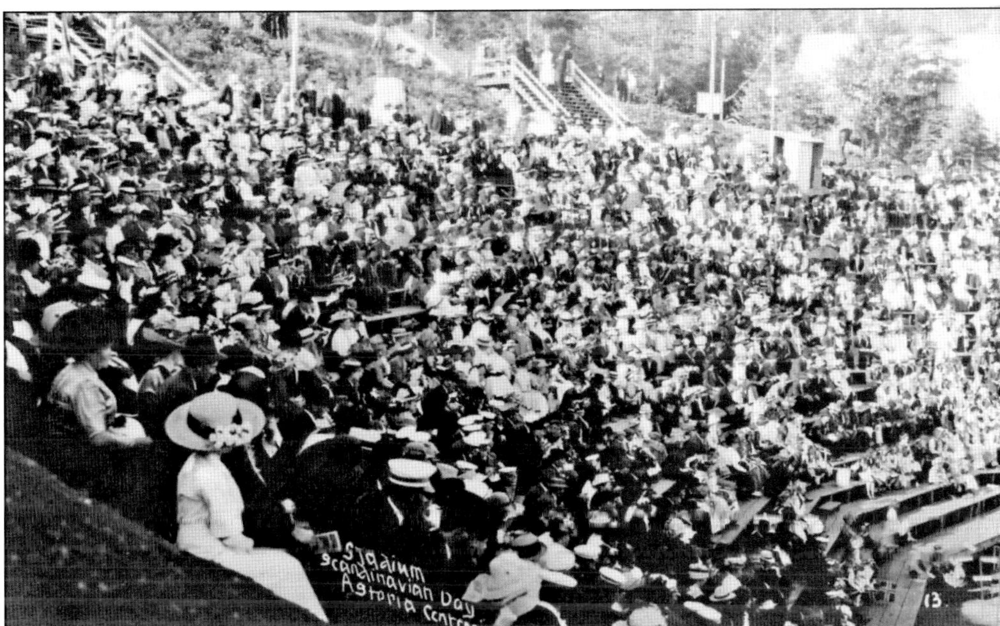

The grand stadium at Centennial Park is seen on Scandinavian Day during the official 30-day centennial celebration that began on August 9, 1911. Funds from the Oregon state legislature, a Clatsop County tax levy, and donations from Col. John Jacob Astor and local businesses made it possible. Visitors from all corners were able to travel to Astoria at reduced railroad rates as well. Centennial Park was in the area of today's Shively Park. Named for John Shively, the land was deeded to the City of Astoria in 1898 and developed for the 1911 anniversary. (Courtesy of Michael Foster.)

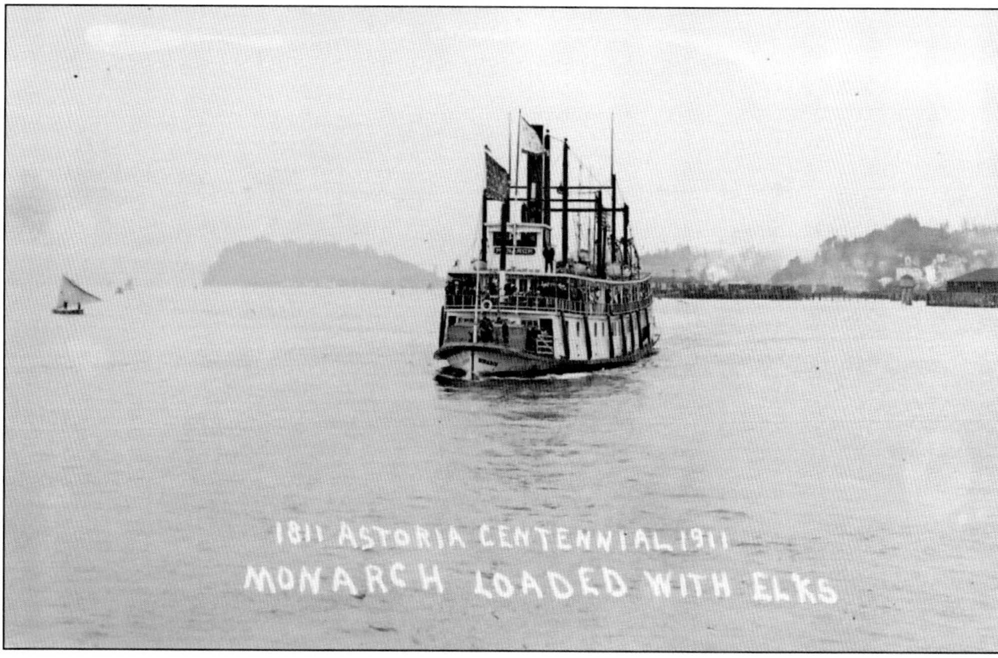

The steamboat *Monarch* arrives during the Astoria centennial with a cargo of Elks. The Elks were a well-established fraternal organization and hosted members from around the region. The *Monarch* had just been recently renamed after being called the *Charles R. Spencer* since its launch in 1901. It was considered one of the elite vessels of its time and was known for its bright red smokestack and extremely loud whistle. (Courtesy of Michael Foster.)

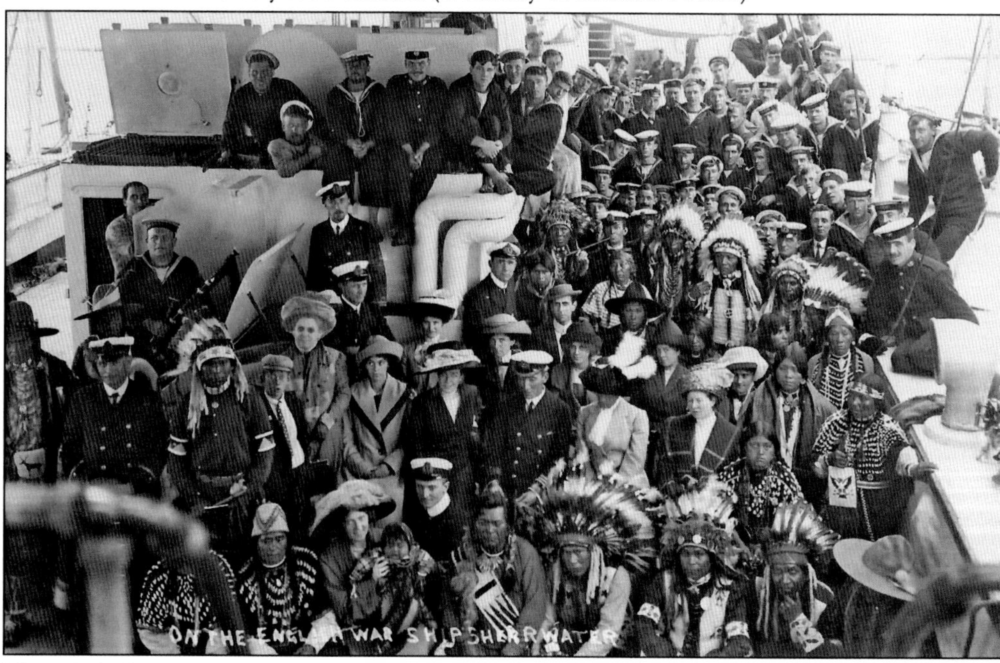

The HMS *Shearwater* was a Condor-class sloop launched in 1900. It served on the Pacific station of the British Royal Navy and participated in Astoria's centennial. Pictured is an interesting and varied group enjoying a tour and possible river voyage aboard the vessel. (Courtesy of Michael Foster.)

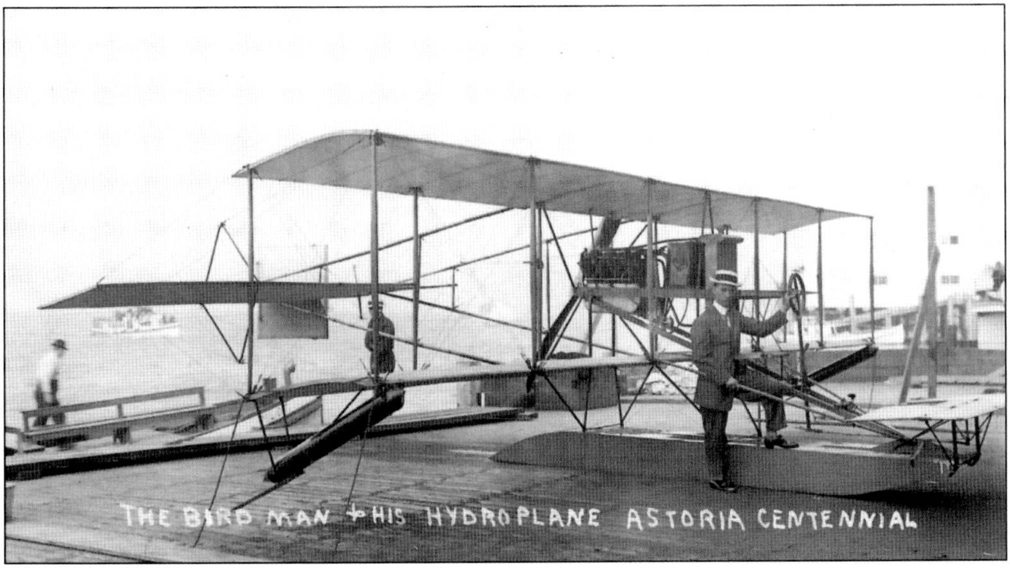

The "Birdman" and his hydroplane, pictured at the river's edge, was another of the many imported entertainment highlights and new-fangled spectacles at the centennial celebration. This is almost certainly Silas Christofferson, who became famous in 1912 for flying his hydroplane from the top of Portland's Multnomah Hotel and landing across the Willamette River in Vancouver, Washington. Silas's brother Harry was also a performer, but to a much lesser degree. The plane could fly at a speed of 50 mph with an 80-horsepower engine. The Curtiss-type plane consisted of steel, wood, and cloth. It carried enough fuel to fly 70 miles. (Courtesy of Michael Foster.)

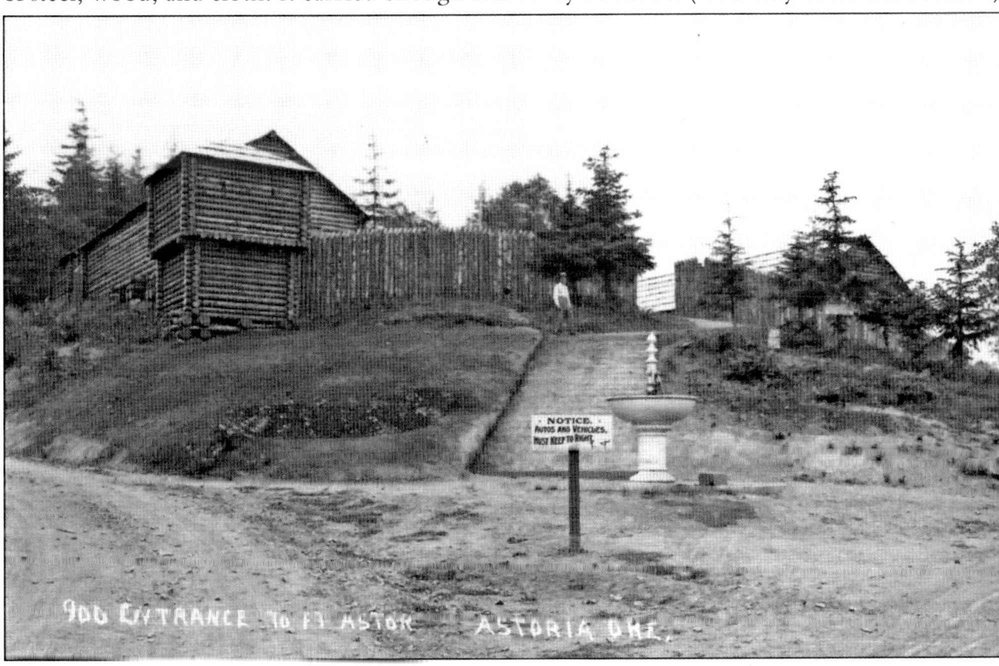

One of the centerpieces of the 1911 celebration was Centennial Park, located in the area that is now Shively Park. Pictured here is the reconstruction of the original Fort Astoria. The fountain in the foreground was saved and recently restored. It can be seen at the Maritime Memorial Park, directly under the Astoria-Megler Bridge in Uniontown. (Courtesy of Michael Foster.)

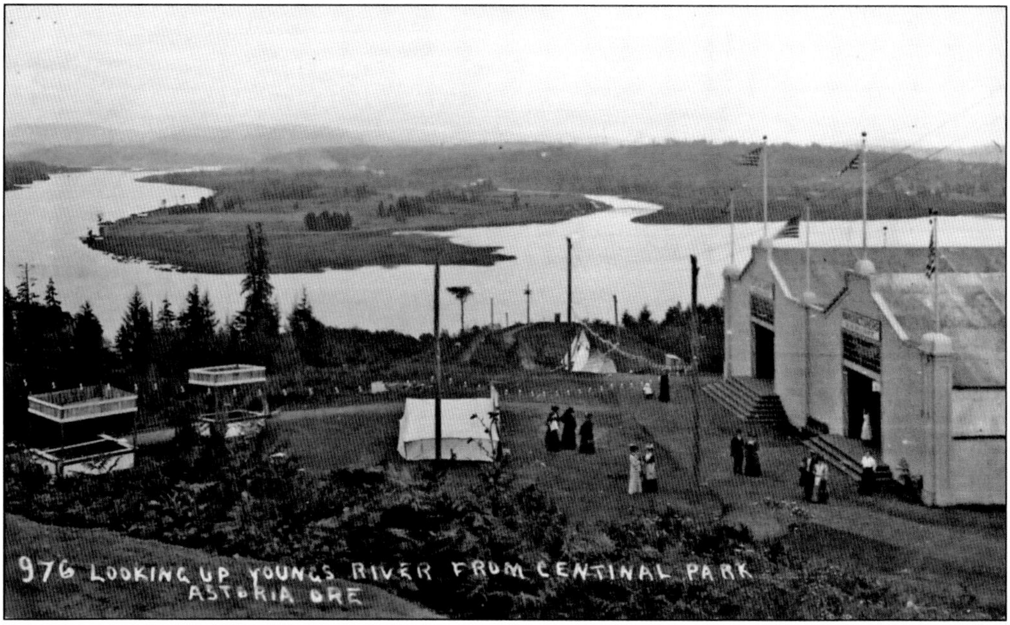

Another view of Centennial Park, in the area of today's Shively Park, shows the display halls, with Indian display teepees beyond. The landscape was designed by Arthur L. Peck, who developed the landscape architecture discipline at Oregon Agricultural College (now Oregon State University). Most of the Centennial Park features fell into disrepair over time and were gone within 20 years. In the 1920s, a meeting hall was constructed and remains in use today. (Courtesy of Michael Foster.)

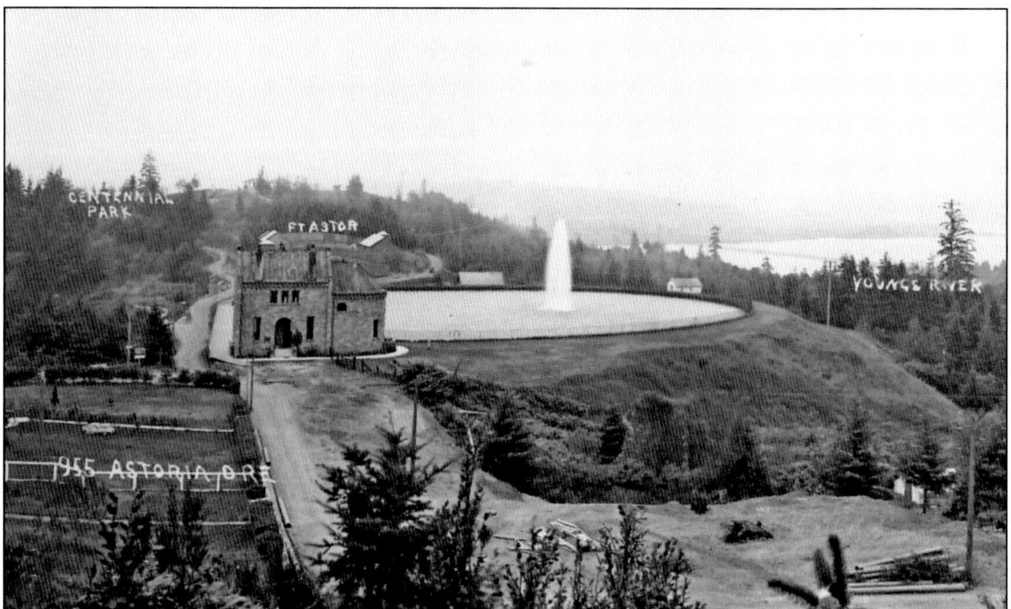

Many postcards have been produced of the Astoria Waterworks. This particular one was made during the centennial to show its proximity to Centennial Park. Still in use today, Reservoir Two (as it known) was completed in 1895 after a volatile strike by Italian stonemasons. The facility stores 5.5 million gallons of water and looks almost exactly like this today. (Courtesy of Michael Foster.)

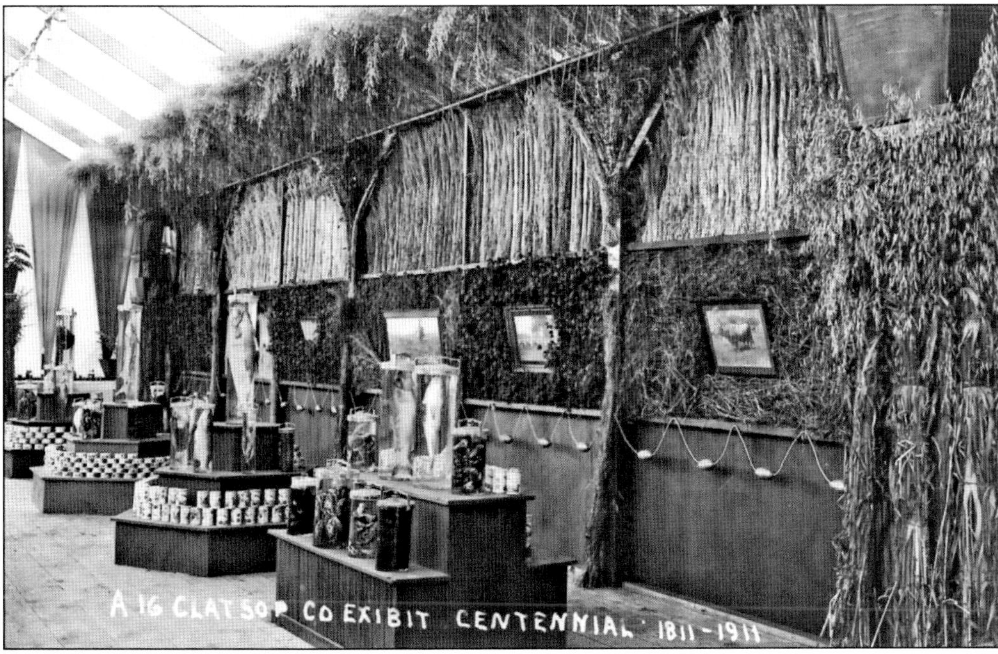

This centennial exhibit hall focused on the local bounty. Displays include fish, crabs, and dairy cows. Note the elaborate decorations on the walls using natural products. (Courtesy of Michael Foster.)

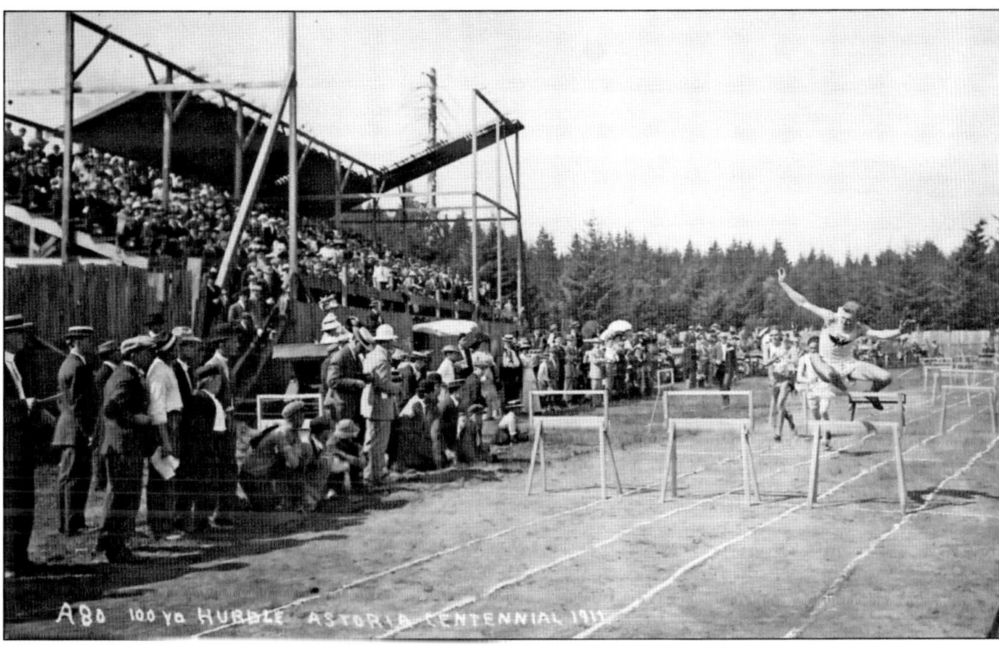

The Astoria track grounds and stands that existed prior to the centennial are pictured here. Displays of athletic ability and competition were always popular features at any event. This location is estimated to be near the area of Third Street and Niagara Avenue, on the top of the hill. (Courtesy of Michael Foster.)

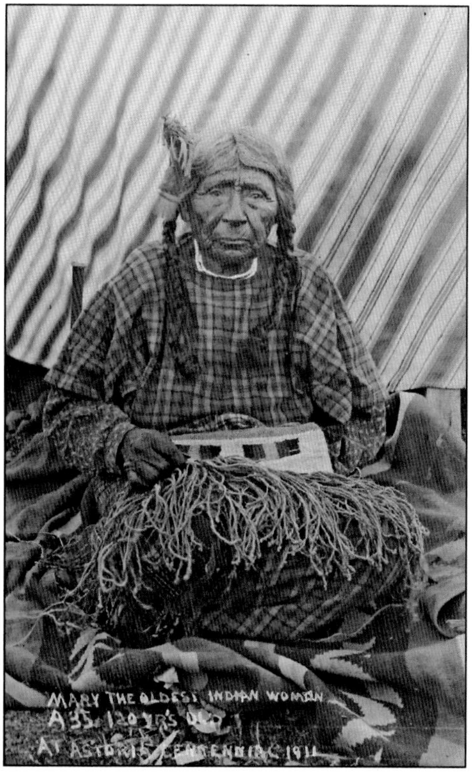

Mary lived in Seaside and was quite the photographed lady during her days. Of course she was very popular at the 1911 centennial. She was said to be a child of the chief of the Clatsops. She is also credited with the identification of the Lewis and Clark salt works and the site of Fort Clatsop. The ancestral village of the Clatsop tribe is said to be on the shore of Young's Bay, just south of the current Astoria High School. No remnants remain. (Courtesy of Michael Foster.)

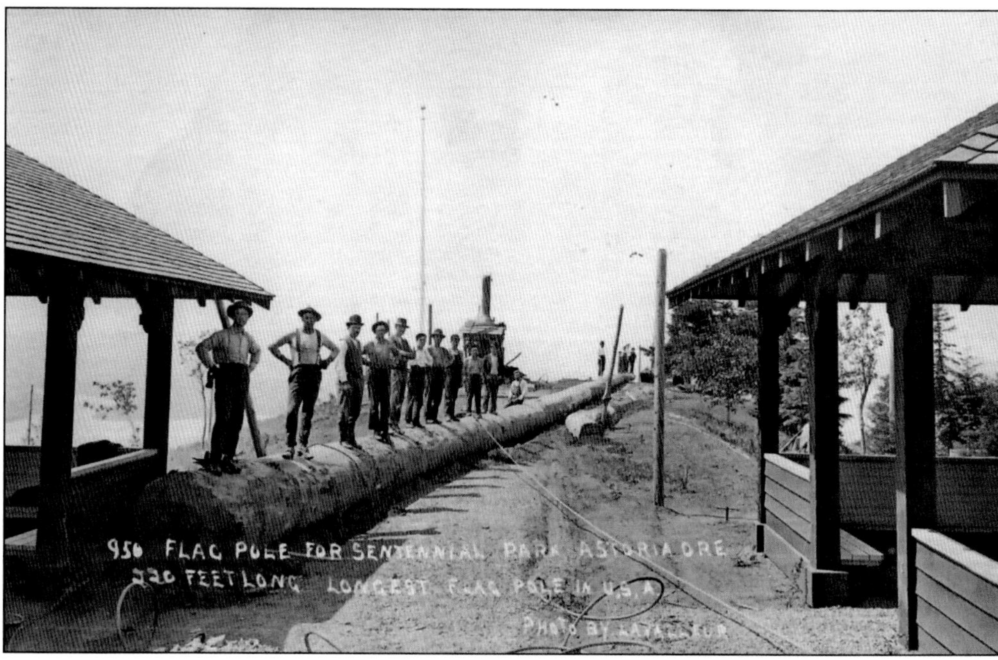

Every effort was made to show off Astoria and its resources during the centennial celebration. Raising a 220-foot-long flagpole seemed like a good idea until an attempt was made place it. It could not be lifted, even with the steam donkey in the picture. It snapped on the way up. The structures on either side are shelters at Shively Park. (Courtesy of Michael Foster.)

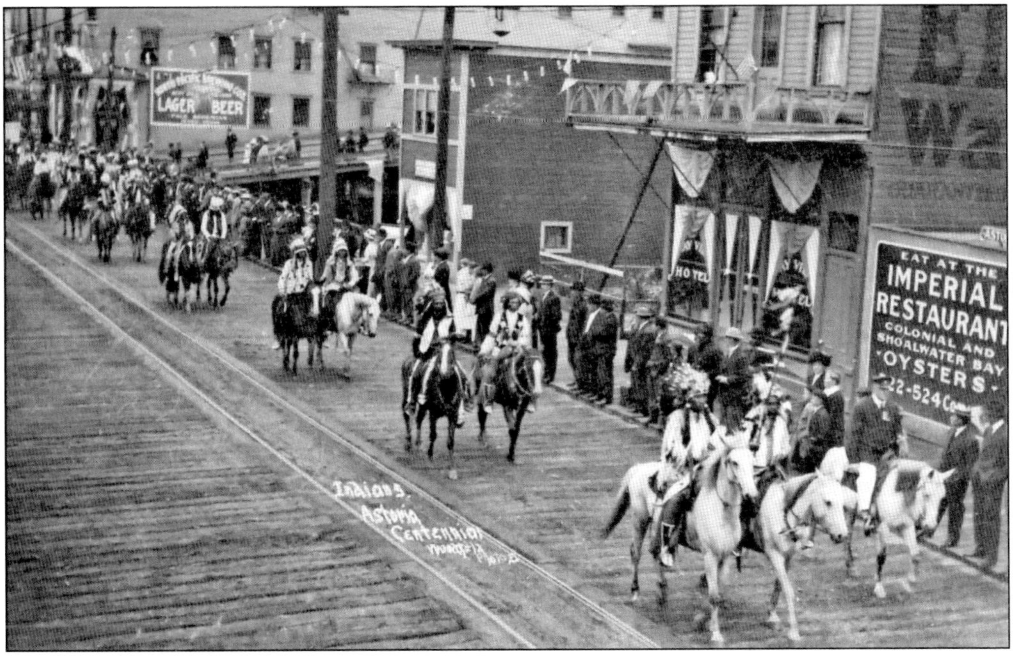

Early Native American culture in the Lower Columbia region included the Chinook on the Washington side and the Clatsops in Oregon. During the centennial, delegations from the Yakima and Nez Perce nations attended. The Yakima had their encampment at Centennial Park. All Native Americans posed in regalia during their stay. Traditionally, neither the Clatsops or Chinook donned feathered headdresses or rode horses. (Courtesy of Michael Foster.)

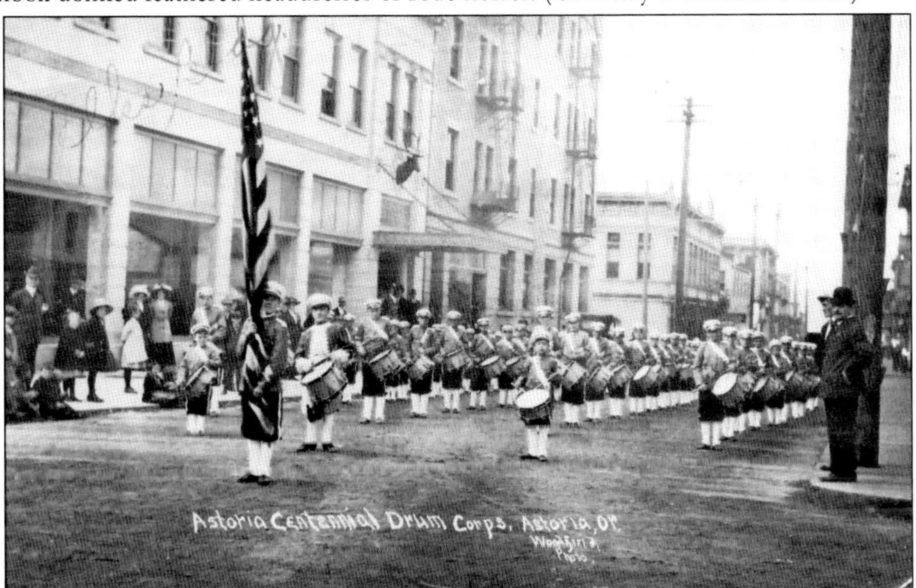

As the centennial parade proceeded, many groups lined up on side streets, much as parades do today. Here, the drum corps waits in front of the Elks building on Eleventh Street. Note the elk bust over the door. The Astoria Elks lodge was the second chartered in Oregon. The building was completed in 1910 and burned in 1922. The message on the reverse of this card reads, "Contrary to the rule, it is a fine, bright day!" (Courtesy of Michael Foster.)

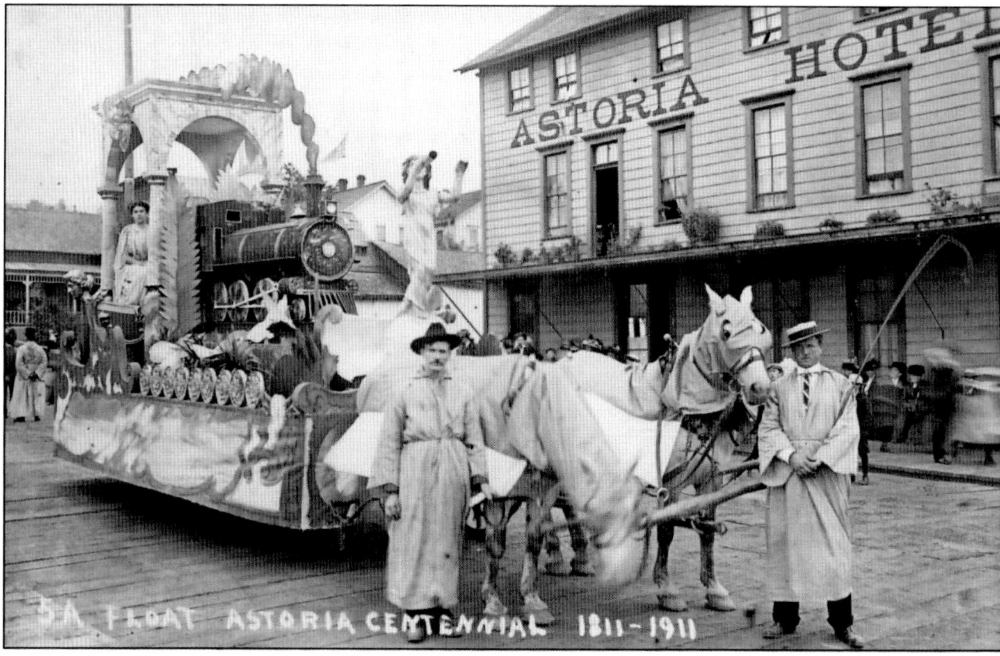

Another elaborate float honors the railroads. The Astoria Hotel was on Seventeenth Street. It was originally called O'Brien's and dates from the 1870s. (Courtesy of Michael Foster.)

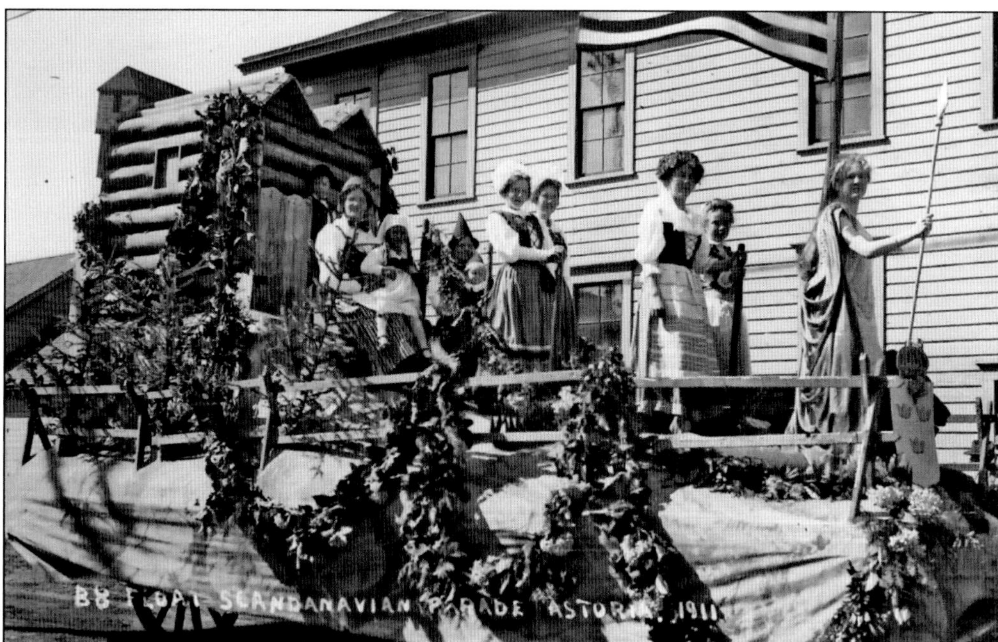

Due to Astoria's deep connections to Scandinavia, it was most appropriate to have a float honoring the heritage of the majority of its residents. These riders wear clothing specific to their country of origin, and a sauna is also aboard, an important aspect of life across Scandinavia. Many homes in Astoria still have saunas. (Courtesy of Michael Foster.)

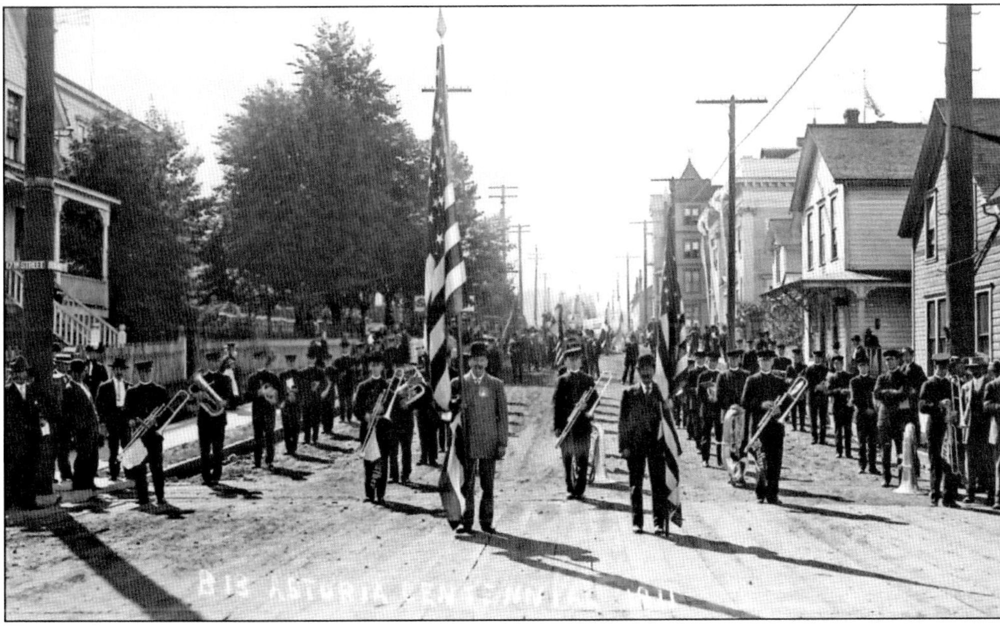

The centennial parade route proceeded down Exchange Street. Here the group stops at the corner of Seventeenth and Exchange Streets. The city hall and St. Mary's Hospital are on the right, a block down. Note the plank roads. As seen in many previous images, much of downtown was built on pilings over tidelands at the river's edge. The pilings, along with the wooden streets and sidewalks, needed constant maintenance. However, this didn't stop promoters from describing Astoria as the "Venice of the West." (Courtesy of Michael Foster.)

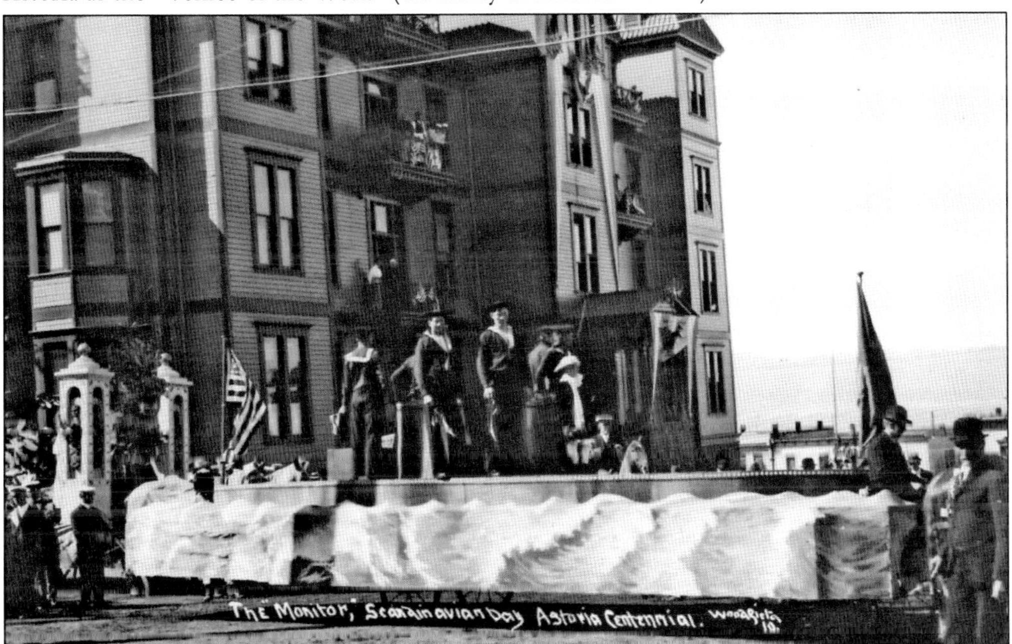

This centennial parade image is included for its clear view of St. Mary's Hospital. Notice the nurses on the balcony and the river to the right, with Washington hills in the distance. This was a very clear day near Sixteenth and Exchange Streets. (Courtesy of Michael Foster.)

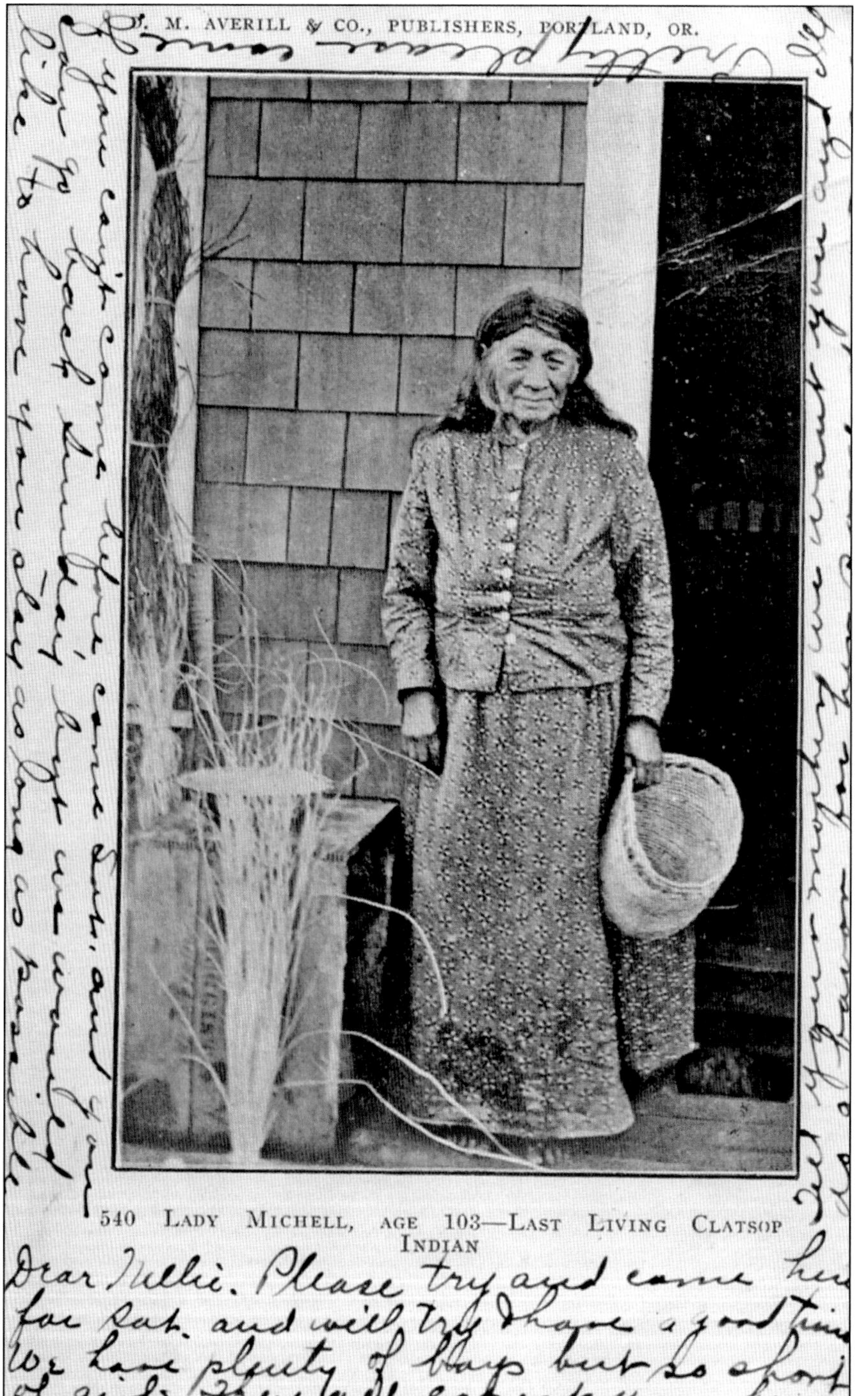

Tsin-is-tum was also known as Jennie Michell. She was said to be the last living member of the Clatsop tribe. She was known for her baskets and for going everywhere barefoot. She was known as Jennie most often in Astoria but "Michelle" in Seaside. She was one of the most photographed people of her day. (Courtesy of Clatsop County Historical Society.)

Begun in 1894, the Astoria Regatta is the oldest celebration hosted in the city. From its humble beginnings as an effort to welcome fishermen home from summers in Alaska, it grew into an annual gathering for boat racing enthusiasts, competitive anglers, and revelers. It has happened annually with breaks only resulting from the Great Fire of 1922 and World War II. Pictured here is the sailboat *CorsAir* in an undated postcard. (Courtesy of Michael Foster.)

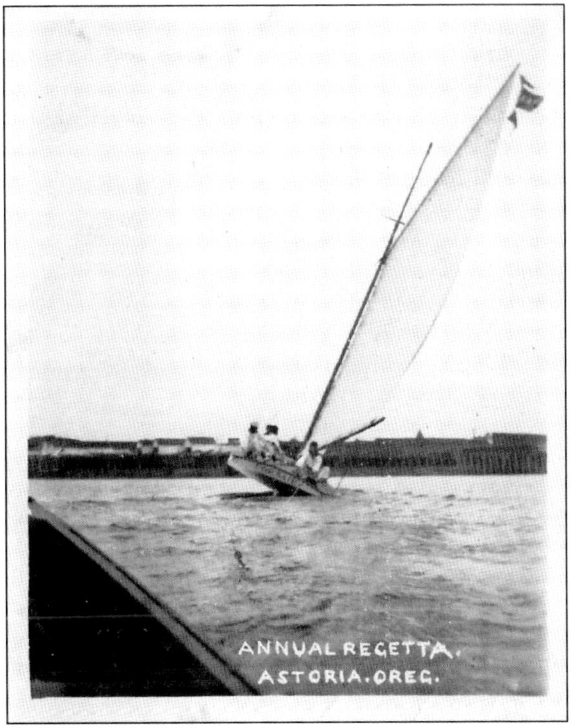

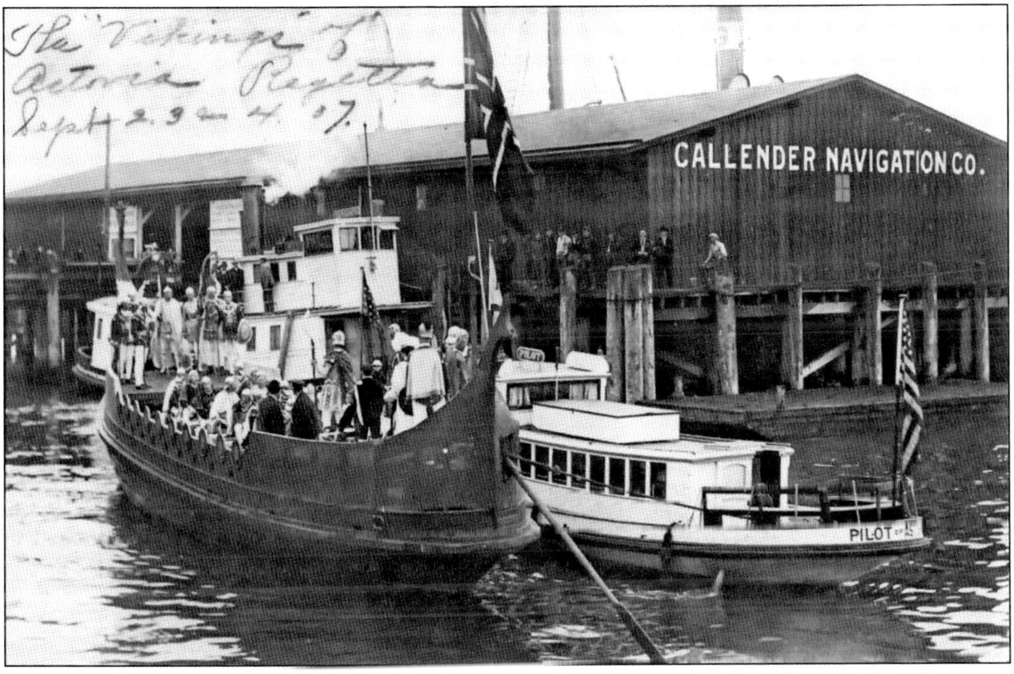

In addition to the competitions on the river, many other opportunities for fun and frivolity were presented, such as this arrival of a Viking ship being guided in by the river pilot boat for the 1907 regatta at the Callender Navigation Co. dock, at the foot of Twelfth Street. This original building was converted to an iron-clad "cribbed sand bunker" in 1922. By 1940, it was being used as a welding shop. (Courtesy of Michael Foster.)

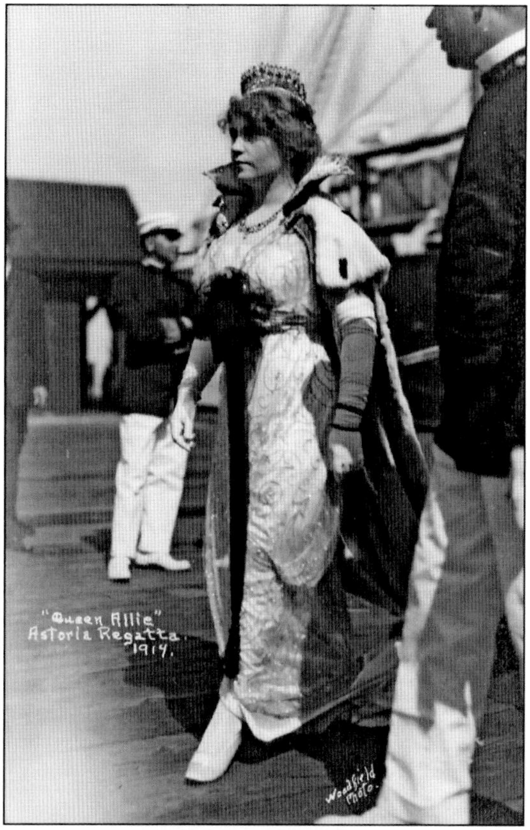

Every year, a Regatta Queen is crowned to begin the festivities, and she and her court reign with dignity and grace during the events, such as banquets, parades, dances, and boat launchings. Over the decades, many local young ladies have enjoyed this honor. (Courtesy of Michael Foster.)

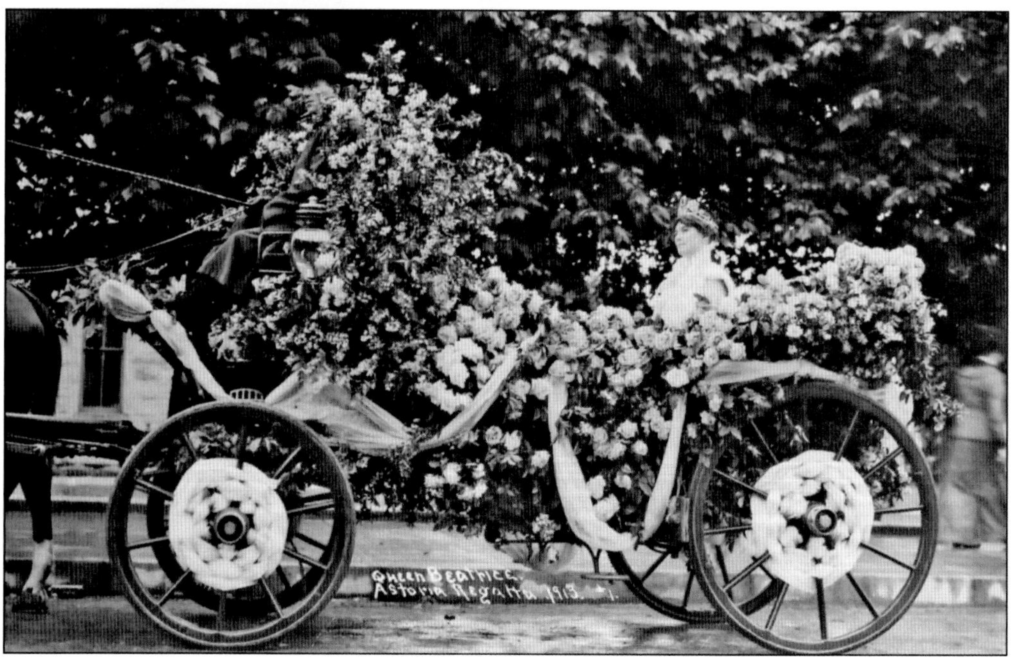

The 1913 Regatta Queen, Beatrice, rides in her splendid horse-drawn carriage, possibly reflecting on the day and giving thanks for good weather. (Courtesy of Michael Foster.)

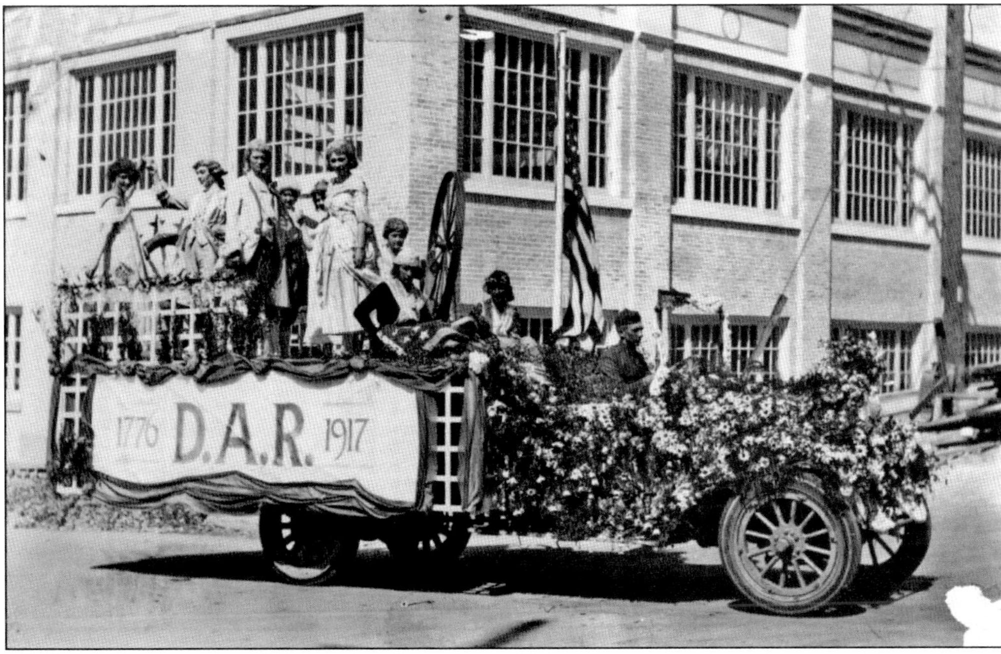

The Astoria chapter of the Daughters of the American Revolution was chartered in 1921 and has worked since then to preserve and highlight the history of the area. Many historic markers and projects exist, and the list is still being added to today. Here is the DAR float in the regatta parade near the Lovell Building on Exchange Street. The Lovell Building was built in 1919 and helps date this image. (Courtesy of Clatsop County Historical Society 96.046.006.WC.)

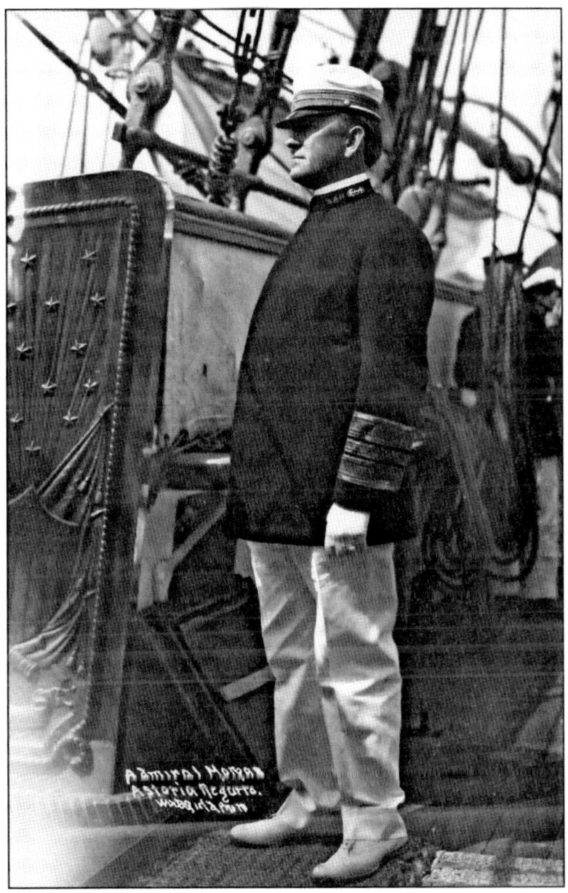

In addition to a Regatta Queen, there must be an Admiral named annually. Today, this honor usually goes to a prominent volunteer, supporter, or organizer for recognition of his efforts on behalf of the community. In the early days, it was often a ship's captain or visiting mariner of some stripe. (Courtesy of Michael Foster.)

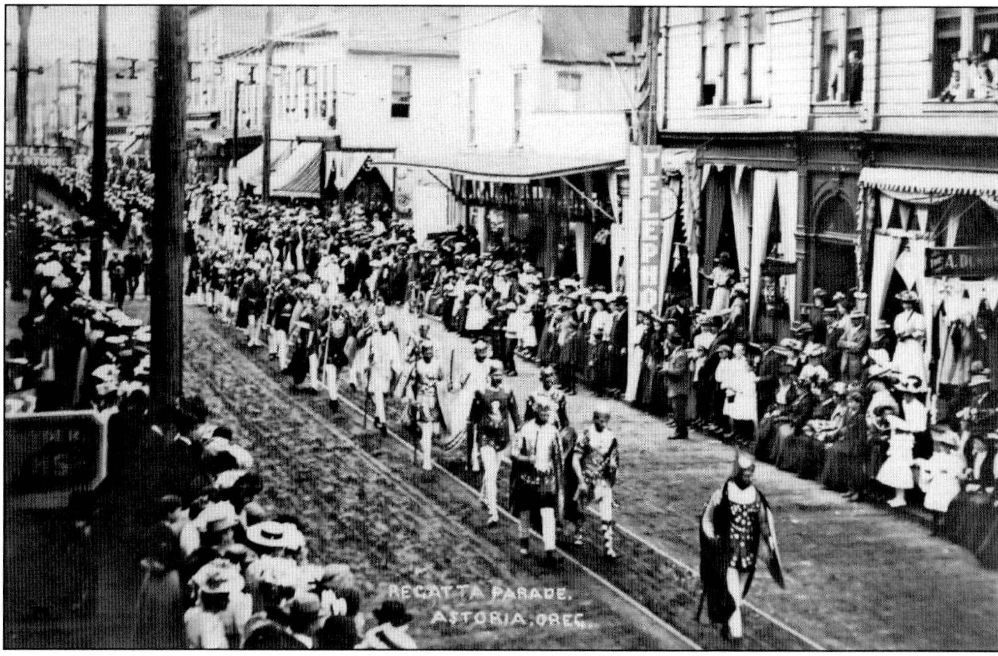

The Vikings have landed and have entered the regatta parade on Commercial Street in this undated image. Noting the planked streets, trolley tracks, and light posts, it is estimated to be the mid-to-late-1890s. (Courtesy of Michael Foster.)

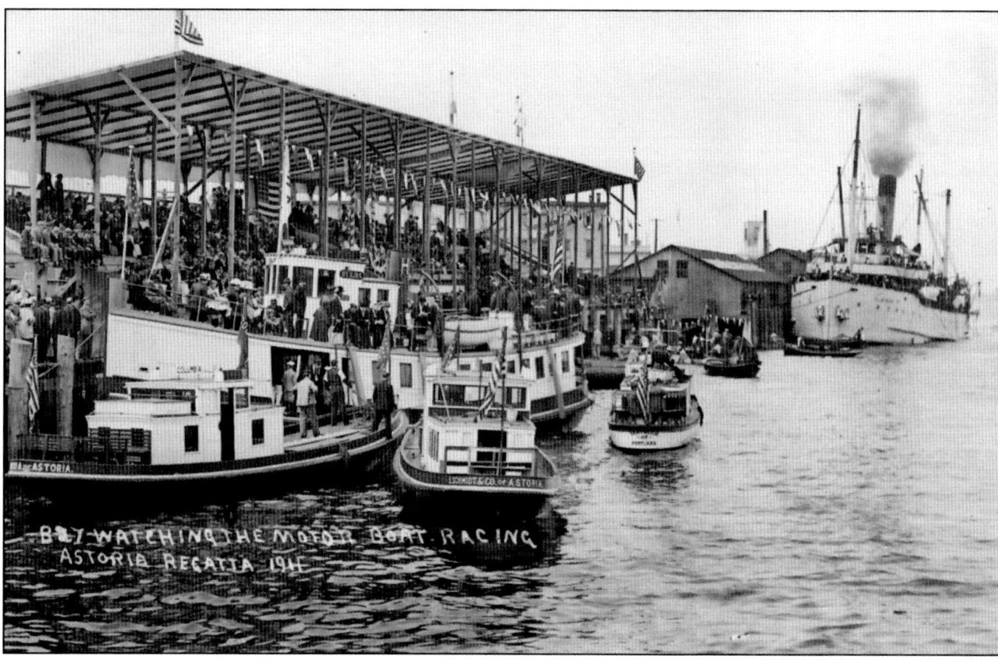

From these viewing stands near the area of today's Columbia River Maritime Museum, regatta attendees could enjoy all the events on the river and possibly jump aboard one of the many watercraft coming by at any time. In this scene from 1911, a cannery tender, a steamboat, various pleasure craft, gillnet boats, and a Navy ship are all available. (Courtesy of Michael Foster.)

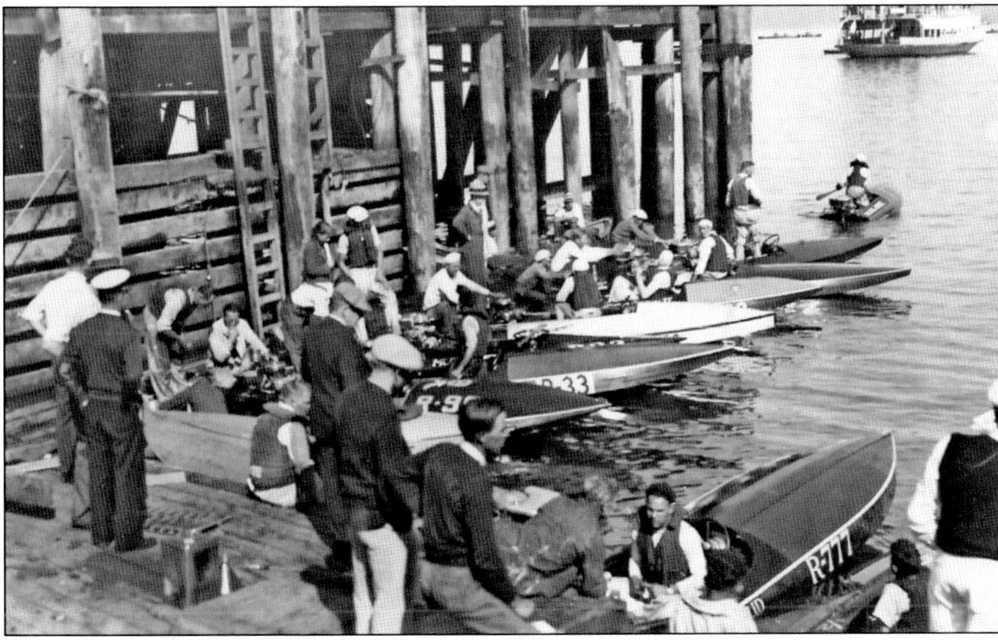

The races of the Pacific Coast Championships were a highlight at the regatta for many years. Here, teams ready themselves and their craft for the competition near the Fourteenth Street ferry launch on the waterfront. Note the ferry heading out in the upper right of this c. 1940 image. (Courtesy of Michael Foster.)

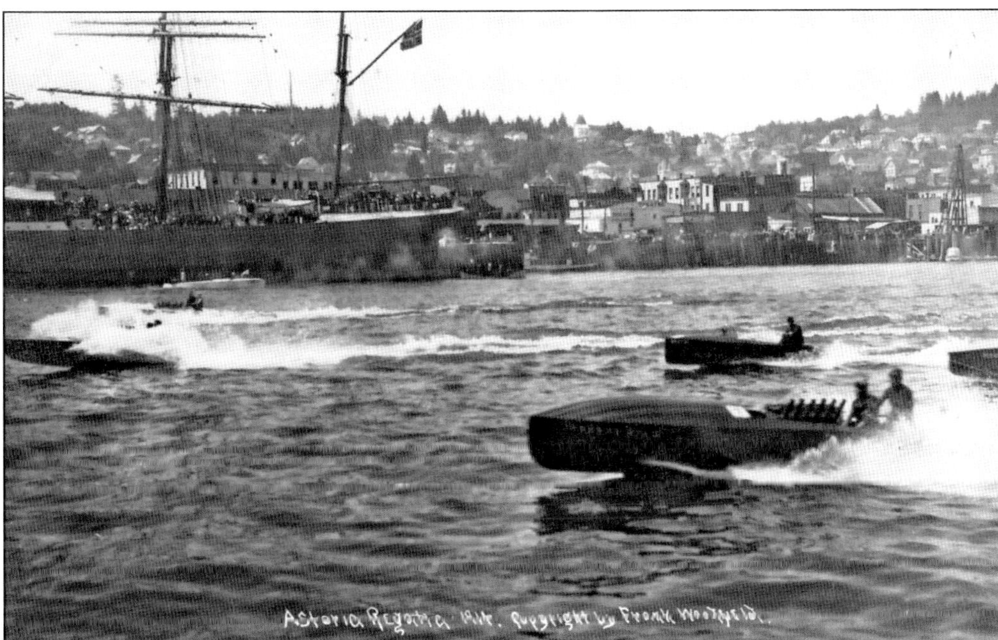

Boat races emerged as the central events at Astoria's annual regatta. Here, in 1914, local photographer Frank Woodfield captures the scene on the river with the bustling waterfront of Astoria in the background. Again, many different types of watercraft are present. (Courtesy of Michael Foster.)

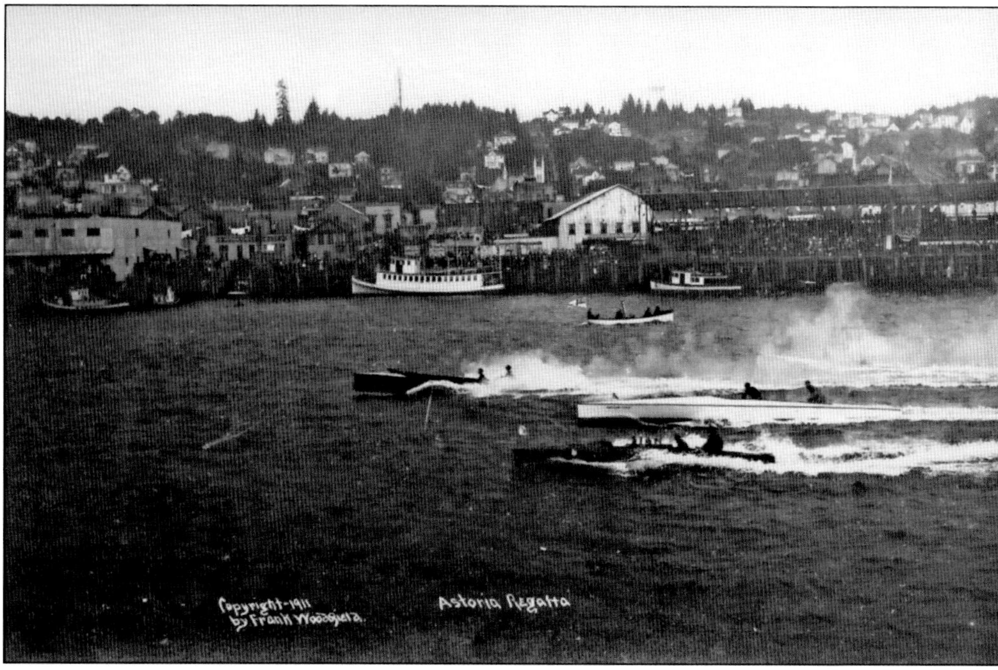

The viewing stands are visible along the waterfront, as is a tight finish for the racers in this 1911 regatta postcard with an image by Frank Woodfield. (Courtesy of Michael Foster.)

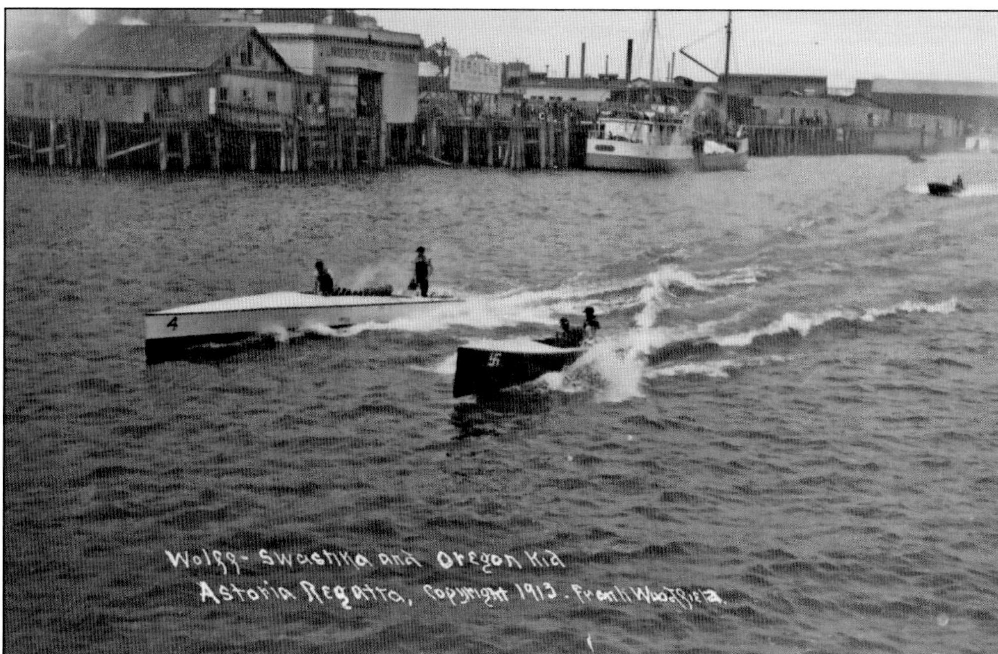

In the last of the racing photographs by Woodfield, one boat emblazoned with a swastika races the *Oregon Kid* at the 1913 regatta. The photograph provides a nice view of the working waterfront of Astoria at the time. (Courtesy of Michael Foster.)

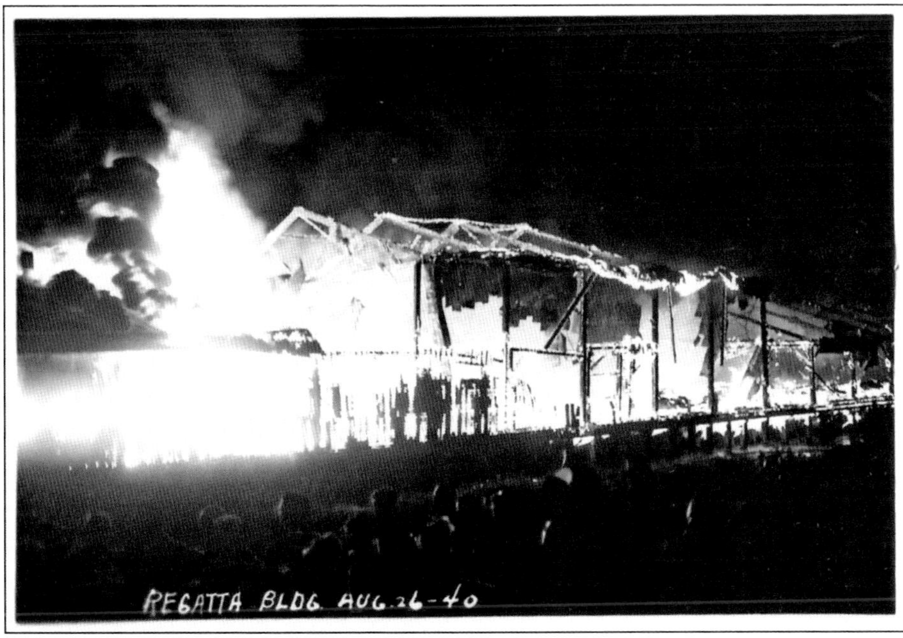

Known by locals as the "Regatta Pavilion," the structure at the foot of Sixteenth Street, used as viewing stands during the regatta and an armory for military and storage purposes otherwise, burned down just around the time of the events in August 1940. (Courtesy of Michael Foster.)

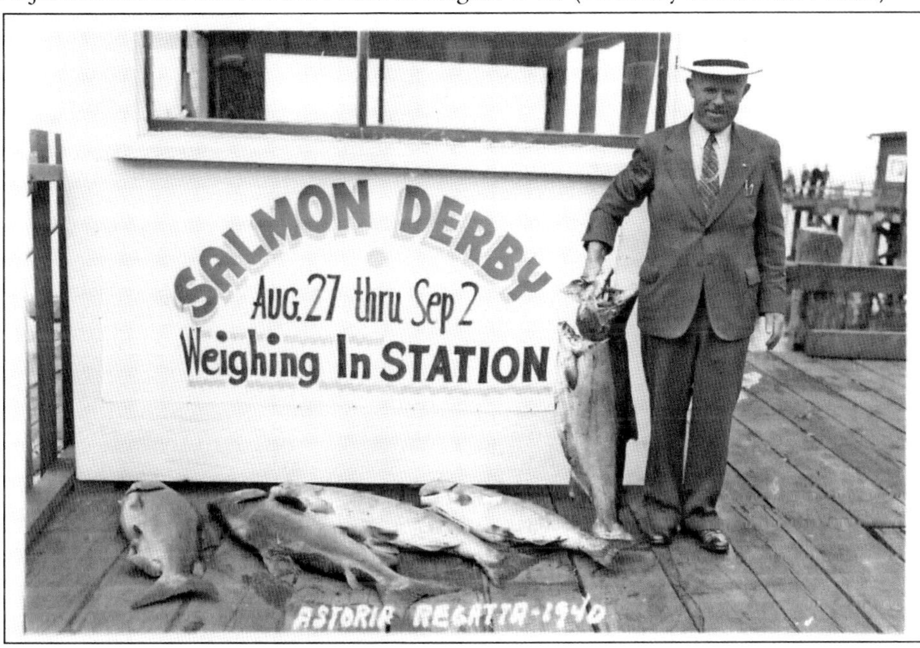

First held in 1922, the annual Salmon Derby at the Astoria Regatta was definitely famous for the fish and also for the sheer numbers of hopeful anglers it attracted. In this image from 1940, an overdressed gentleman, possibly an official, displays a prized chinook salmon. Cash prizes of up to $1,000 were on the line and certainly added to the frenzied competition on the river. In the 1960s, the event was curtailed significantly by Oregon Fish and Game Department regulations. (Courtesy of Michael Foster.)

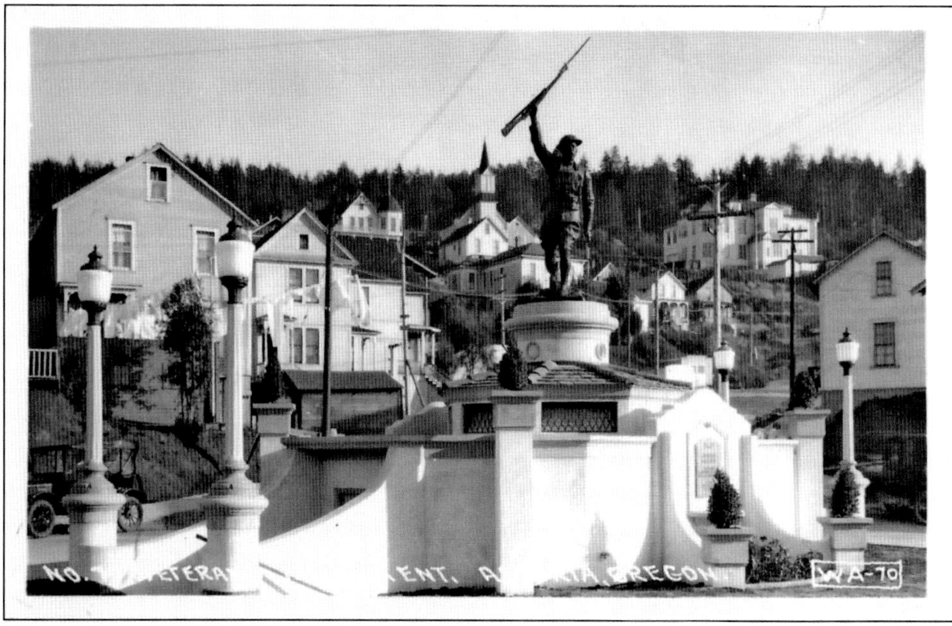

This real-photo postcard shows today's Uniontown-Alameda Historic District and the Doughboy Monument honoring veterans of World War I. Designed by Charles T. Diamond, it was listed in the National Register of Historic Places in 1984. The dedication of the Doughboy Monument took place on July 21, 1926, one day before the Astoria Column. Less grand, but no less important, the Doughboy Monument also functioned as a "comfort station," offering the first public restrooms in Astoria. (Author's collection.)

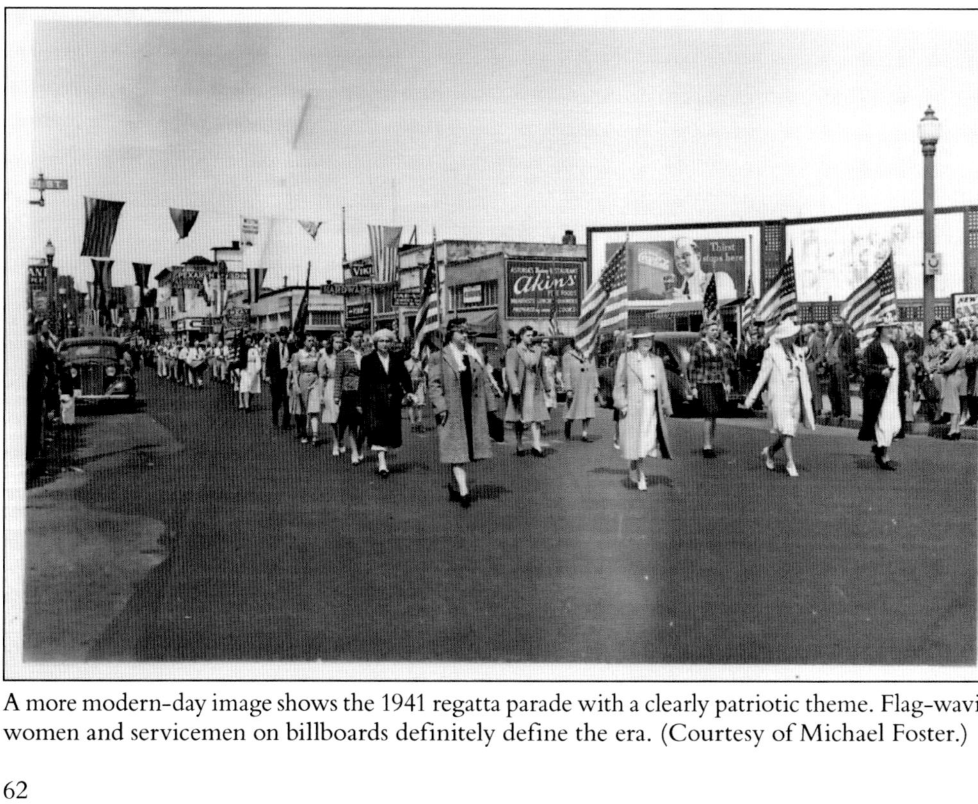

A more modern-day image shows the 1941 regatta parade with a clearly patriotic theme. Flag-waving women and servicemen on billboards definitely define the era. (Courtesy of Michael Foster.)

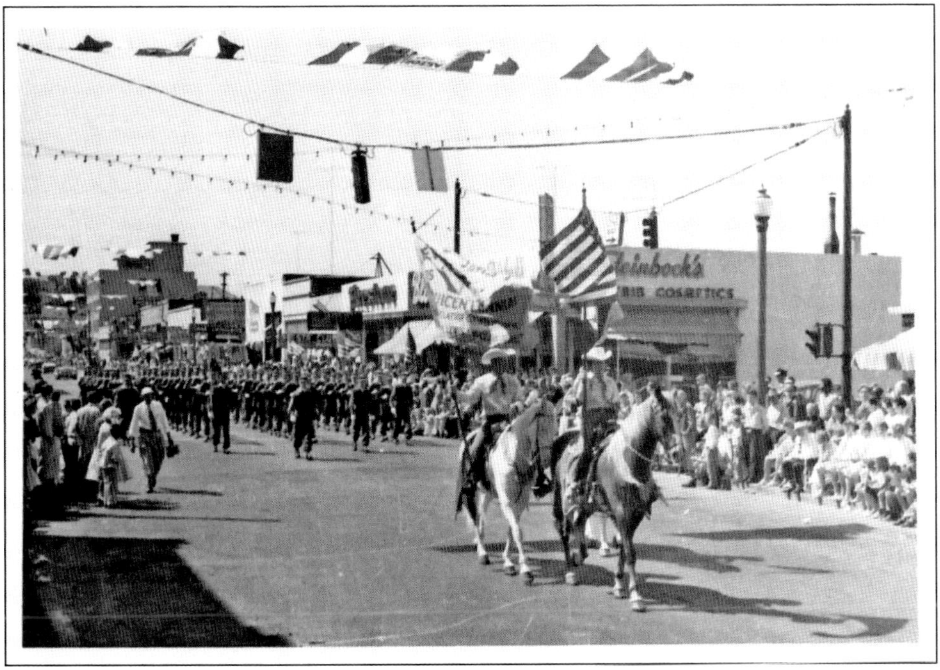

The Astoria sesquicentennial was celebrated in 1961. The parade headed east down Commercial Street past the corner of Eleventh Street, flags flying. The Spexarth Building at Eighth and Commercial Streets is in the background. (Courtesy of Michael Foster.)

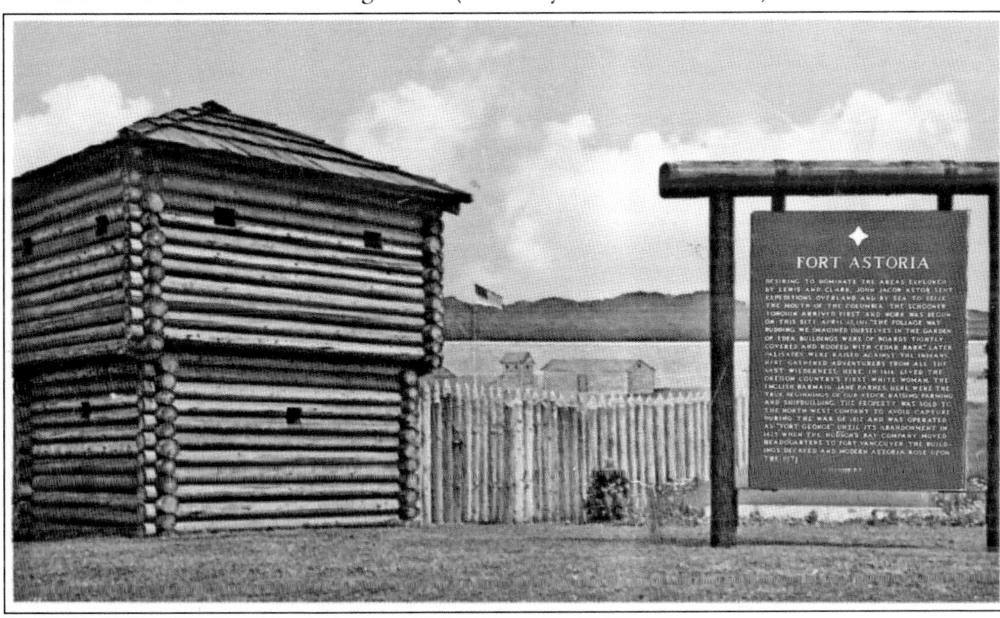

A partial replica of Fort Astoria stands at the corner of Exchange and Fifteenth Streets downtown. In addition to the DAR marker placed on the site on October 6, 1924, an Oregon historical marker begins with "Desiring to dominate the areas explored by Lewis and Clark, John Jacob Astor sent expeditions overland and by sea to seize the mouth of the Columbia . . ." and as they say, the rest is history. Today, green lines on the pavement outline the original footprint of the structure. (Courtesy of Michael Foster.)

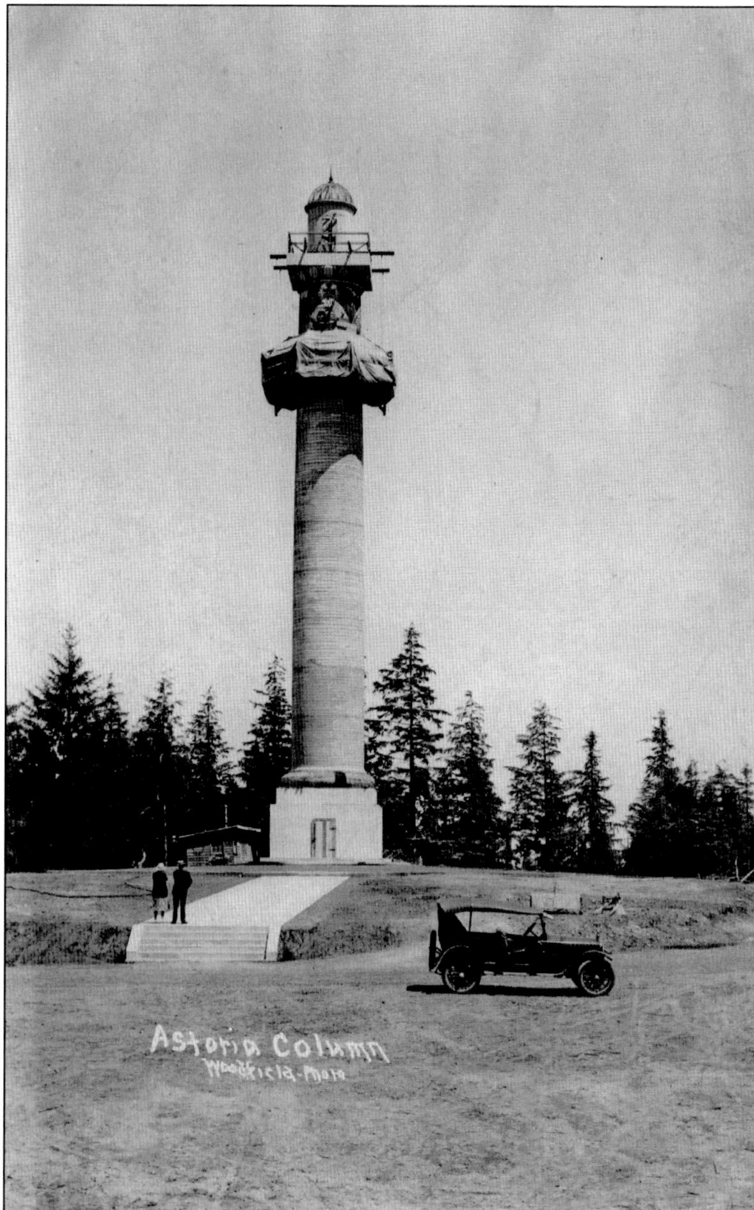

Dedicated on July 22, 1926, the Astoria Column is the city's most recognizable symbol. A monument was long desired by locals, and in 1925, the Astor family and the Great Northern Railroad agreed to donate the seed funds for the project. The 125-foot monolith was designed by New York architect Electus Litchfield and fashioned after Trajan's Column in Rome dating from 113 AD. It sits atop the 700-foot summit of Coxcomb Hill and gives a commanding view to those who climb its 164 steps. The land had been purchased after the Astoria centennial in 1911 as a legacy gift to the community. Its spiral design has 14 scenes depicting historical events of the area. The artwork (shown being applied in this image) on the surface is sgraffito—a process by which layers of pigmented cement are applied and scraped to create the design. It was designed and applied by Attilio Pusterla, an Italian immigrant and New York artist. The cost for the column was $32,500. (Courtesy Clatsop County Historical Society 101 92.045.019.)

Six

Business

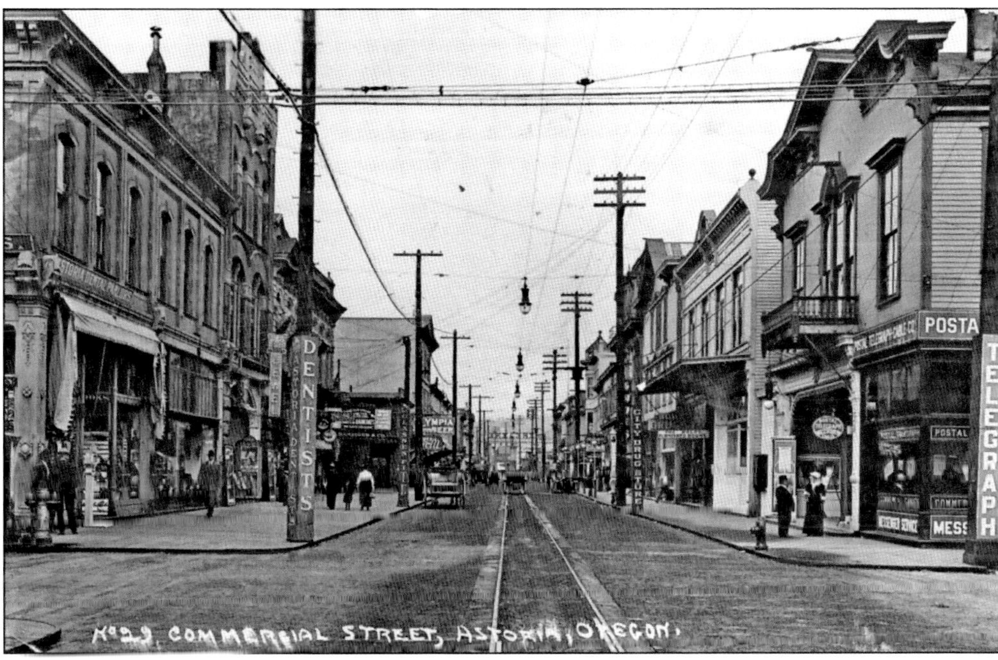

The aptly named Commercial Street has always been the heart of the downtown district in Astoria. This c. 1912 photograph taken at the corner of Eleventh Street shows a city in transition, with horse-drawn carriages, automobiles, trolley tracks, and electric lines. The planked streets and sidewalks made this area usable, as it was built above the river at the time. (Courtesy of Michael Foster.)

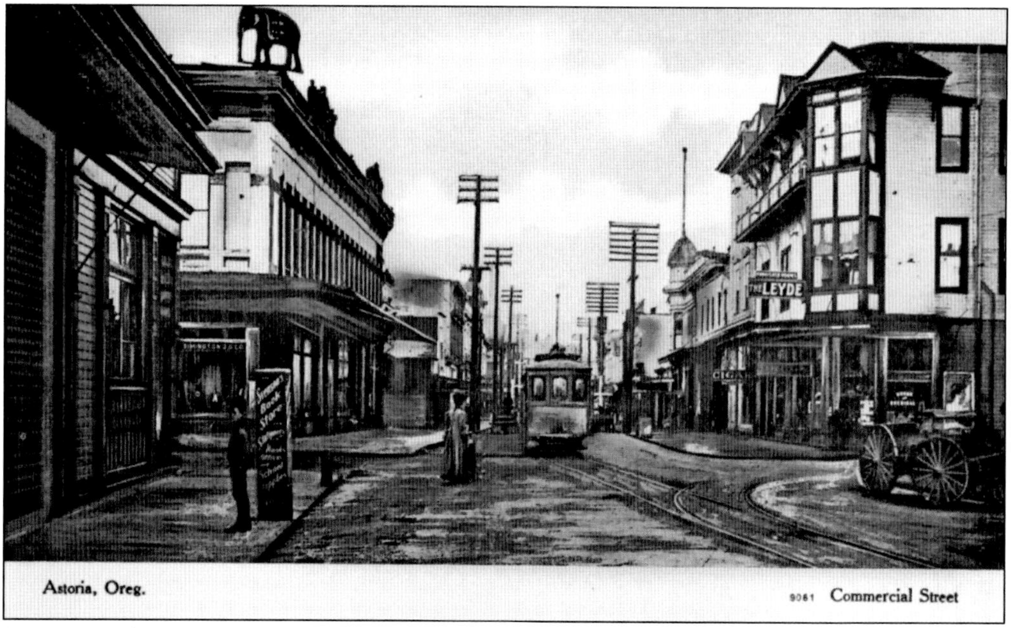

Commercial Street is pictured in 1908 looking west, with Foard & Stokes at the corner of Fourteenth Street. Its rooftop elephant was a local landmark. The Leyde Hotel stood at the site of today's Young Building until it burned down in 1916. Trolleys were introduced in 1888 and were horse-drawn until 1892, when electricity was introduced. Fares were 5¢ and it ran daily from 5:45 a.m. to 11:00 p.m. A carriage is still in use at the time, as seen at right. The card was published by Utzinger & Son of Astoria; this much-beloved business still exists on Business 101 toward Miles Crossing. (Courtesy of Michael Foster.)

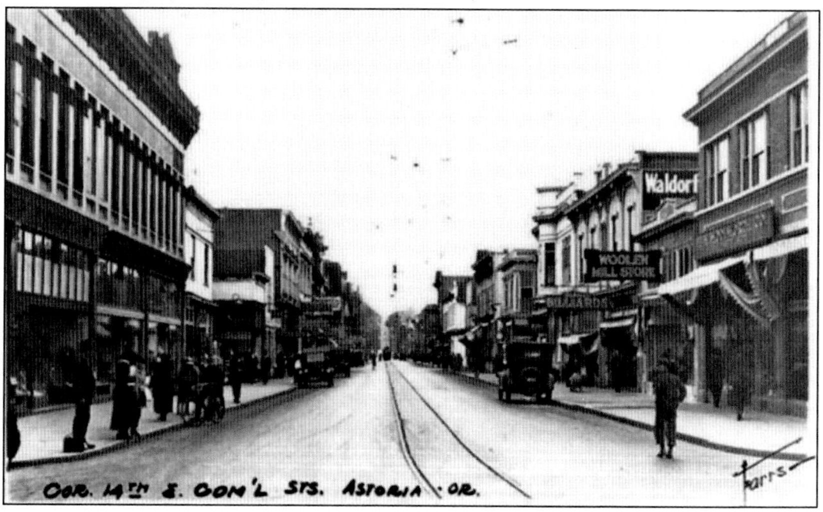

Commercial Street continues to modernize, as shown in this image from about 1920. Automobiles are abundant, but the trolley tracks are still in use. The storefronts are upgraded and more uniform. The Young Building (built in 1916), on the right, would be one of only two buildings between Fourteenth and Eighth Streets on Commercial to survive the Great Astoria Fire of 1922. The Young Building was designed by "Astoria's Architect," John E. Wicks. Wicks was prolific in the area and is credited with the design of at least 34 structures in downtown Astoria. (Author's collection.)

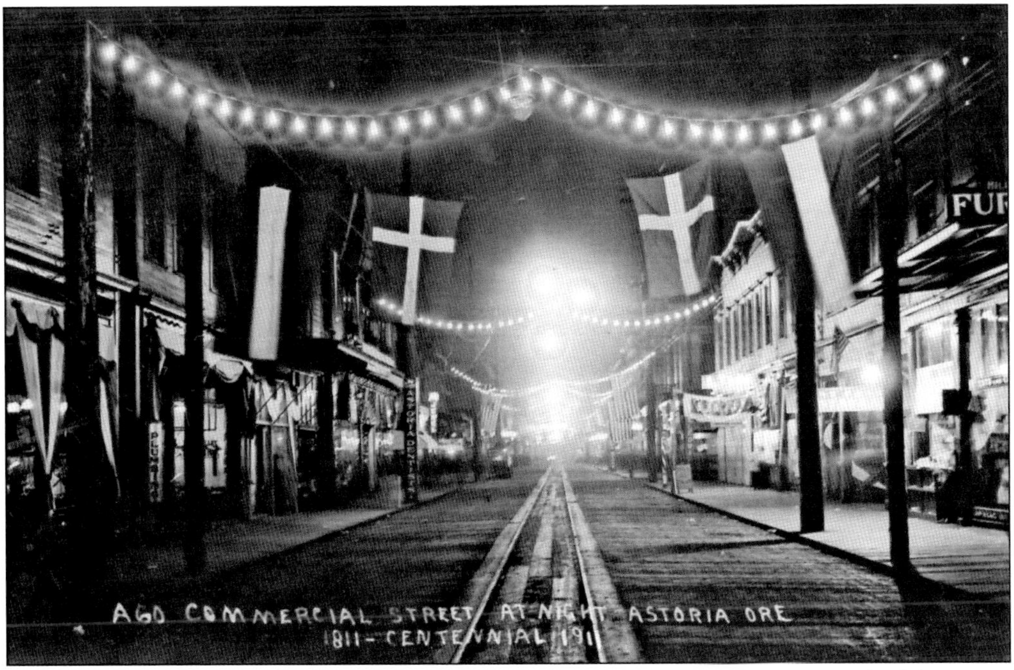

This nighttime view of Commercial Street on the occasion of the Astoria centennial celebration is significant, because the strings of lights were donated by Pacific Power and Light to commemorate the milestone—and promote its newly available and expanding services, of course. (Courtesy of Michael Foster.)

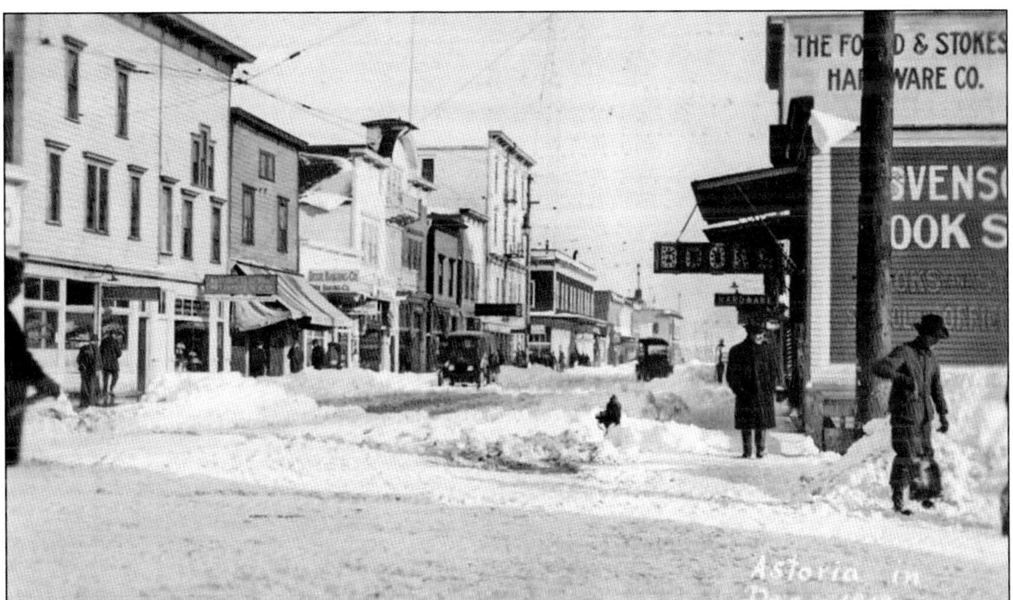

Dated December 1919, this snowy view of Commercial Street looks east at the corner of Fourteenth Street. Svenson's Book Store is the current location of the Hotel Astoria. (Courtesy of Sara's Old Photos.)

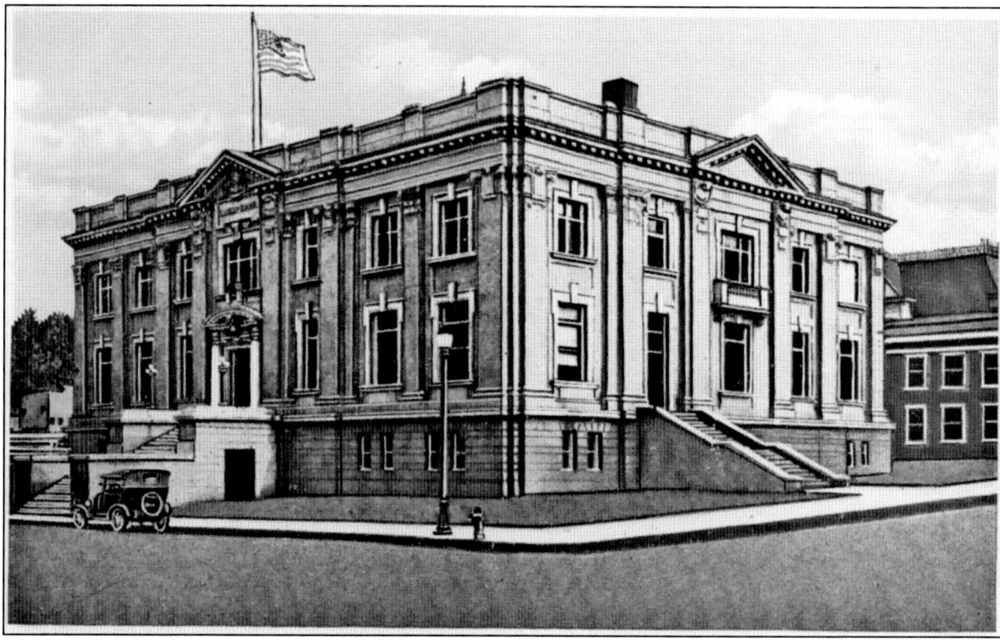

The first Clatsop County Courthouse was built in 1855 at the corner of this block between Seventh and Eighth Streets and Commercial and Duane Streets. The new, and present, building was completed in 1908. Portland architect Edgar M. Lazarus designed the American Renaissance style building, which took four years to complete due to ongoing labor disputes. It is listed in the National Register of Historic Places. (Courtesy of Sean Fitzpatrick and Anne Carpenter.)

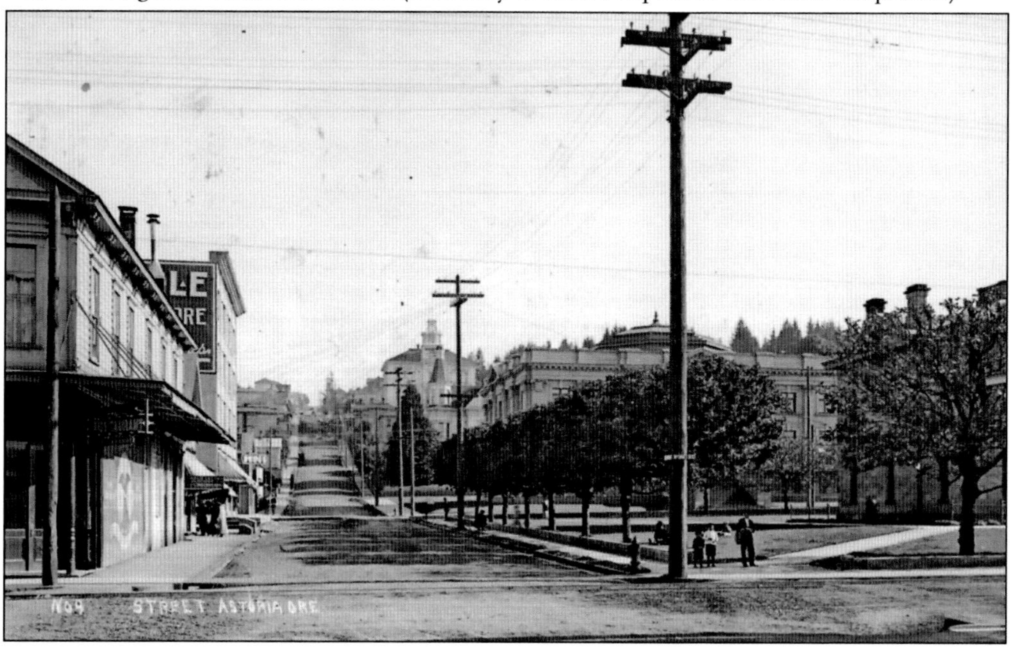

This c. 1912 real-photo postcard looking south is a great street-level view of one of the busiest corners in Astoria today, Eighth and Bond Streets. The old post office is on the right, leading up to Commercial Street. The courthouse and the Spexarth Building are to the right and left, respectively. McClure School is up the hill. (Courtesy of Ray Hakala.)

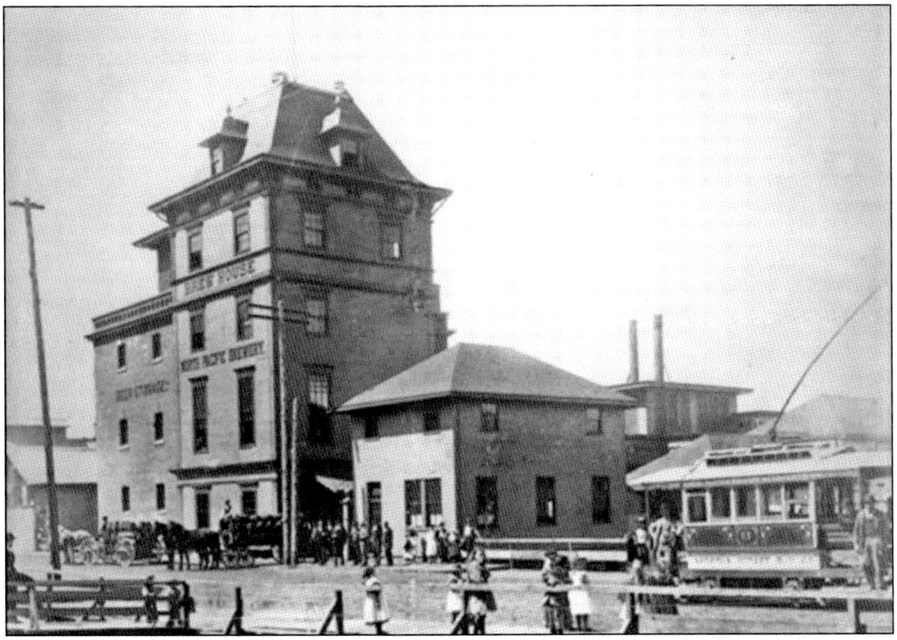

From the 1880s through 1915, when Prohibition began in Oregon, Astoria had several successful breweries. North Pacific Brewery, founded in 1893, was the largest. The building pictured here was built in 1896, and the brick storage building is still standing. It now houses the Uppertown Firefighters Museum at the corner of Marine Drive and Thirtieth Street. Today, many new breweries are popping up in Astoria to meet the current demand for craft beers. (Author's collection.)

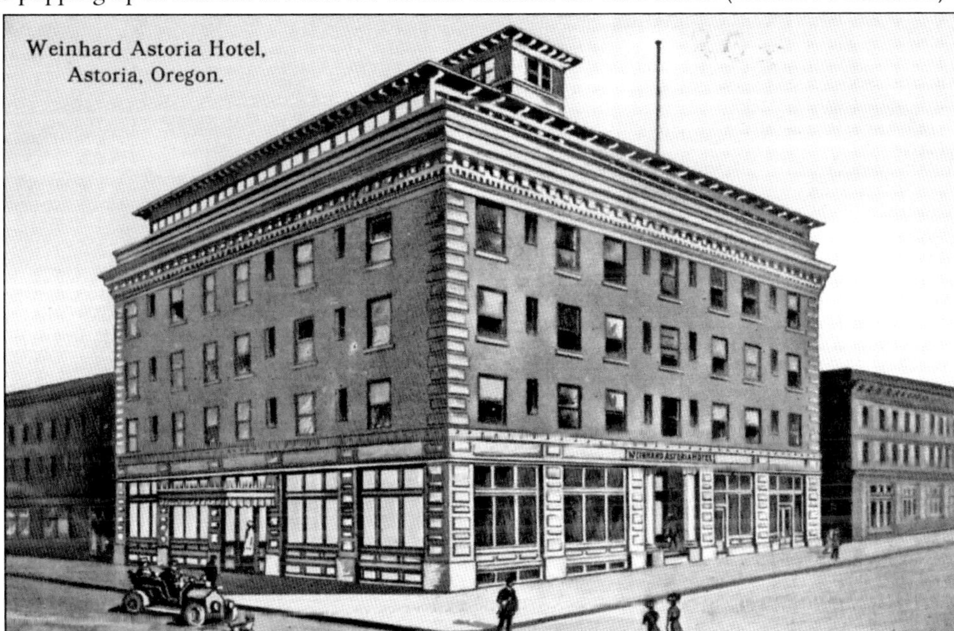

The Weinhard Hotel was built about 1910 and offered first-class accommodations for travelers until it burned down in the 1922 fire. It stood at the corner of Twelfth and Duane Streets. The entryway of the hotel was salvaged following the fire and placed at Shively Park to mark the start of a popular hiking trail. (Courtesy of Michael Foster.)

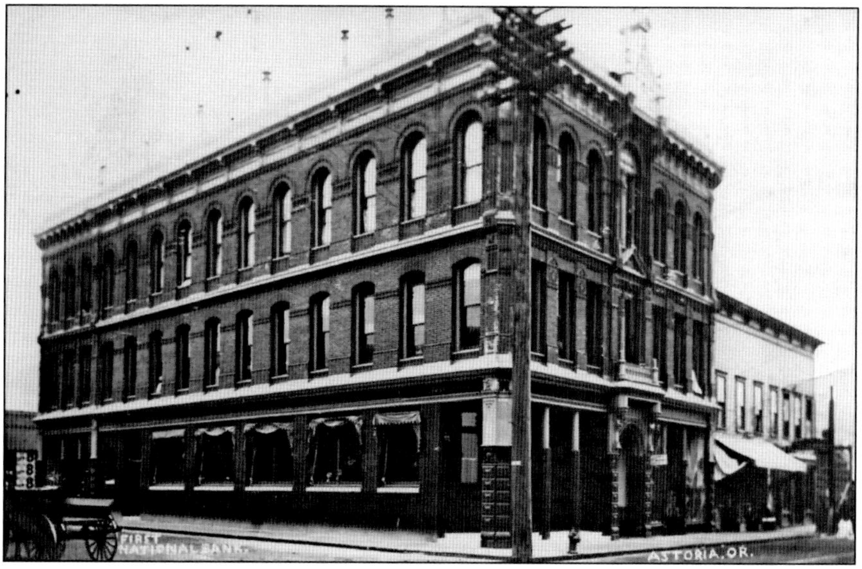

Founded by Capt. George Flavel in 1885, the First National Bank, pictured around 1915, stood at the corner of Tenth and Bond Streets. After it burned in 1922, the second version was built at the corner of Ninth and Commercial Streets. The building has had many tenants after the bank closed and currently serves as Clatsop County's Judge Guy Boyington Building public meeting space. (Courtesy of Michael Foster.)

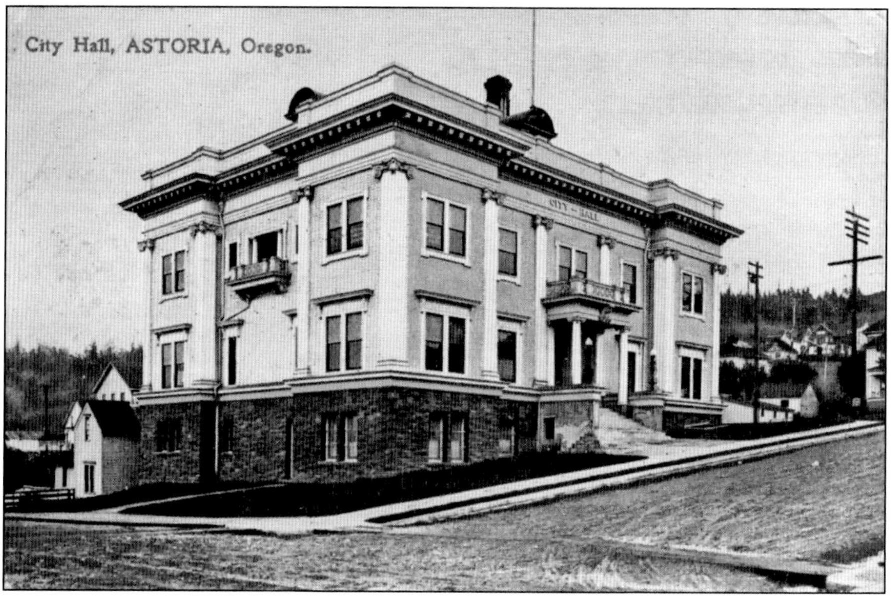

The city hall was built in 1905. The Neoclassical style building also housed the jail. Municipal administration and services were housed here until 1939, when they were moved to their current location at Eleventh and Duane Streets. Beneath the structure is Fort George Cemetery, the oldest European cemetery in the Northwest. Some residents of the original Fort Astoria and other early settlers were buried here. Some graves were moved, but others remain on the site. During World War II, the building served as the USO and later the first Columbia River Maritime Museum. It became the home of the Clatsop County Historical Society in 1985. (Courtesy of Michael Foster.)

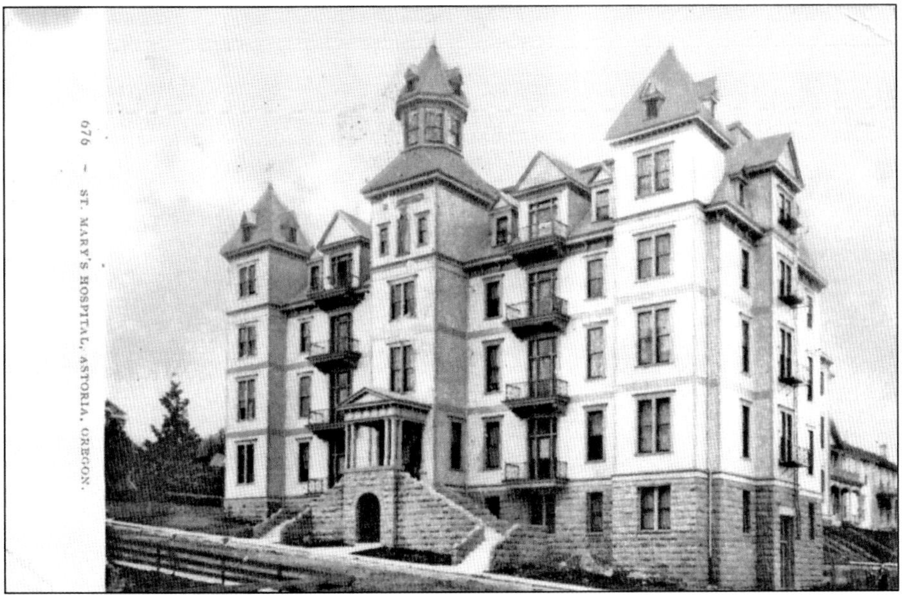

The first hospital in Astoria was established by the Sisters of Providence in the former Arrigoni Hotel around 1888. When it outgrew that facility, the four-story wooden structure pictured here was built in 1905 near the original on Sixteenth Street between Duane and Exchange Streets. It was expanded in 1931, and the wooden structure was eventually taken down. The foundations seen here remain as a parking lot. While excavating the foundation, remnants of the Pacific Fur Company's stockade were unearthed. The brick addition now serves as the Owens-Adair Apartments. (Courtesy of Michael Foster.)

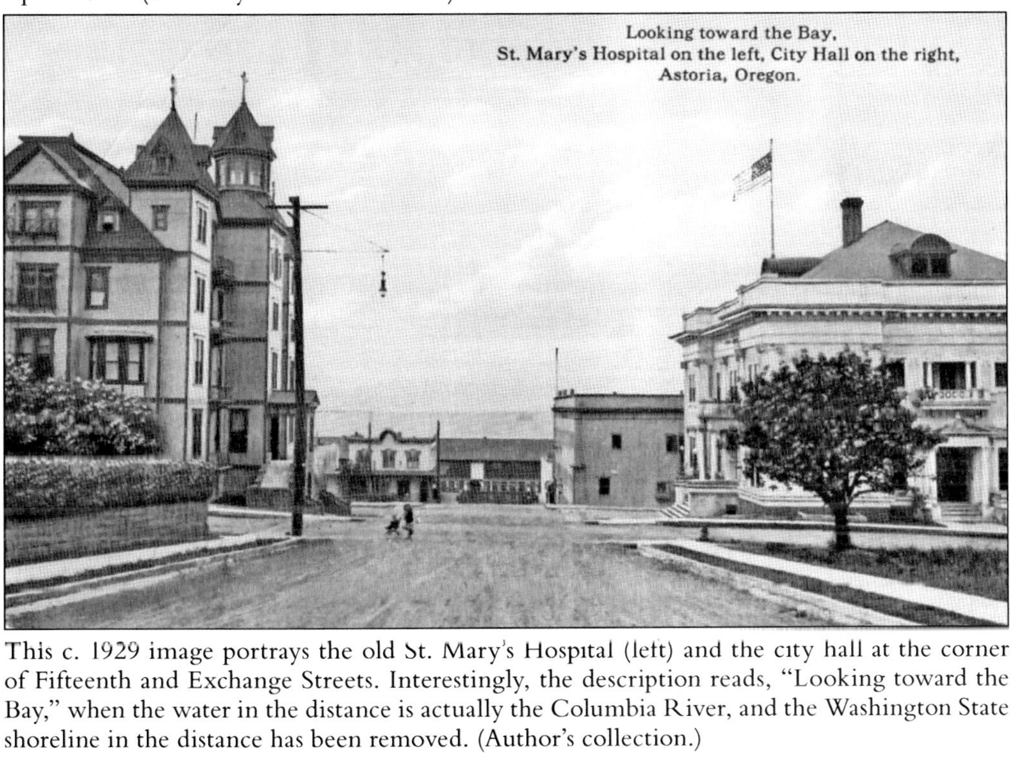

This c. 1929 image portrays the old St. Mary's Hospital (left) and the city hall at the corner of Fifteenth and Exchange Streets. Interestingly, the description reads, "Looking toward the Bay," when the water in the distance is actually the Columbia River, and the Washington State shoreline in the distance has been removed. (Author's collection.)

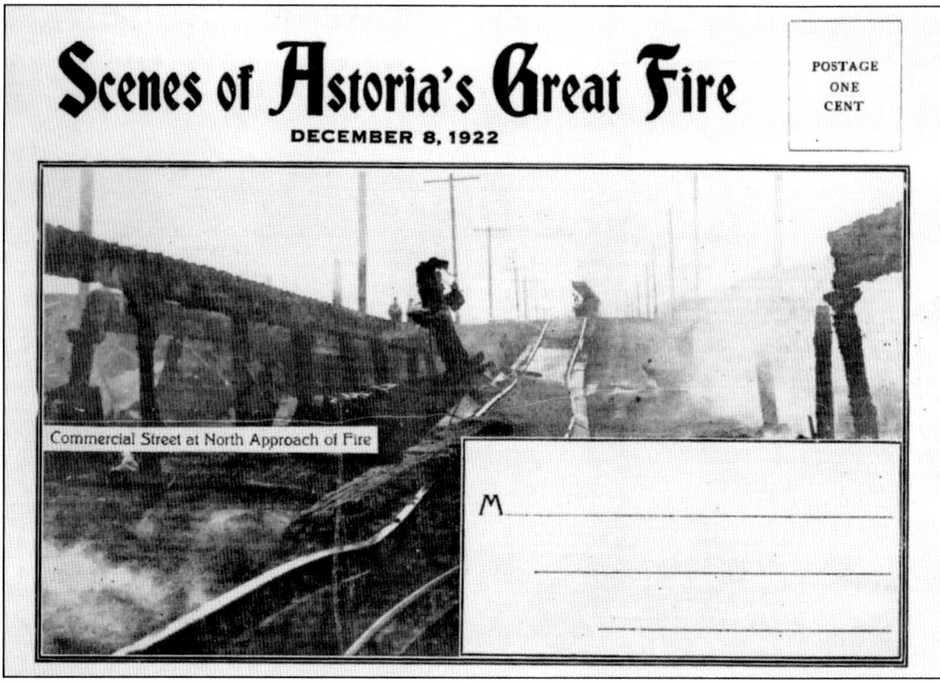

On December 8, 1922, a large section of downtown Astoria burned to the ground. It is referred to as "Astoria's Great Fire" and was, in fact, the second time the town had burned. Postcards capturing the devastation were sent all around the world. They are very collectible today and serve as excellent points of reference for the rebuilding that occurred immediately following the fire. Twenty-four city blocks were completely destroyed. The financial loss at the time was more than $15 million. This card was published by Louis Scheiner of Portland. (Courtesy of Michael Foster.)

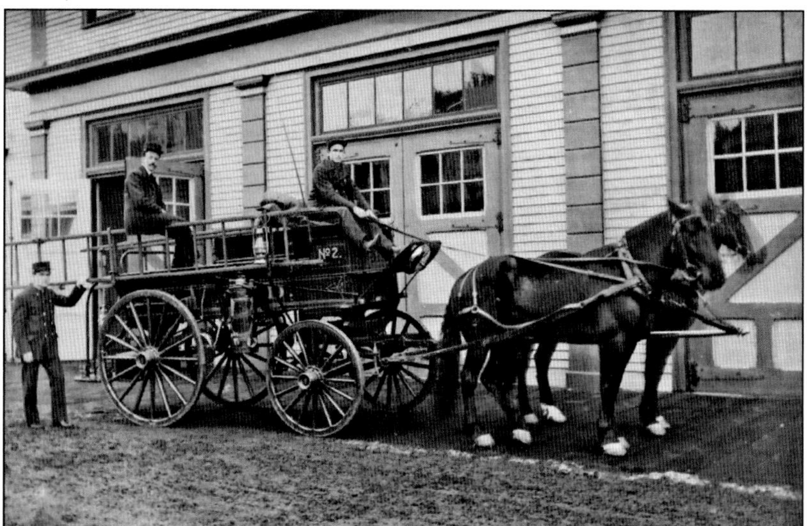

Even though the city of Astoria had suffered from fire devastation previously and fire departments tried to prepare, the equipment and horse teams, like those pictured here around 1905, were inadequate to control the inferno that consumed the downtown core. Several buildings were dynamited to stem the spread of the flames. (Courtesy of Michael Foster.)

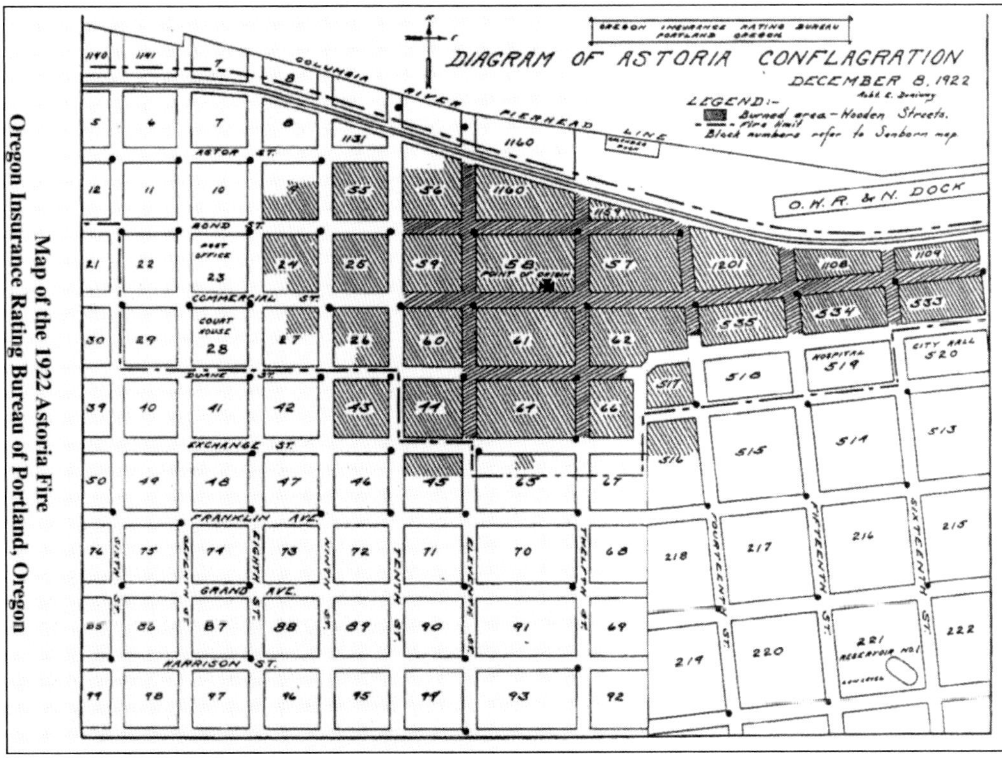

This map illustrates the areas affected during the December 8, 1922, fire. (Author's collection.)

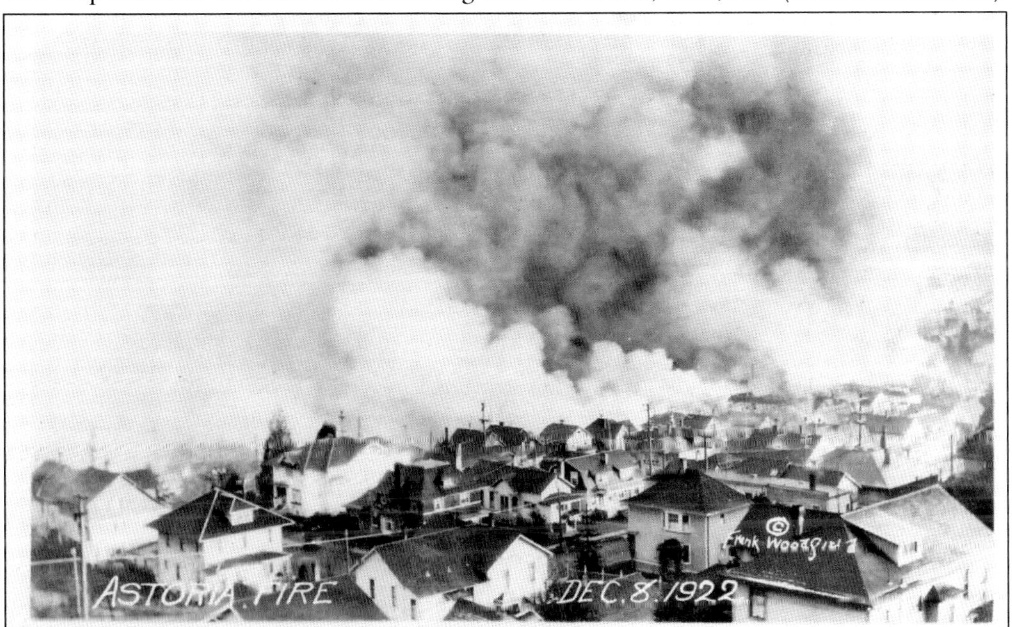

The fire started near Eleventh and Commercial Streets and quickly spread. This photograph was taken by Frank Woodfield looking north from Third and Harrison Streets. He rushed this image to Portland for publication in the newspapers, and it quickly became quite famous. (Courtesy of Sara's Old Photos.)

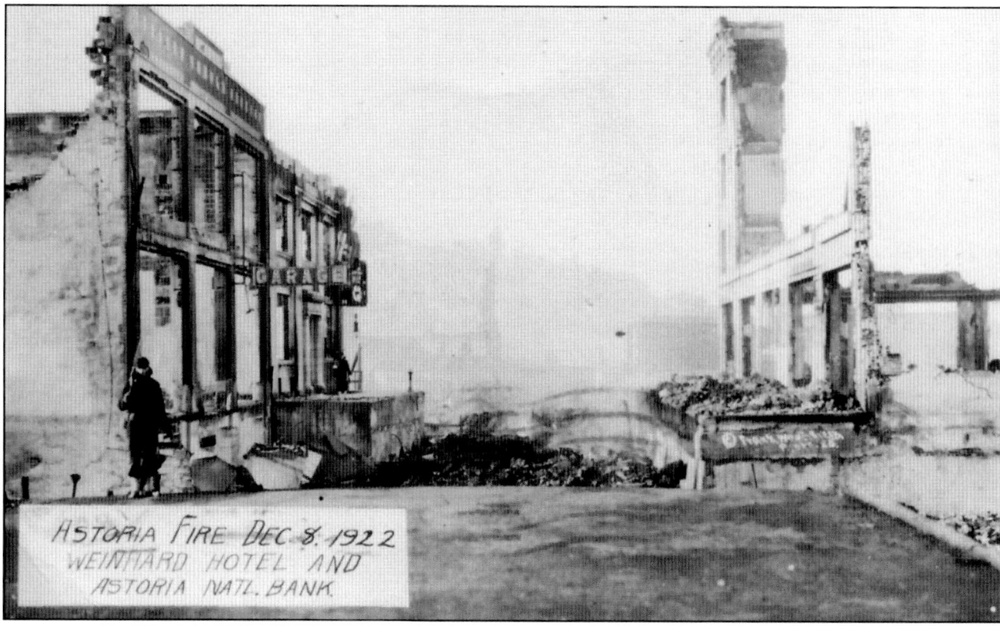

In another image of Astoria's Great Fire, the shell of a building in the background is the once-posh Weinhard Hotel. The grand marble columns that framed the entrance of the hotel were salvaged and now mark the beginning of a nature trail in Shively Park, up the hill near the city Reservoir. (Courtesy of Michael Foster.)

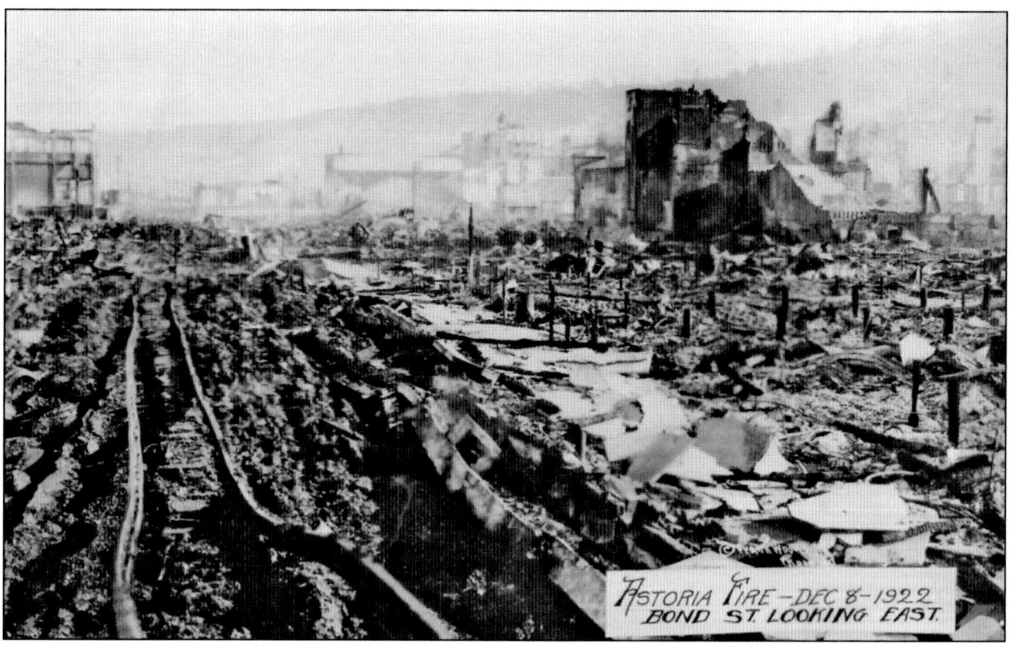

The twisted and melted trolley tracks on Bond Street, looking east, indicate the intensity of the heat during the fire. It was nearly a perfect storm of conditions: a wooden-structure town built above the water on pilings, streets made of creosoted planking, and a draft underneath that acted like a giant bellows. (Courtesy of Michael Foster.)

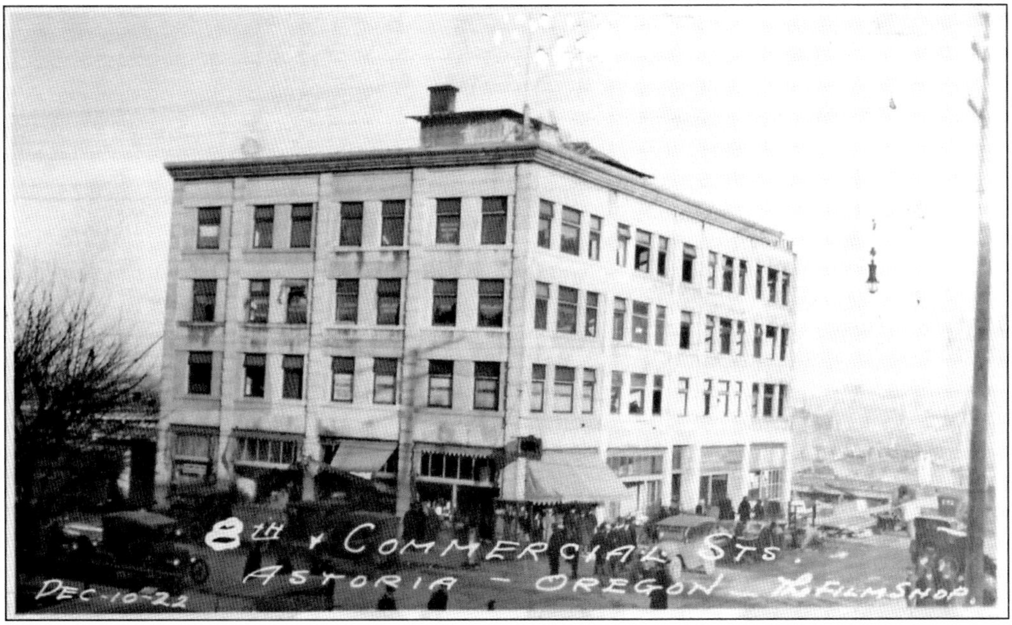

The Spexarth Building was constructed in 1911 of reinforced concrete at the corner of Eighth and Commercial Streets. It was one of the first of its kind in Astoria and the first location of JC Penney in town. During the 1922 fire, the windows blew out and the east side was charred, but the building withstood the fire, as is shown in this real-photo postcard immediately following the event. It was quickly repaired and housed many businesses as the town rebuilt. The Spexarth looks much the same today. (Courtesy of Michael Foster.)

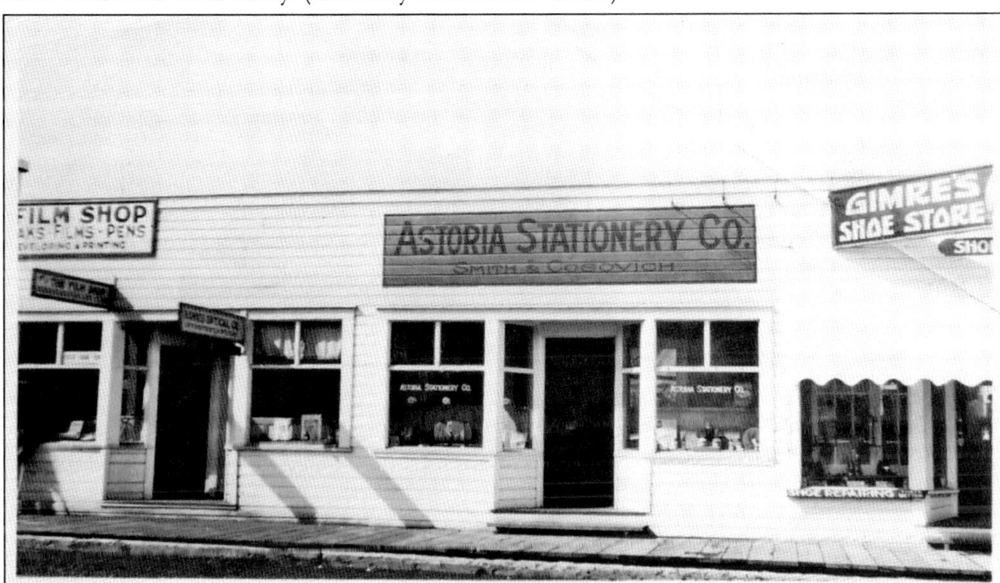

Following the fire, temporary structures were quickly built downtown to allow some return to normalcy as soon as possible. These were on Thirteenth Street between Duane and Exchange Streets. Established by Sven Gimre in 1892, Gimre's Shoe Store is still a family-owned business in Astoria. It is the oldest shoe store west of the Rockies, currently located on Fourteenth Street, just up from the river. (Courtesy of Michael Foster.)

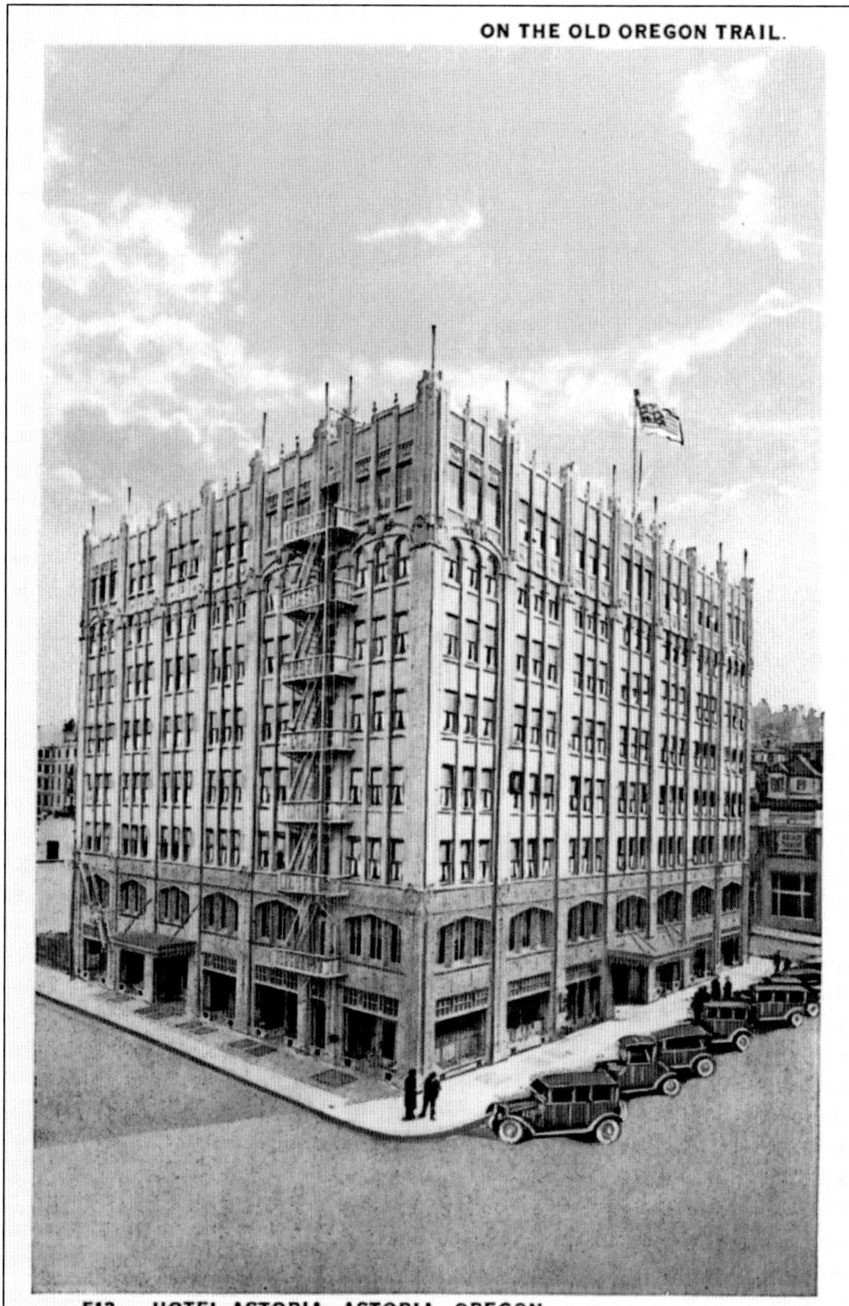

Construction began on the Hotel Astoria in November 1922 at the corner of Fourteenth and Commercial Streets. At the start of the project, the plans called for the hotel to be five stories tall, but only a month later, the Great Fire destroyed almost all of downtown Astoria. The resulting severe shortage of housing prompted the Columbia Hotel Company to revise the design to increase the planned height to eight stories. The Gothic-style skyscraper designed by Tourtellotte & Hummel was the tallest building in Oregon outside of Portland when completed. (Courtesy of Sean Fitzpatrick and Anne Carpenter.)

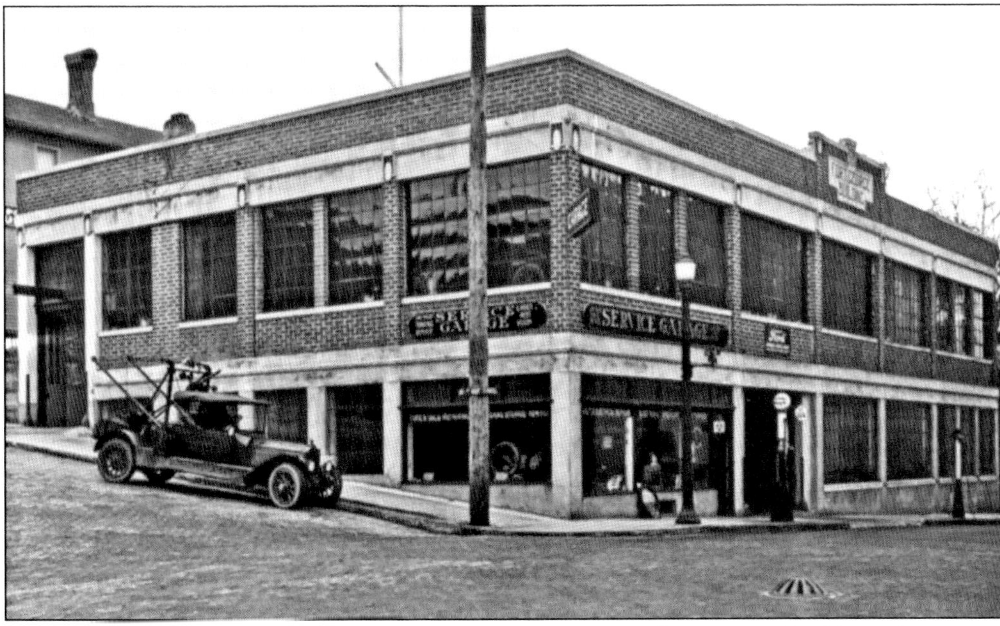

The Fort George Building, pictured around 1925, was one of many new buildings that sprang up after the fire during the rebuilding of Astoria. Built in 1924, it still stands at the corner of Fifteenth and Duane Streets and houses two very popular establishments today: the Fort George Brewery and the Blue Scorcher Bakery. (Courtesy of Sara's Old Photos.)

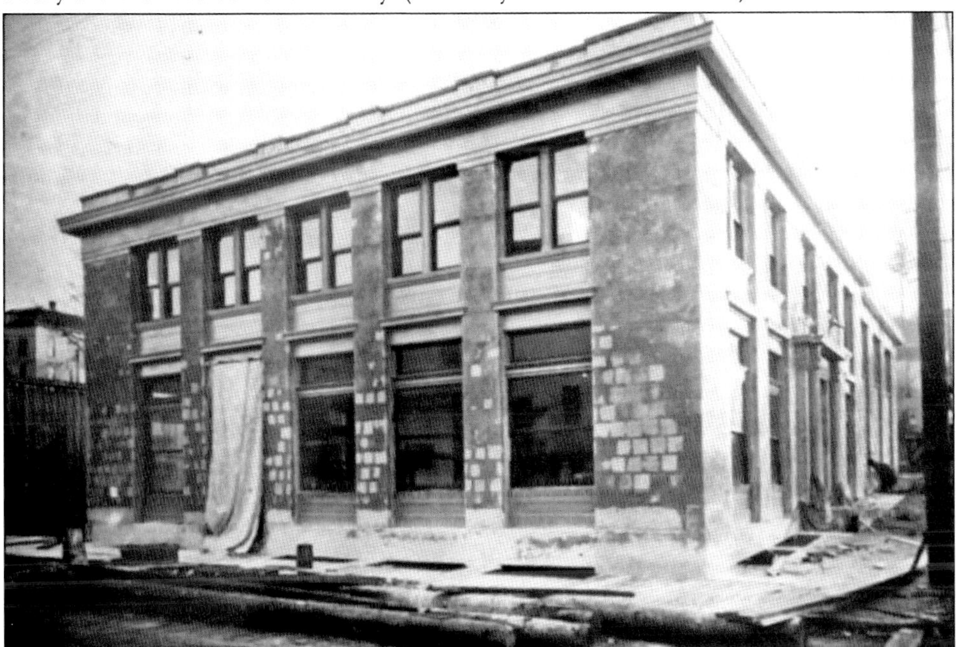

Designed by Portland architects MacNaughton and Raymond, the new YMCA building at Twelfth and Exchange Streets opened in 1914 and served the community until 1987. Being outside the 1922 fire zone, the structure served as the headquarters for many social service agencies that were displaced and in critical demand. The building is currently under renovation. (Author's collection.)

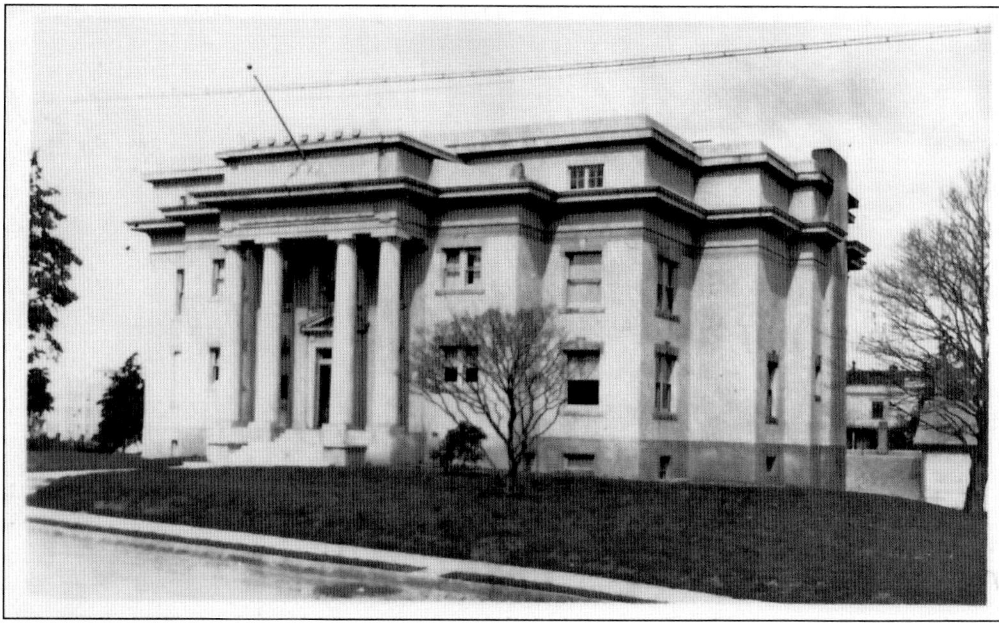

Located at the corner of Fifteenth Street and Franklin Avenue, the magnificent Masonic lodge, pictured around 1923, was rebuilt following destruction in the fire. It is still in use by local Masons as well as many other community organizations. Designed by architect C.T. Diamond, images of the building were used in advertisements for Union Metal Mfg. Co., makers of the prominent Greek Doric–style columns. (Courtesy of Michael Foster.)

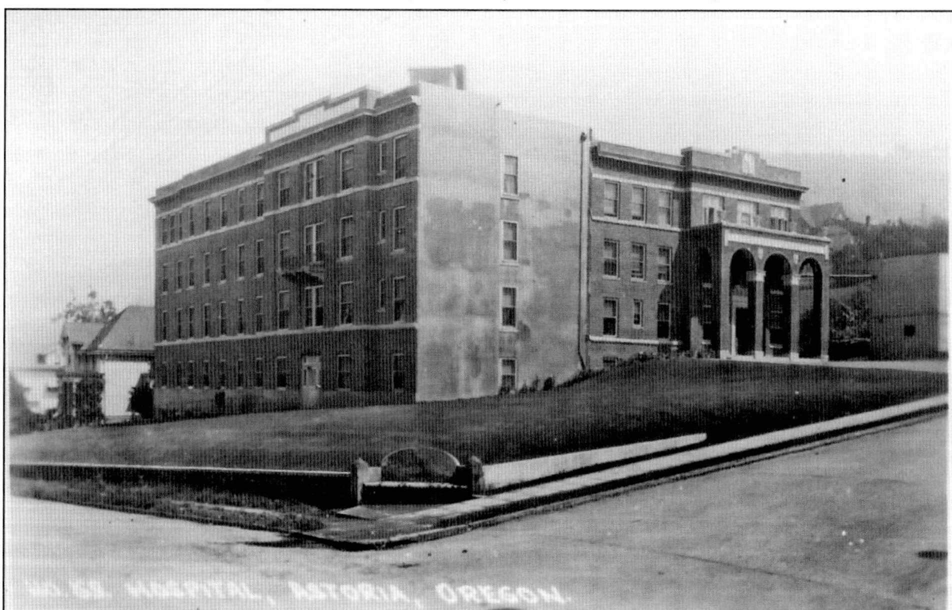

The Columbia Hospital was completed in 1927 by local Lutheran organizations as the medical needs of an expanding population increased. Work was started in 1922 using a design by Astoria architect John E. Wicks, but the project was shuttered after the 1922 fire and due to a lack of funds. It is located at the corner of Sixteenth Street and Franklin Avenue and currently serves as an elderly rehabilitation and care facility called Clatsop Care. (Courtesy of Michael Foster.)

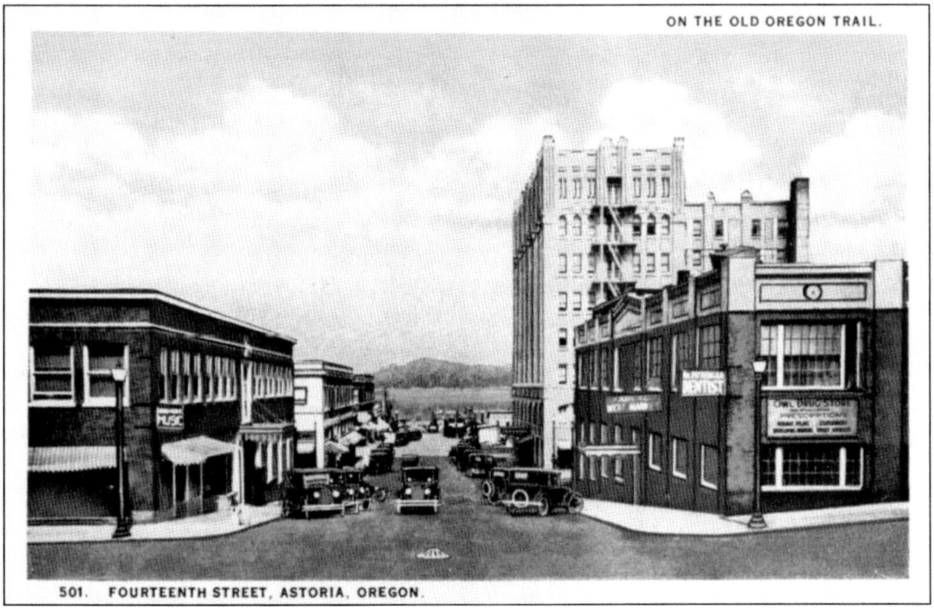

This great view of Fourteenth and Exchange Streets can be immediately recognized today with many thanks to local historic preservation efforts. The Lovell Building on the right was owned by Sherman Lovell during the fire. He would not allow his car dealership to be dynamited, and it was saved. It served as the temporary home to many businesses during the rebuild. This street is a thriving commercial hub in today's Astoria. (Courtesy of Sara's Old Photos.)

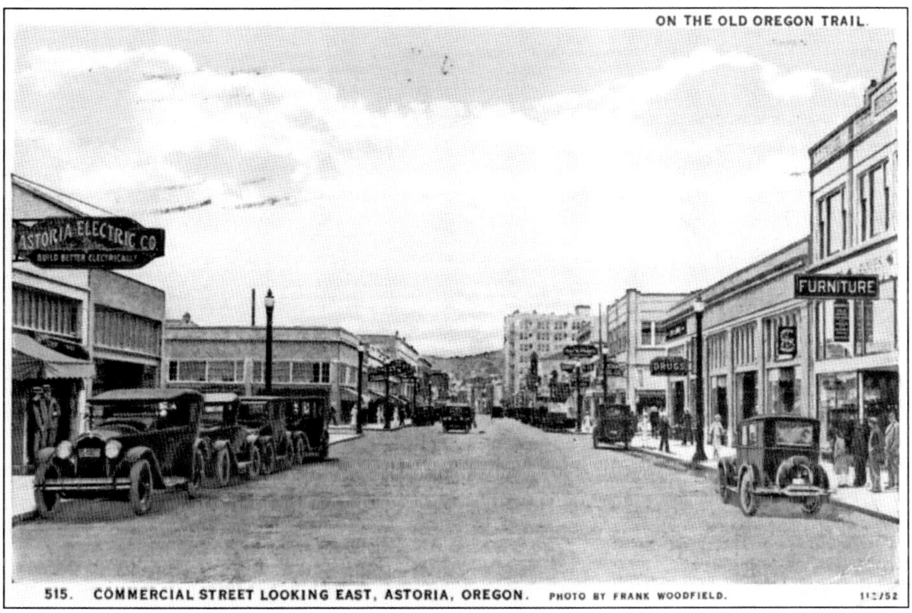

The new look of Commercial Street after the fire began to emerge in the late 1920s. This postcard view is from Ninth Street looking east. Most of these same buildings are in use today and can be easily recognized. Note the two way automobile traffic, no trolley tracks, and underground electric wires. Trolley service ended by 1925. Light posts similar to those seen here were reintroduced recently. Salvaged originals can be seen around town in front yards and the occasional residential street corner around town. (Courtesy of Michael Foster.)

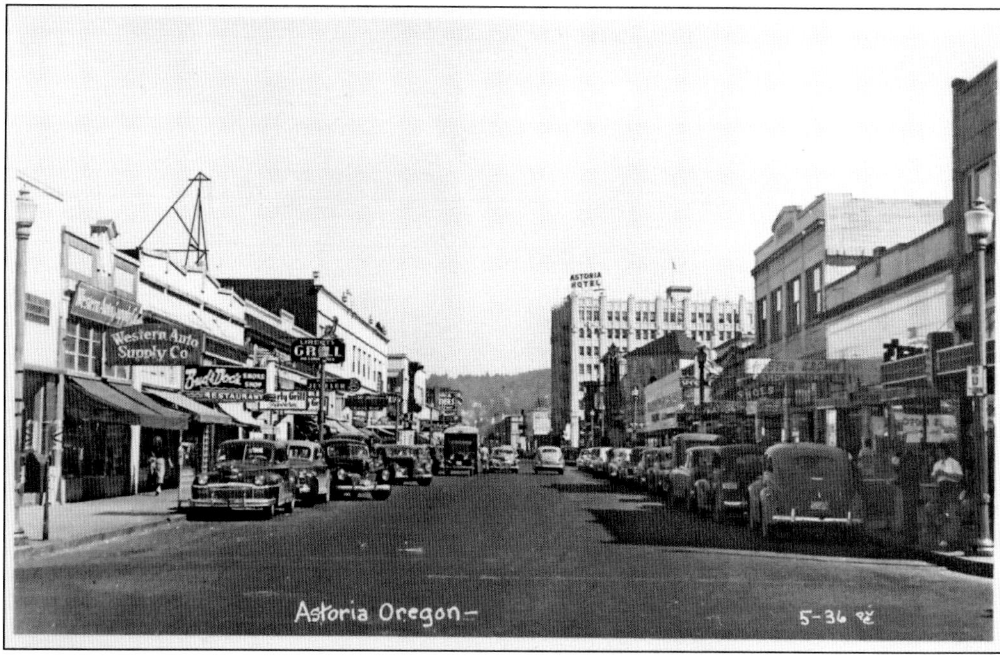

A much more recognizable Commercial Street is pictured looking east around 1936. The location is close to the previous image. (Courtesy of Michael Foster.)

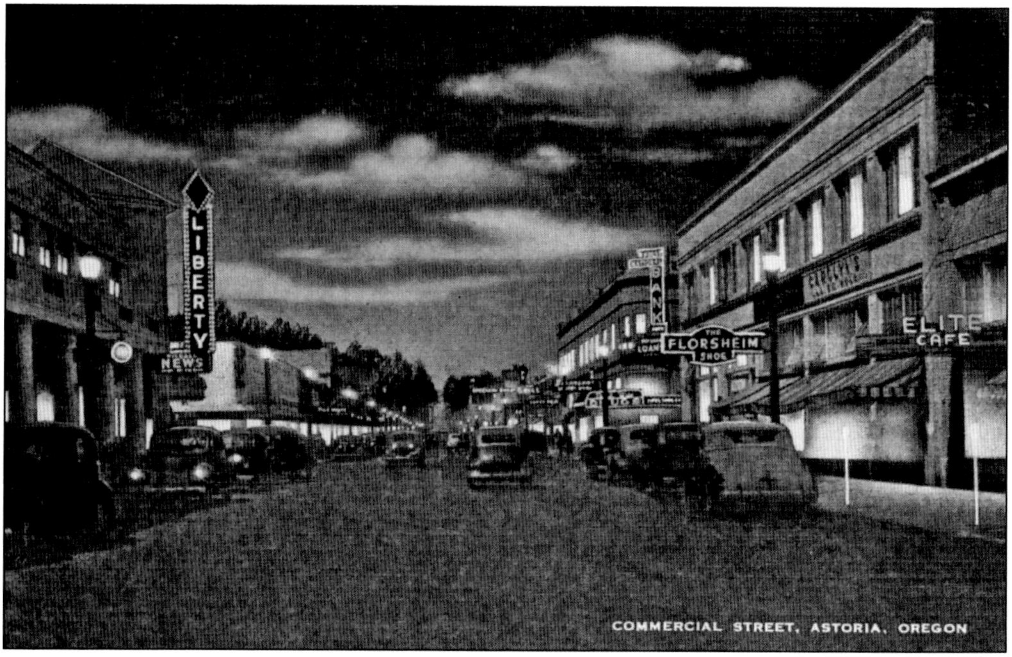

Here is Commercial Street looking west about 1940. The building on the right is today's Wells Fargo Bank, with the Liberty Theater on the left, directly across the street. The Liberty opened in 1925 and hosted vaudeville, live music, and film over the decades. Boasting dramatic Mediterranean-style design throughout, the Liberty Theater is the centerpiece of Astoria's cultural scene, and has been beautifully restored and serves as a top notch performing arts and events venue today. (Courtesy of Michael Foster.)

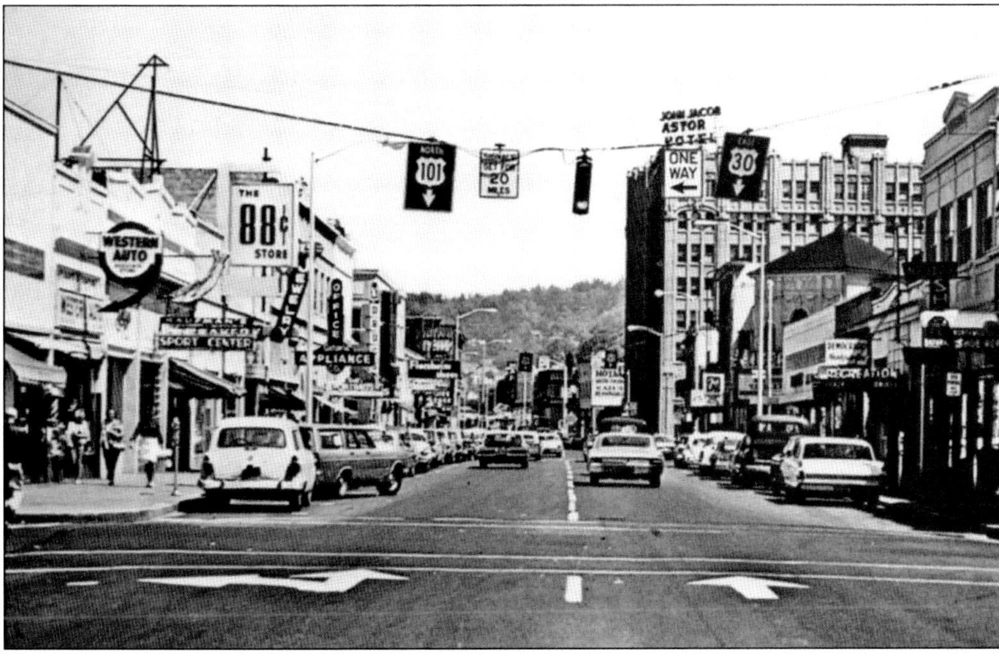

Pictured around 1960, a bustling Commercial Street now has one-way traffic. The John Jacob Astor Hotel was painted pink during this era and known locally as "Big Pink." (Courtesy of Sara's Old Photos.)

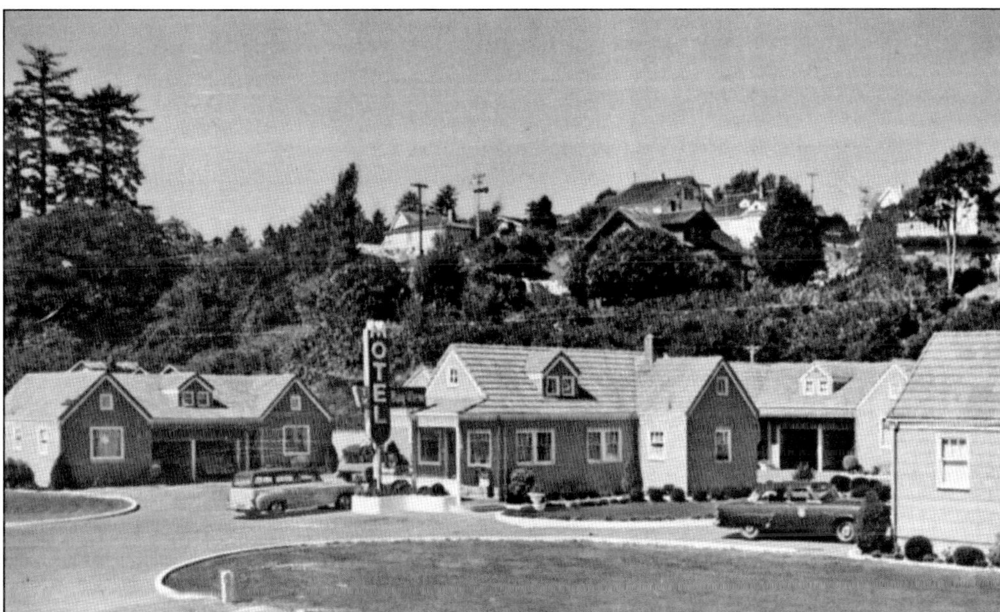

The Bay View Motel, built in 1940 on the shores of Young's Bay, is still around today. Its most recent claim to fame was being a key location for the movie *Kindergarten Cop*, starring Arnold Schwarzenegger, filmed in Astoria in 1990. At one time, there were five such classic motor hotels with a three-mile stretch of Highway 101. (Courtesy of Sara's Old Photos.)

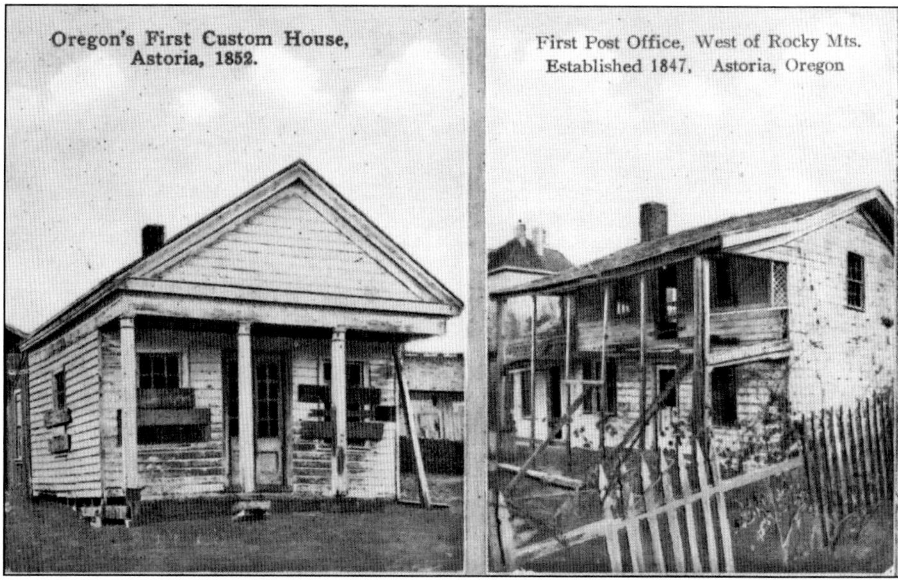

Astoria's first customs house was built in 1852 in response to the expanding shipping economy in the area. Appointed by President Taylor, Gen. John Adair was the first customs agent in the Northwest. It is rumored that Abraham Lincoln had turned down the position. A replica of the customs house stands near its original location at Thirty-Fourth Street and Marine Drive. Also pictured is Astoria's first post office. (Courtesy of Michael Foster.)

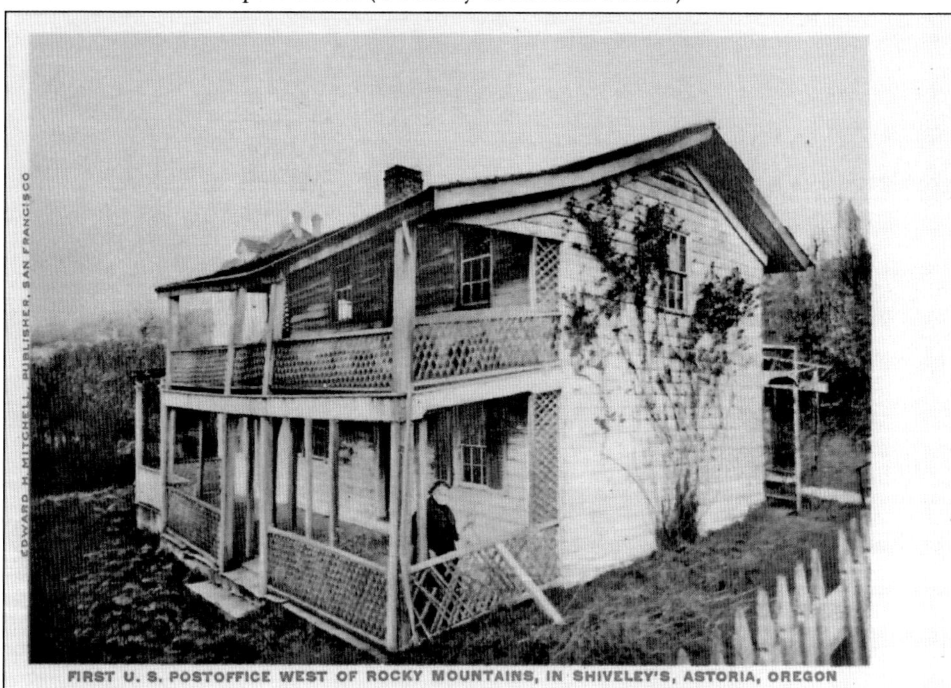

Upon his arrival in 1847, John Shively applied to be the postmaster for the territory. He was appointed to the position and opened the first post office west of the Rockies in his home. An obelisk stands on the site where the pictured home once stood on Fifteenth Street between Exchange Street and Franklin Avenue. (Courtesy of Michael Foster.)

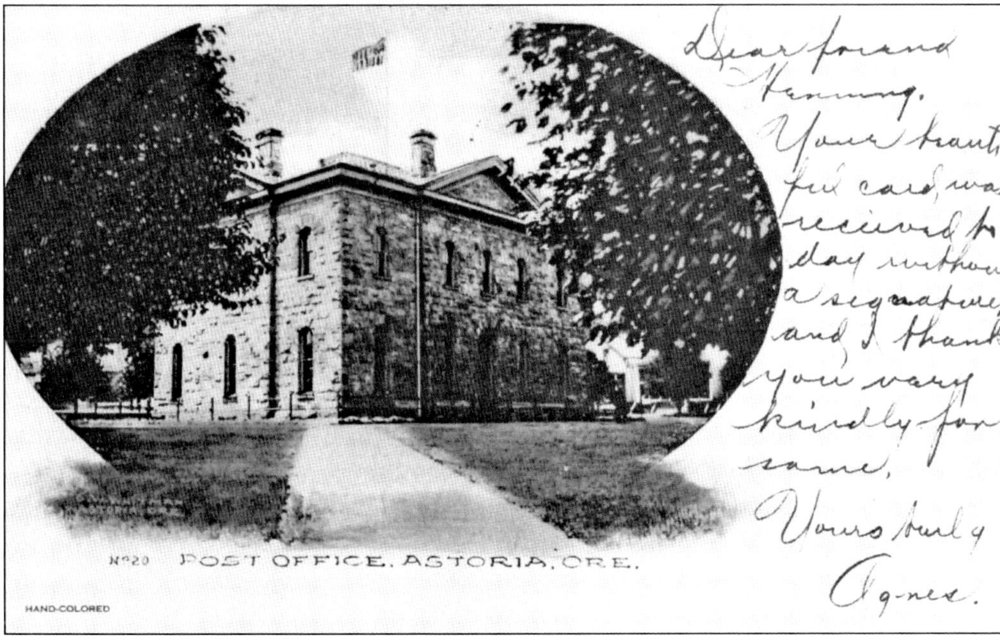

This post office building was completed in 1878 and housed the customs operations as well. A long-time landmark downtown, the building was taken down in 1930–1931. The stones from the building are said to make up many retaining walls around the city. Postmarked 1907, this hand-colored postcard has some lovely handwriting. (Courtesy of Michael Foster.)

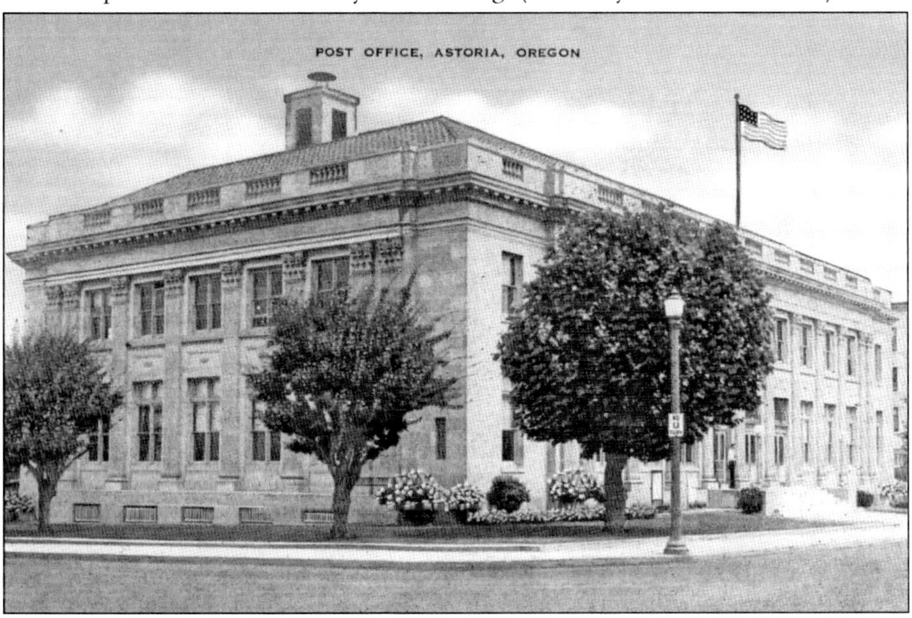

Built with Work Progress Administration funds, the new Beaux Arts style post office designed by Edgar M. Lazarus, who also designed the Clatsop County Courthouse directly across the street, was completed in 1933. The trees surrounding the building remain and have been on site for more than 100 years. It is located on Commercial Street between Seventh and Eighth Streets and is in full use today. It is also listed in the National Register of Historic Places. (Courtesy of Michael Foster.)

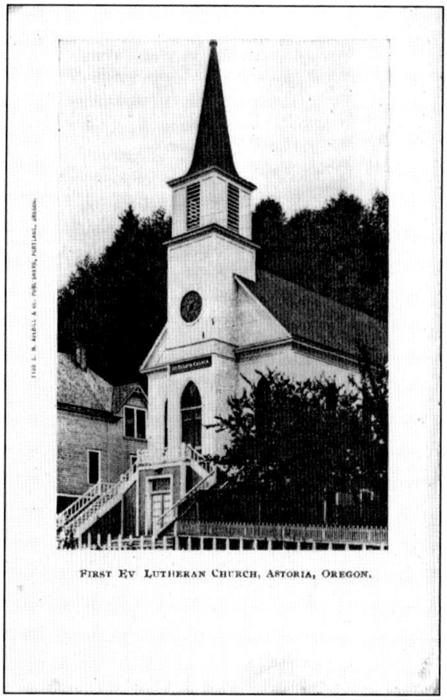

The First Evangelical Lutheran Church is pictured around 1900 in its (at least) second location at Thirty-Fifth and Duane Streets in Uppertown. This congregation began as a group of Scandinavian Lutherans. At some point, a more specifically Norwegian Lutheran congregation emerged and continued at First Lutheran Church. It is currently located very near this spot on the east end of town, although it is a much more modern structure. (Courtesy Bill Young.)

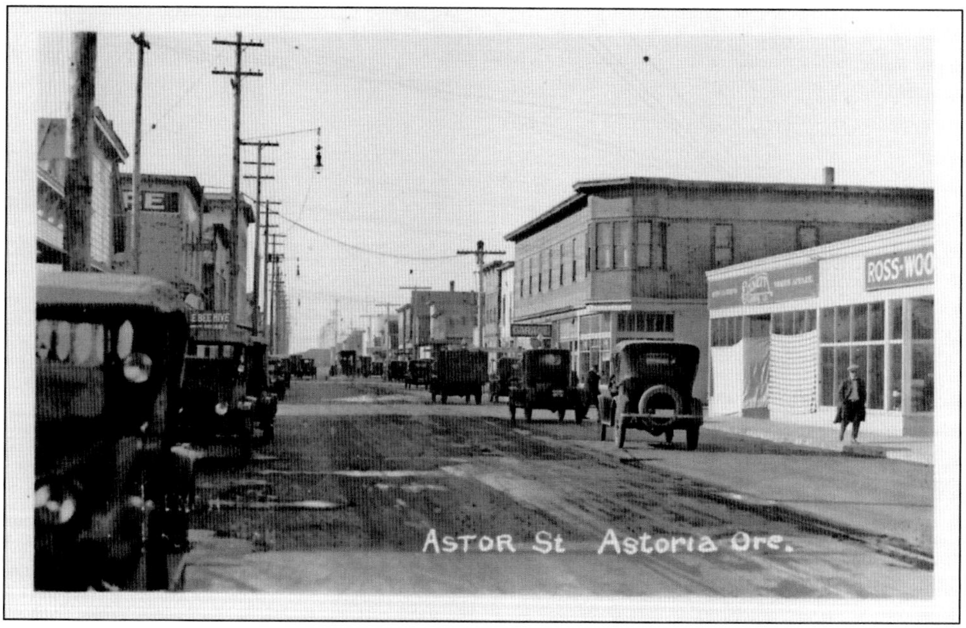

Jumping to the other end of town with a distinctly different culture, Astor Street was known as the red-light district. It was the site of numerous establishments euphemistically referred to as "female boarding houses." While seeking such entertainment and a good stiff drink at one of the many saloons in the area, a young man could easily be shanghaied—kidnapped and forced to crew on a "slow boat to China." This image is from about Fifth Street looking west around 1920. On the left, the tallest building is August Erickson's famous Louvre on the corner of Seventh Street, built in 1896. The river is to the right. Much to the chagrin of many disapproving Astorians, this area was untouched by the Great Fire of 1922. (Courtesy of Ray Hakala.)

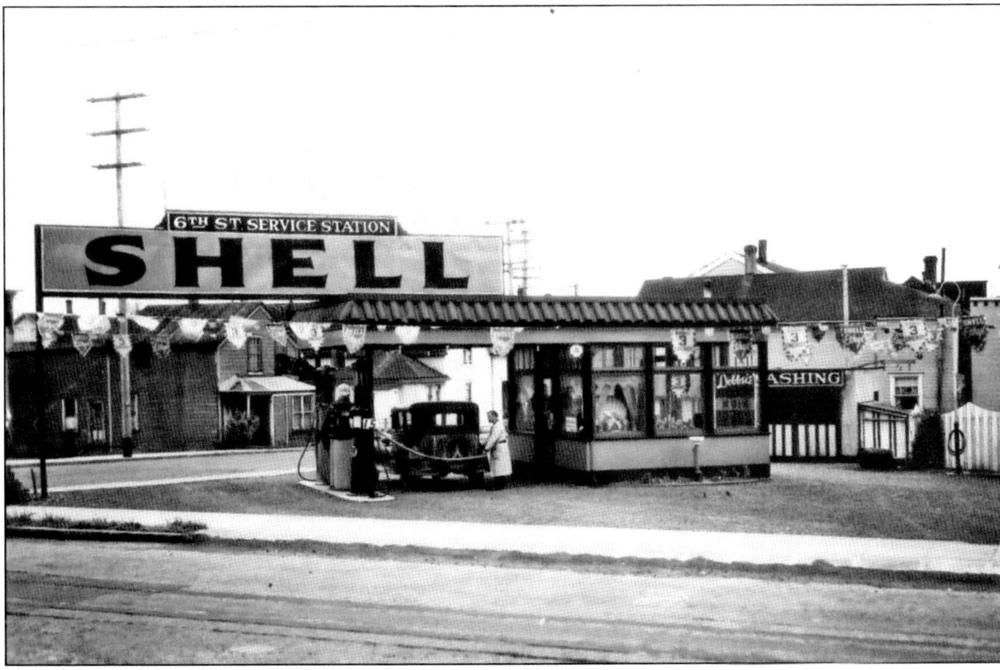

The west end of Astoria, near the river, was a diverse working-class neighborhood. This image from about 1930 promotes the increasing services available to the automobile driving public. Commercial Street is in the foreground with Sixth Street to the left. Today there is a park on the site. (Courtesy of Ray Hakala.)

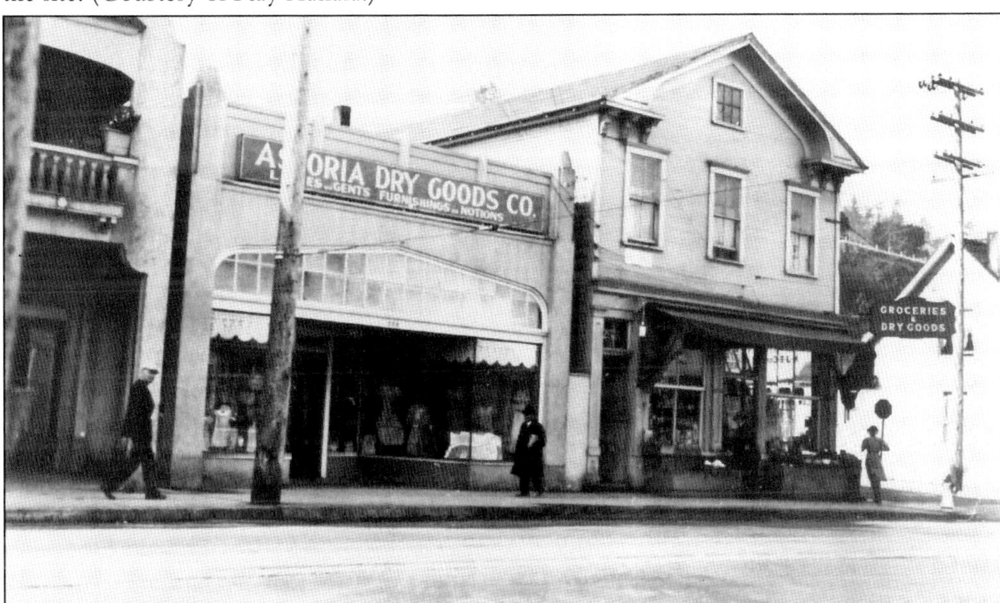

Bond Street is seen between Sixth and Seventh Streets. For many years, this was Astoria's "China Town." After the fishing industry excluded them, some remained and maintained thriving businesses and raised families. This postcard shows just such activity around the 1920s. Decades before, it was quite densely packed with the burgeoning Chinese population of the era. The Chinese tong is to the left. (Courtesy of Ray Hakala.)

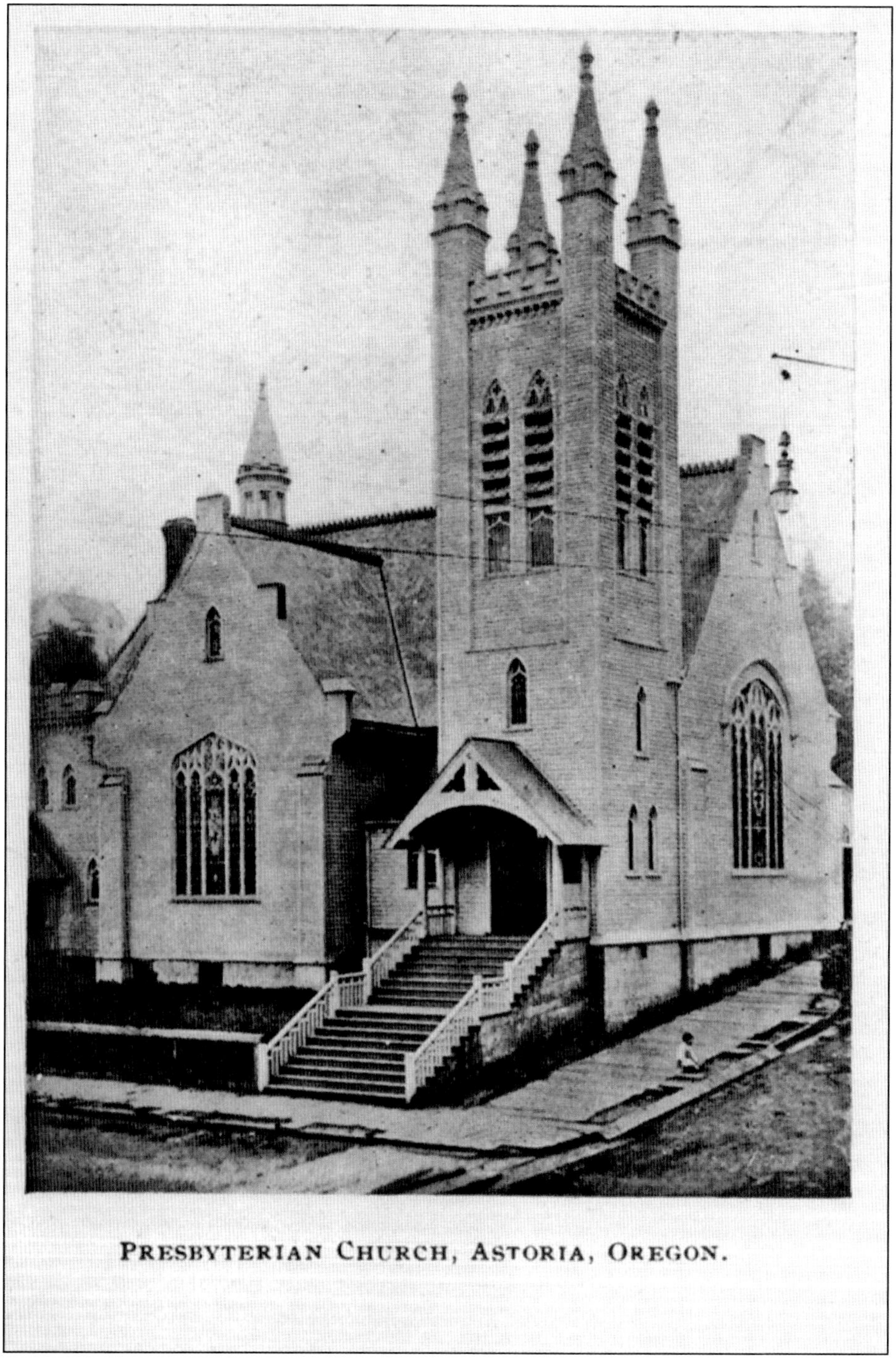

The First Presbyterian Church in Astoria is located at Eleventh Street and Grand Avenue. The Carpenter Gothic–style church was constructed in 1903 with money from its congregation, including Capt. George Flavel and his family. It features stained glass windows by the Povey brothers of Portland. It is a landmark widely visible from many points in downtown. Its appearance today is much the same as in this image from the early 1900s. (Courtesy of Sara's Old Photos.)

Seven

WATERCRAFT AND TRANSPORTATION

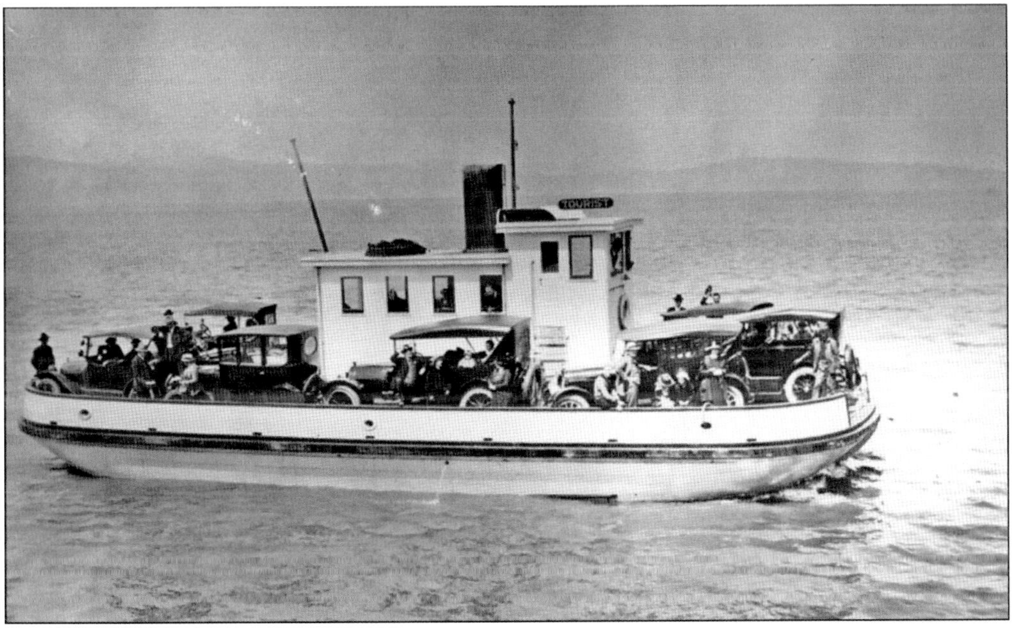

The first ferry service from Astoria across the Columbia was an improvised scow. In the summer of 1920, Capt. Fritz Elfving recognized the need, or opportunity, and transported over 700 cars. As the automobile gained in popularity and affordability, traditional modes of transportation had to evolve and adapt. Elfving knew his new business would continue to grow, so he contracted with Wilson Shipbuilding in Astoria to build a new diesel ferry. It was called the *Tourist* (pictured here). It was 60 feet long and could carry 15 automobiles and 30 people. It was launched as part of Elfving's Astoria-McGowan Ferry Company in May 1921. Some of the first passengers were members of a Model T club enjoying a motorcar excursion to the coast. (Courtesy of Sara's Old Photos.)

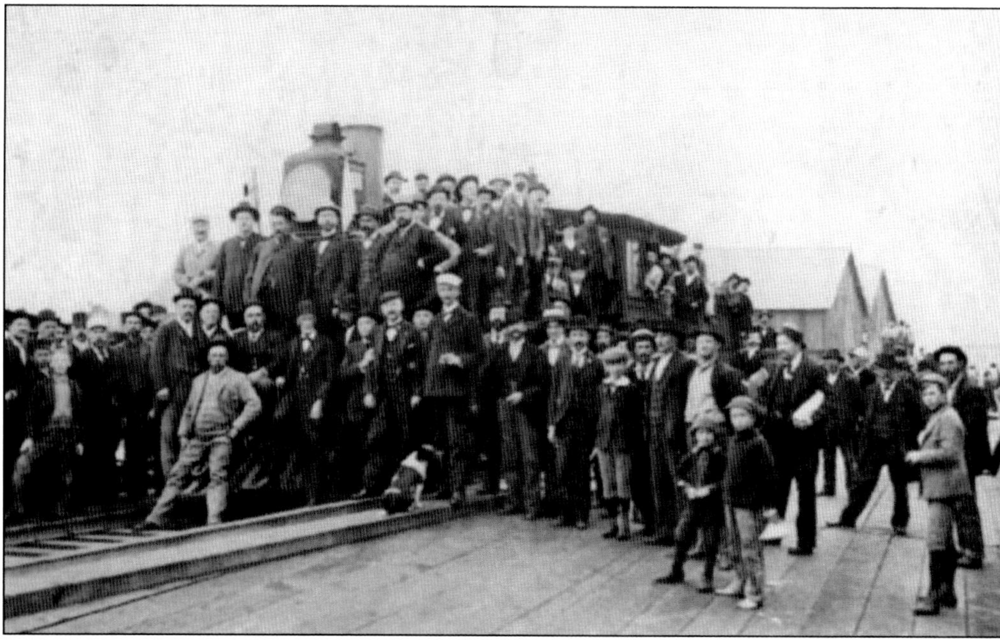

Astorians offered incentives to get the railroad to town. After several failed attempts, in December 1894, Astoria city leaders accepted a proposal from Montana businessman Andrew B. Hammond, who had both the construction experience and the financial backing to bring rail service to Astoria. At the time, the transcontinental railroad ended at Goble, making Portland the western terminus of the line. Finally, after half a century of anticipation, the Astoria & Columbia River Railroad (A&CR) line was completed on April 4, 1898. The first train arrived on May 16, 1898, and this postcard commemorated the event. (Courtesy of Michael Foster.)

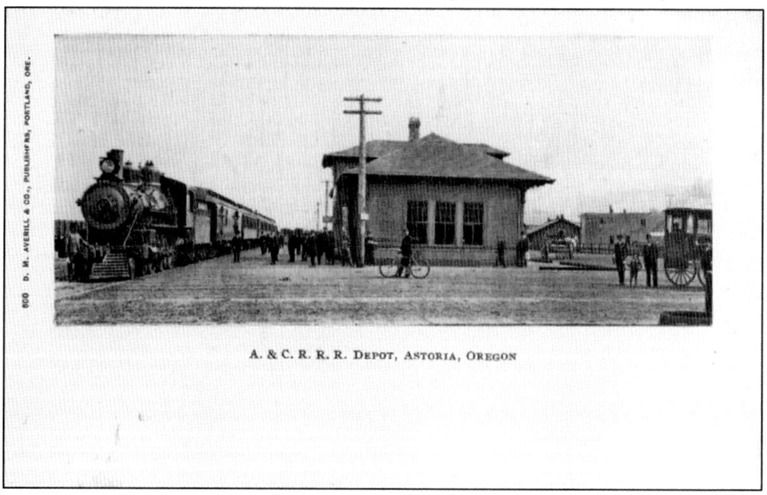

Some of the earliest postcards promoting tourist destinations were produced and distributed by the railroad companies. This image shows the original wooden depot at Astoria's waterfront. The Spokane, Portland & Seattle Railway (SP&SR) bought the A&CR on February 24, 1911. In 1925, the SP&SR constructed a brick depot at Twentieth Street. The new depot was just east of the original and handled passenger traffic until service ended in 1952. After standing empty for decades, it was donated to the Columbia River Maritime Museum in the 1990s by the Burlington Northern Railroad. (Author's collection.)

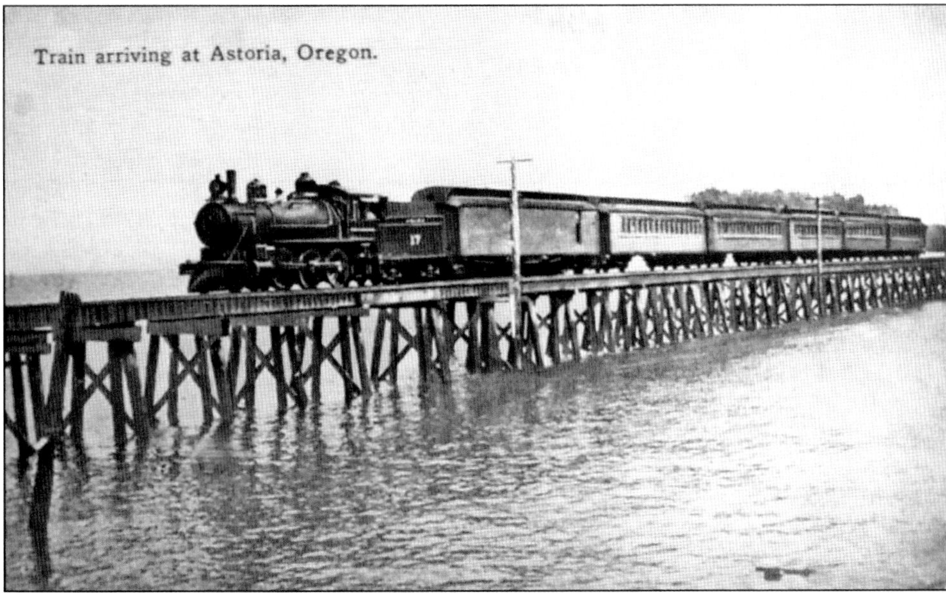

At the peak of rail activity, there were eight passenger trains a day, including a "daddy train" that brought fathers to spend the weekend with families along the coast. Although freight traffic was booming, it was the tourist trade that was successfully established during this era. The middle class was expanding, and escaping from the valley heat was a true luxury, much as it is today. (Author's collection.)

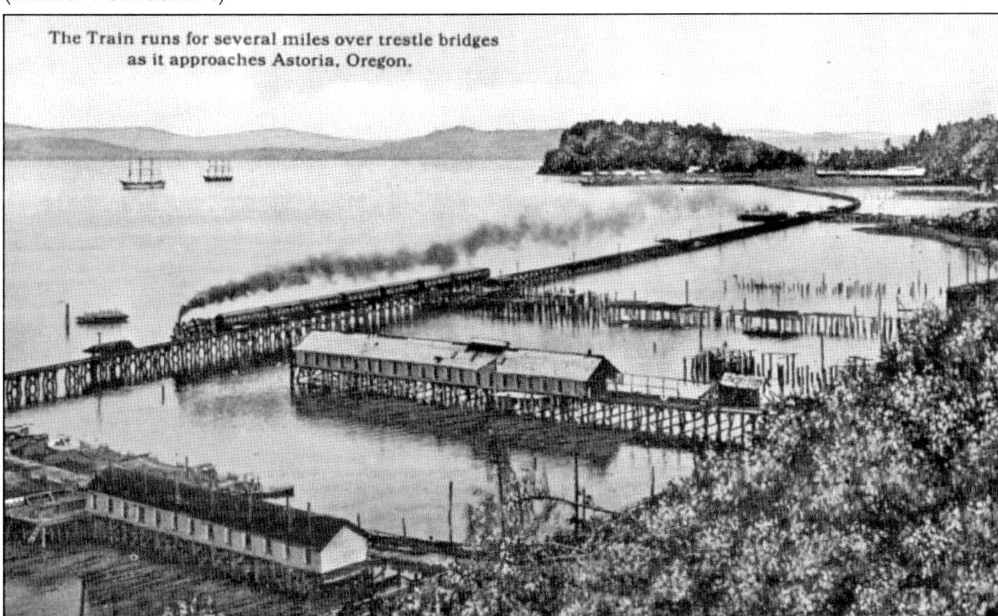

Astoria, in this view of Uppertown leading east to Tongue Point, has always been imagined as a booming commercial port. From the early days, the railways were seen as the means to reach that goal. Once it was completed, the SP&SR connected all centers of industry, aiding in economic development throughout the Lower Columbia region. The railroad once crossed Young's Bay on a long trestle and went to Warrenton and Seaside. The path of the current Young's Bay bridge to Warrenton follows the general path of the trestle. (Courtesy of Michael Foster.)

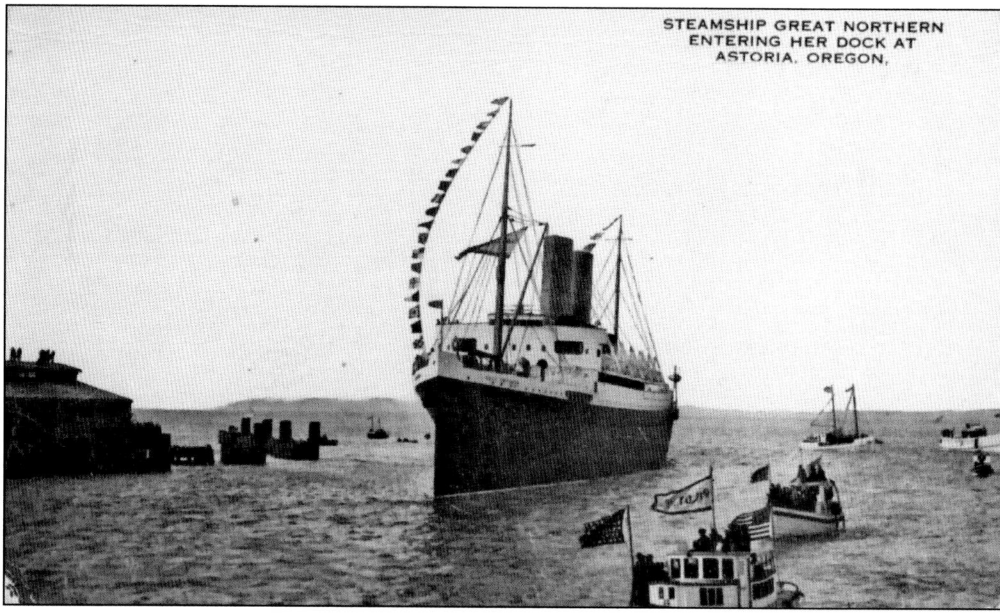

Transportation links between land and sea were being continuously streamlined. In 1914, the Great Northern Pacific Steamship Company was born. It had two ships, the *Great Northern*, pictured here, and the *Northern Pacific*. They ran between Astoria and San Francisco regularly, carrying passengers and freight between the port cities. During the winters, they had voyages to Hawaii. Once arriving in Astoria, passengers on the SP&SR could board a luxury steamer heading south beginning in 1915. It was not profitable however, and was put up for sale shortly before America entered World War I. (Courtesy of Sara's Old Photos.)

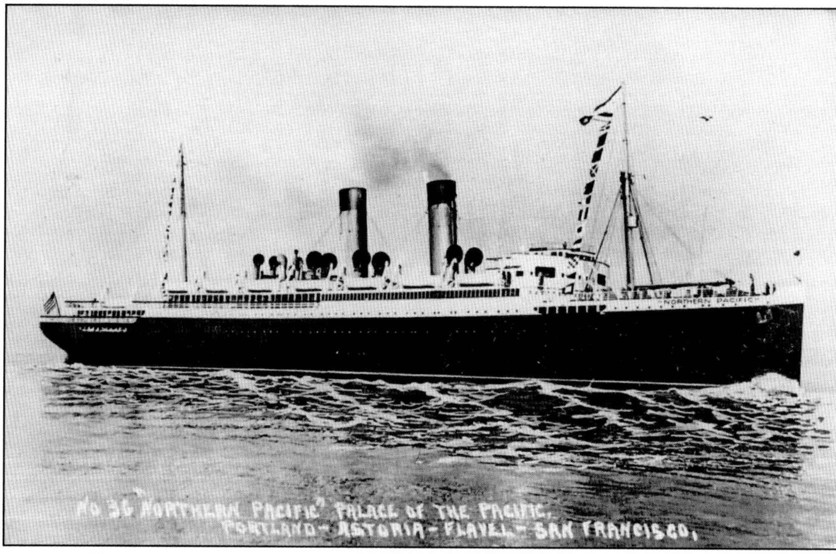

The promotional caption on the reverse of this 1915 postcard reads, "The first stop is at Astoria, Oregon, at the mouth of the Columbia River. There is not a more charming water trip on the continent than the 100 mile voyage up the Columbia between this point and Portland. On a clear day, at the junction of the Willamette and Columbia, five snow-capped mountain peaks are clearly visible: St. Helens, Jefferson, Adams, Rainier-Tacoma and Hood. The company operates its fleet as far south as Los Angeles (San Pedro)." (Courtesy of Bill Young.)

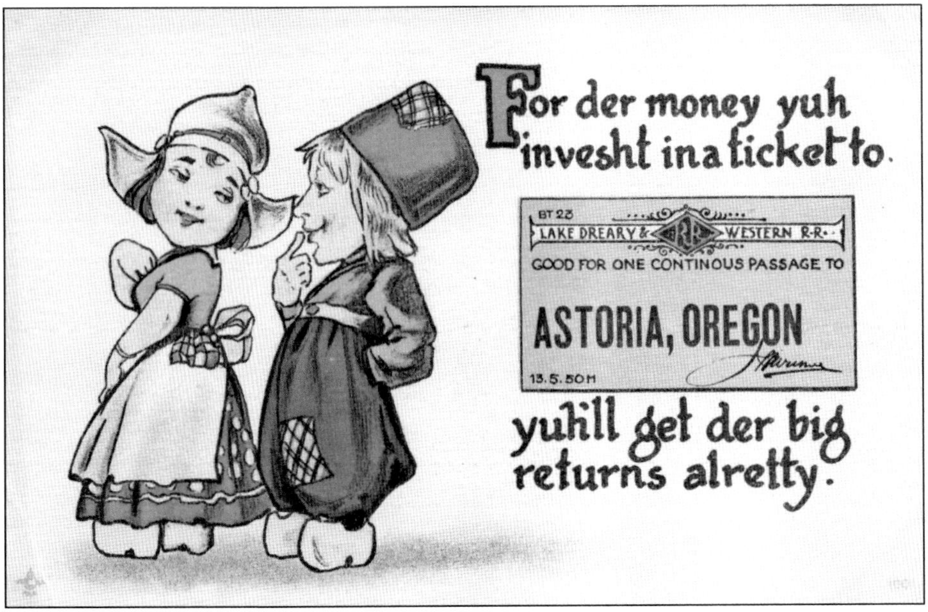

Playing on the Scandinavian heritage of Astoria and its surrounding communities, other railroad companies promoted trips to destinations west. This postcard is from the Lake Erie & Western Railroad—a service area with another high Scandinavian concentration. Upon closer inspection, one might notice a play on the name of the line—"Lake Dreary & Western R. R."—possibly encouraging people to leave home and take a trip! (Courtesy of Michael Foster.)

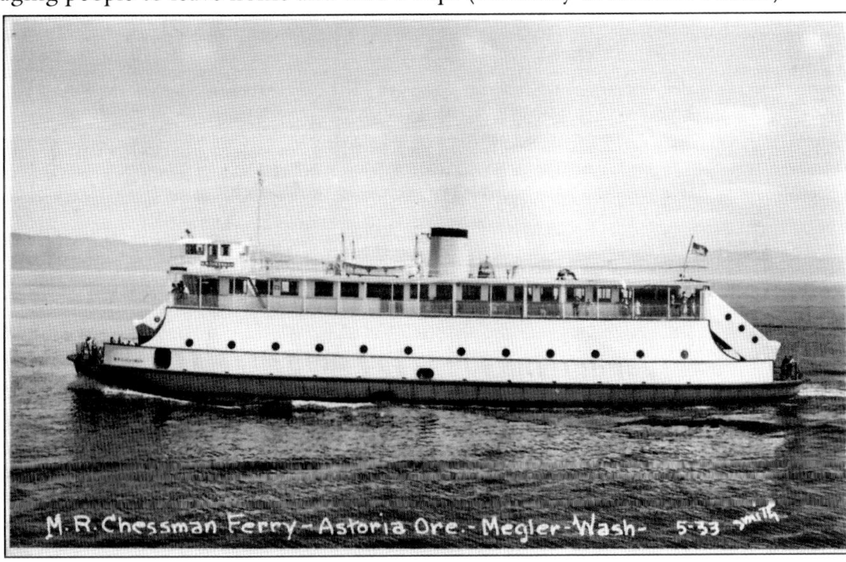

After many years of success, Captain Elfving retired and sold the ferry business to Astoria resident Merle R. Chessman in 1946. Chessman had been publisher of Astoria's daily newspaper and served as an Oregon state senator. It is said that Chessman planned to sell the operation to the Oregon Highway Department, but he died suddenly before the sale. The steel ferry *M.R. Chessman* was launched in 1947 and remained in service until the 1960s. In 1966, the US Navy bought the *M.R. Chessman* for $300,000 and transferred the vessel to Vietnam. The Navy had originally intended to use the vessel as a ferry on the Mekong River; instead, it was employed as a machine shop for river patrol craft. (Courtesy of Michael Foster.)

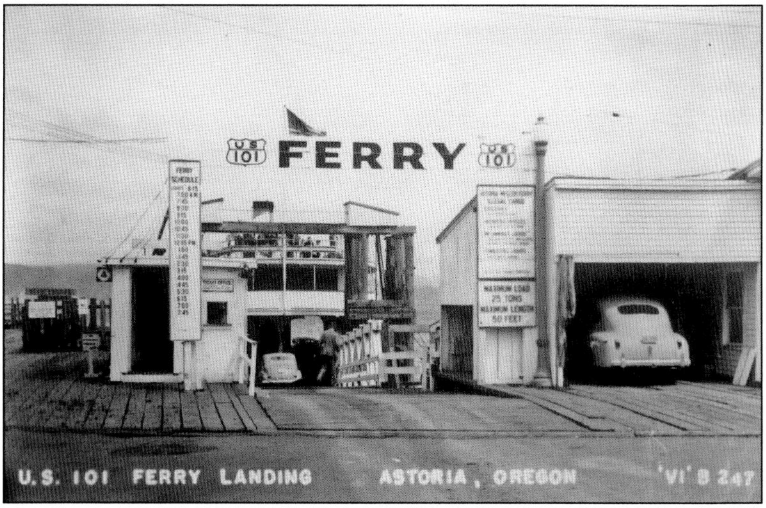

As Astoria grew, Elfving commissioned a larger wooden-hulled ferry, *Tourist II* (with a capacity of 22 automobiles and 155 passengers), which was launched at Astoria on June 17, 1924. The ferries departed from a specially built dock at Fourteenth Street (pictured here, with cars loading onto the *Tourist II*) in Astoria. Elfving had persuaded the Astoria City Council to use municipal funds to build this dock. Today, it is home to tug and pilot boats, and scenes from the movie *Free Willy* were filmed on it, but it may be welcoming back the *Tourist II* at some point in the future. An enthusiastic community group has organized to bring the original vessel back to Astoria. (Courtesy of Sara's Old Photos.)

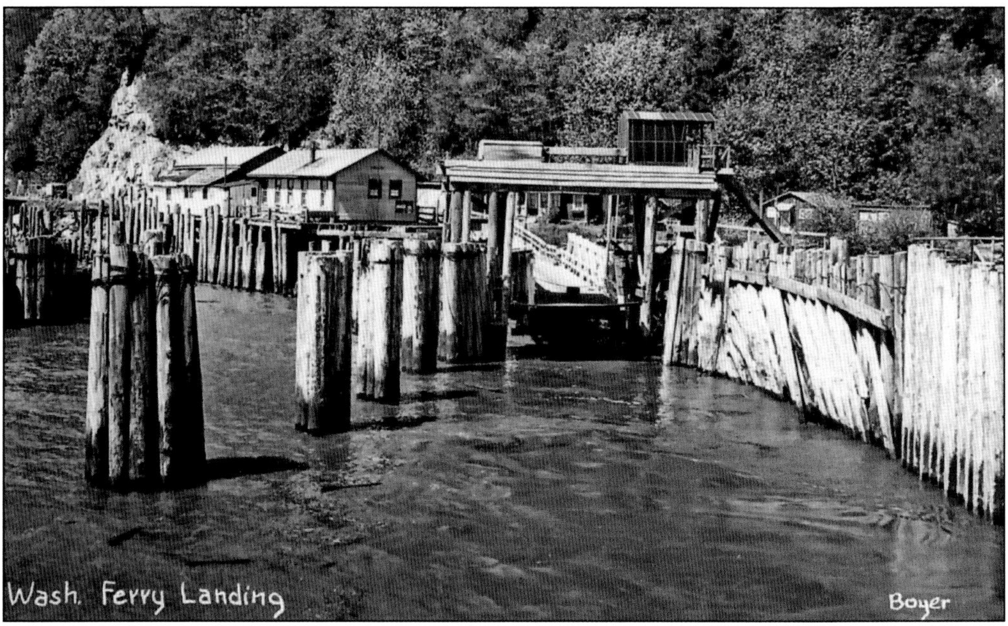

Here is an excellent view of the ferry landing in Megler, Washington. Captain Elfving worked both sides of the river to secure the facilities needed for his ferry operation. Pacific County built a road from the town of Chinook to McGowan, and a ferry slip was built at the end of the dock owned by the P.J. McGowan Cannery. In good weather, the ferry trip took about 30 minutes. The remains of these pilings can be seen east of the Washington side of the Astoria-Megler Bridge. (Courtesy of Sara's Old Photos.)

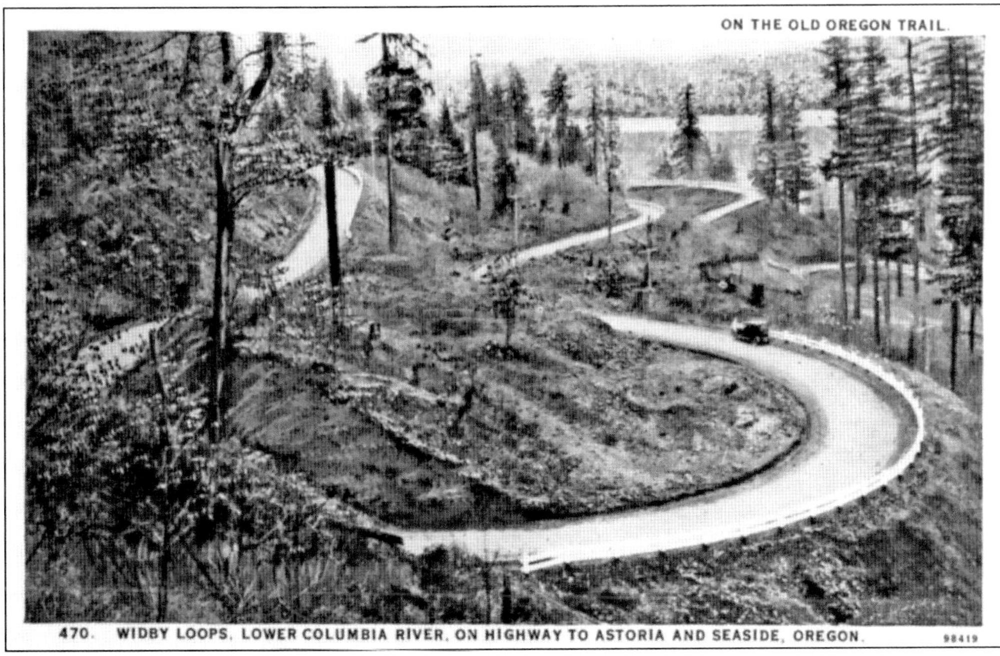

The Columbia River Highway—also known by its federal designation, Highway 30—first opened between Portland and Astoria on August 12, 1915. The new highway was the first major road in the area at a time when Oregon and other states were rushing to develop infrastructure to accommodate the automobile boom. When it opened, it was graveled in some areas but not paved. It had many curves (as shown on this postcard), but the new highway served its purpose well. The location of the Widby Loops on (Old) Highway 30 is near the area of Bradley Summit, towards Wauna Mill. (Courtesy of Sean Fitzpatrick and Anne Carpenter.)

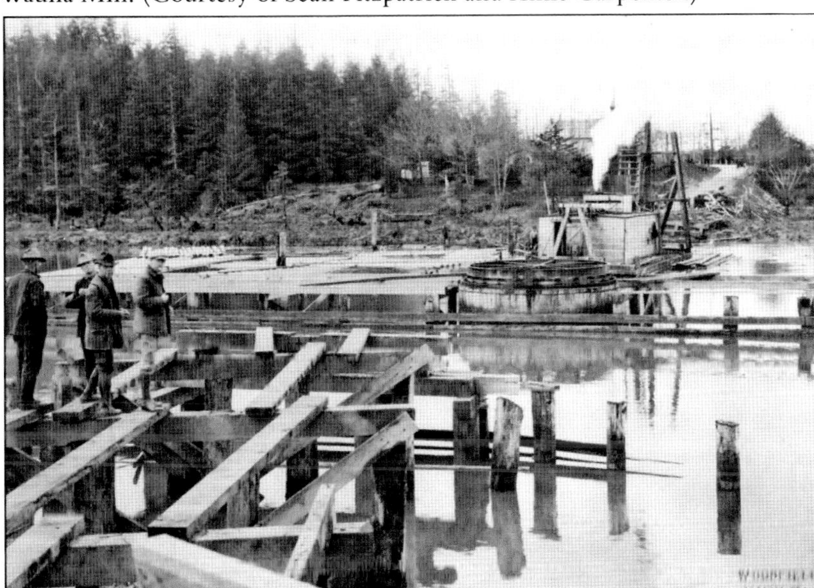

This 1926 Frank Woodfield photograph shows the building of the Walluski River Bridge near the present-day Clatsop County Fairgrounds on Highway 202. Daniel Young, son of Andrew and nephew of Benjamin, is in the dark hat looking back. (Courtesy of Bill Young.)

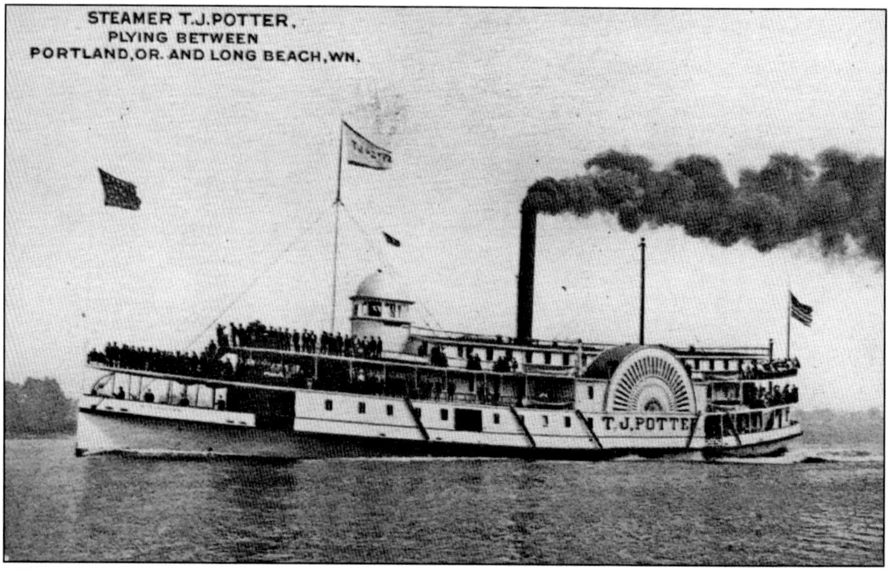

Owned by the Oregon Railway & Navigation Company (OR&N), the *T.J. Potter* was one of the few side-wheeled steamboats that operated on the Columbia. It was built entirely of wood and launched in 1888. The *Potter* was known as the fastest and most luxurious steamer on the river and held the speed record for the fastest trip between Portland and Astoria for a time. Upgraded several times, the *Potter* was used for passenger transport until 1916, then served as barracks for Wilson Shipyard workers. After being stripped by salvagers in 1925, the last remains of the *T.J. Potter* are visible at low tide on the northeast shores of Young's Bay, near Astoria High School. (Courtesy of Michael Foster.)

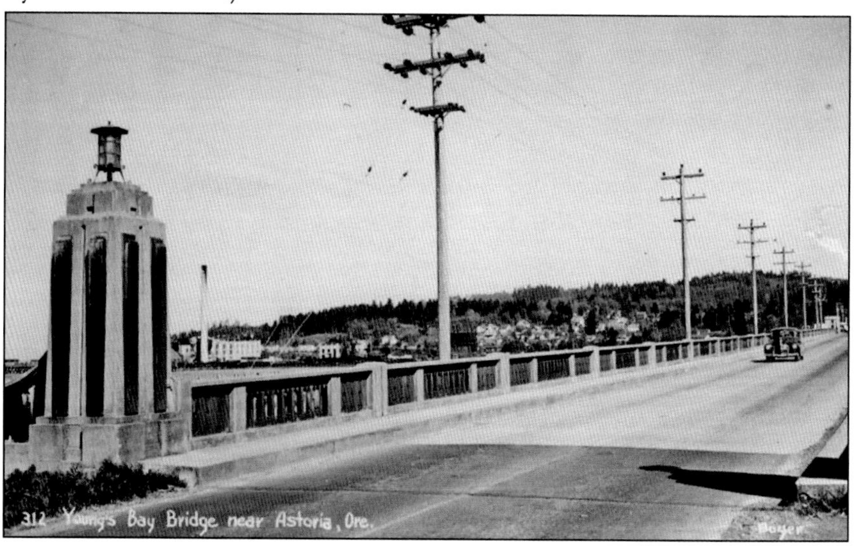

The "old" Young's Bay Bridge, as it is now called by locals, was new and modern in 1921. The bridge features accent elements from its designer, Conde McCullough. The Art Moderne pylons topped by light fixtures, pictured on this postcard, flank the landings on both ends of the bridge. McCullough (1887–1946), an assistant professor at Oregon Agricultural College (Oregon State University), designed many of the bridges along the Coast Highway (101) and became the head of the bridge division of the Oregon Department of Transportation. His designs are known for their architectural beauty. (Courtesy of Sara's Old Photos.)

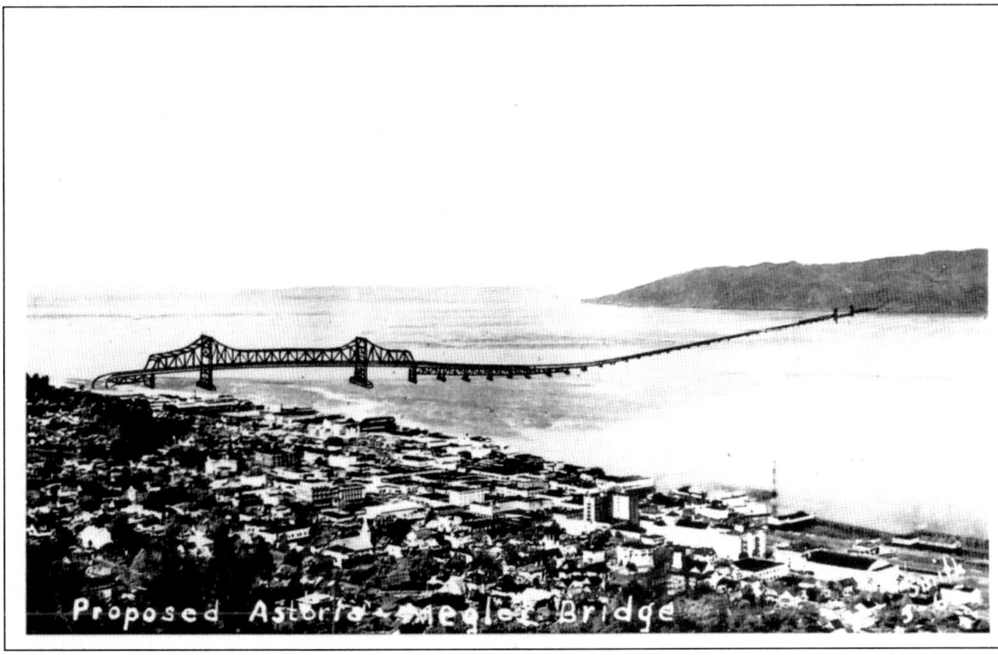

With the automobile gaining popularity, more demand for roads and access was inevitable. Motorists turned away from the railroads to reach the Oregon and Washington coast. Imagining a bridge across the river was easy—no long lines, missed ferries, or waiting for good weather. This postcard illustrated the proposed Astoria-Megler Bridge in the early 1960s as an aid to visualize the project and promote it. The 4.2-mile bridge was completed in 1966 and was the longest continuous truss bridge in North America at the time. The toll was $1.50 each way and was discontinued in December 1993 after the "Bridge to Nowhere" was paid for completely. (Courtesy of Michael Foster.)

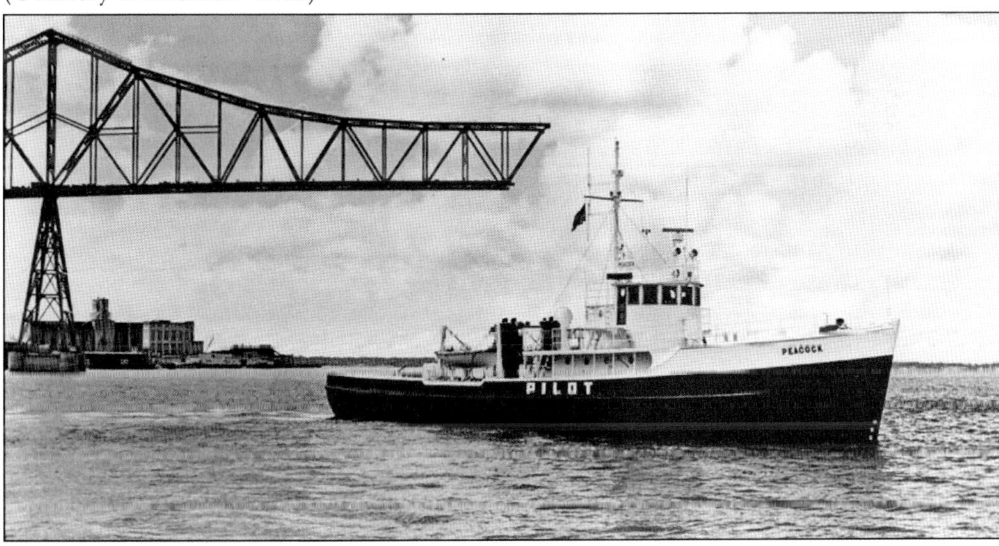

While this image is not a postcard, it tells many stories. It was taken during the construction of the Astoria-Megler Bridge, when life on the river was changing. The flour mill no longer exists, the bridge ended ferry service, and the Peacock has been replaced by a newer version. (Courtesy of Sara's Old Photos.)

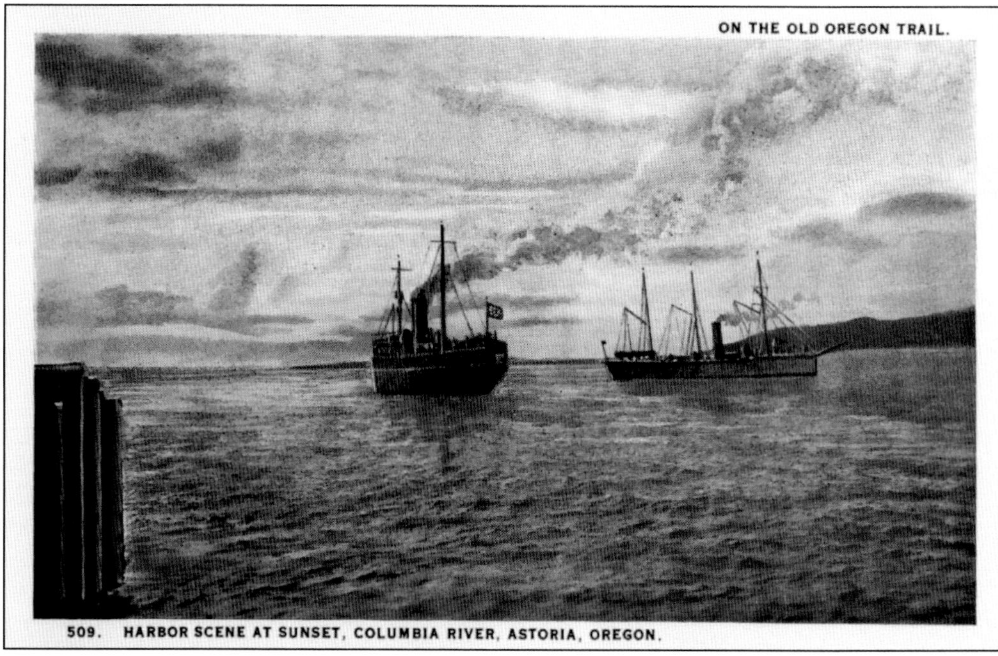

Commerce on the river never stops, but it sometimes slows down. Here is a lovely evening scene with just two ships heading to sea. (Courtesy of Sean Fitzpatrick and Anne Carpenter.)

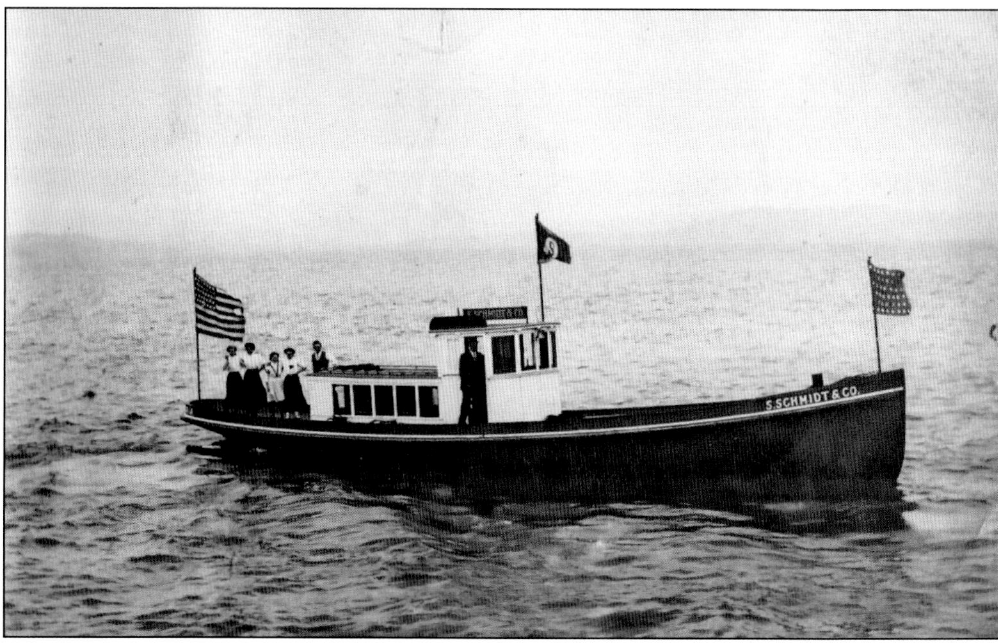

The cannery launch *S. Schmidt Co.* worked on the Columbia River collecting fish from fishermen or fish-buying scows and took the fish directly to the Schmidt Cannery for processing. A cannery launch was a common style of boat used for ferrying passengers and fish on the river locally. Karl E. Soderberg (great-grandfather of native Astorian Michael Soderberg) is at the wheel, with his children along for the ride, in this c. 1915 image. (Courtesy of Michael Soderberg.)

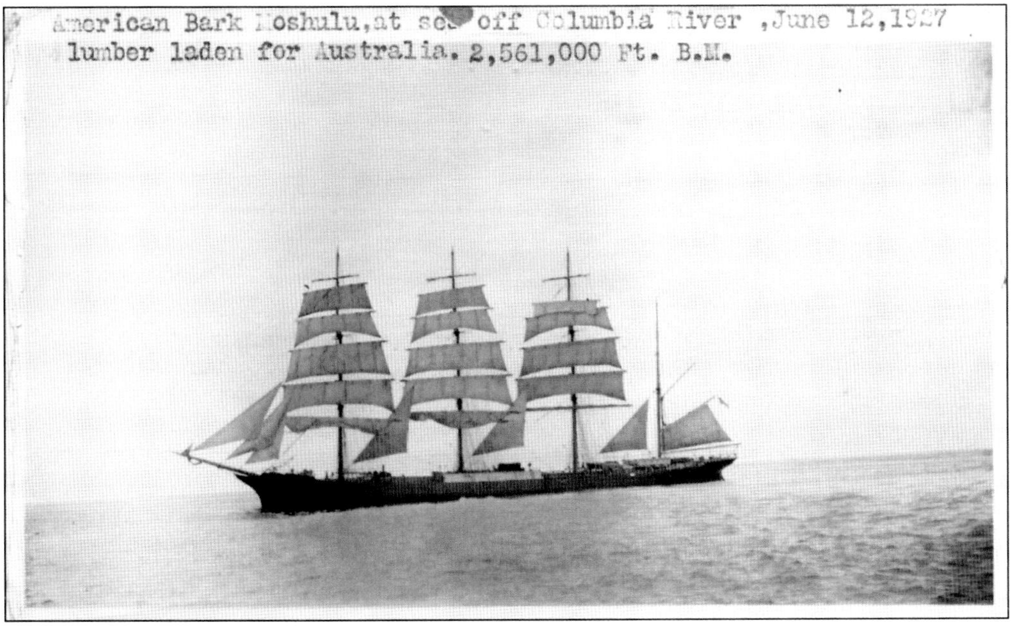

Originally named the *Kurt*, this four-masted steel barque was built in 1904 under German ownership. Its significance to Astoria begins in 1917, when it was seized and held here by the United States when it entered World War I. It was renamed *Dreadnought*, but another ship already had the name, so *Moshulu* was selected by First Lady Edith Wilson. It went on to a varied and distinguished sailing career. The *Moshulu* is now berthed at the Philadelphia waterfront and serves as a restaurant and event venue. (Courtesy of Michael Foster.)

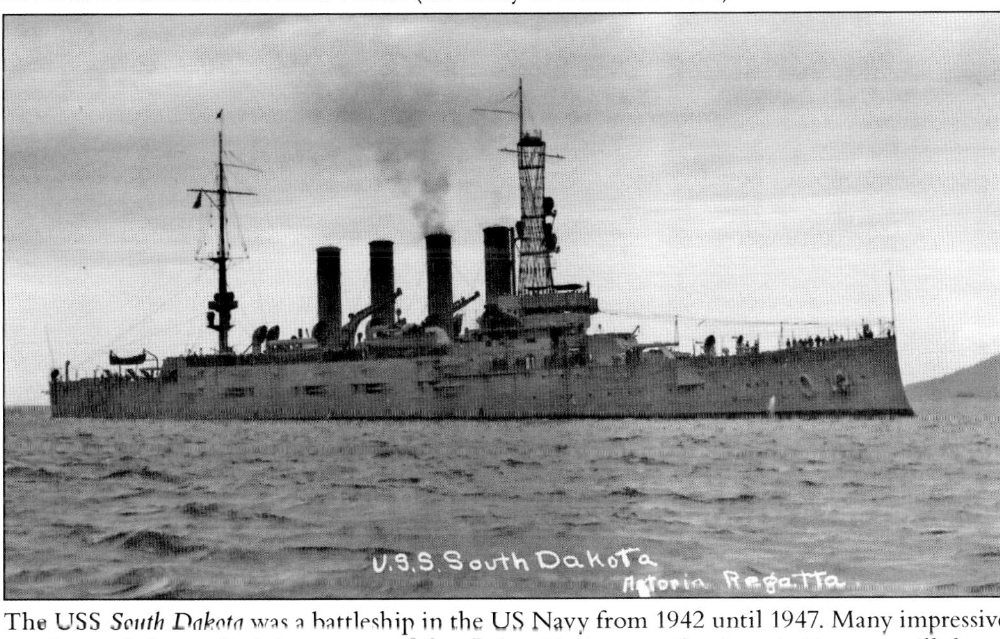

The USS *South Dakota* was a battleship in the US Navy from 1942 until 1947. Many impressive naval vessels have plied the waters of the Columbia River. The Astoria Regatta still draws Navy ships to the celebration, as it did here in the late 1940s. Impressive military ships can be seen parading past Astoria every year headed to Portland's annual Rose Festival. (Courtesy of Michael Foster.)

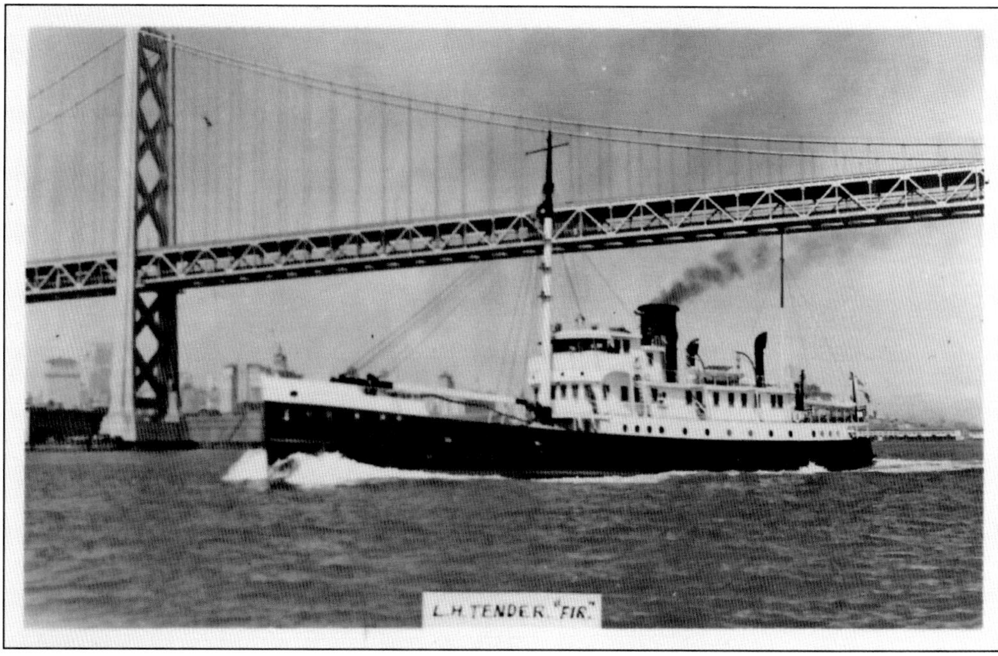

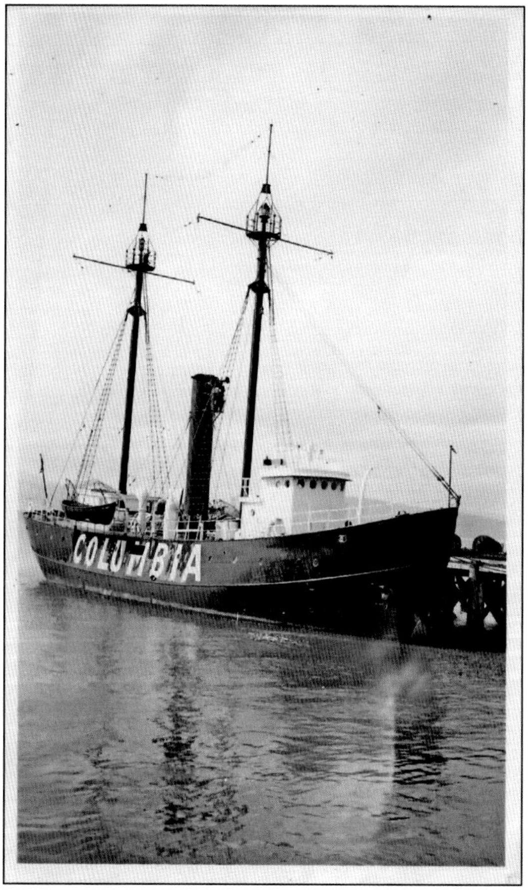

The lighthouse tender *Fir* was launched in 1939 as part of the Lighthouse Service. Shortly after, it was commissioned as a Coast Guard cutter when the Lighthouse Service became part of the Coast Guard. During World War II, its duties were to patrol the Oregon and Washington coasts. It was later reclassified as a coastal buoy tender until it was decommissioned in 1991. Its successor cutter, also named *Fir*, is in active use by the Coast Guard and based in Astoria. (Courtesy of Michael Foster.)

Lightship *Columbia*, decommissioned in 1979, is the last of five lightships with that name and is permanently docked in Astoria at the Columbia River Maritime Museum. Lightships have a long history of providing safe navigation along ocean and lake coastlines, effectively marking dangerous areas, narrow channels, and harbor entries. Guided tours are available through the museum. (Courtesy of Michael Foster.)

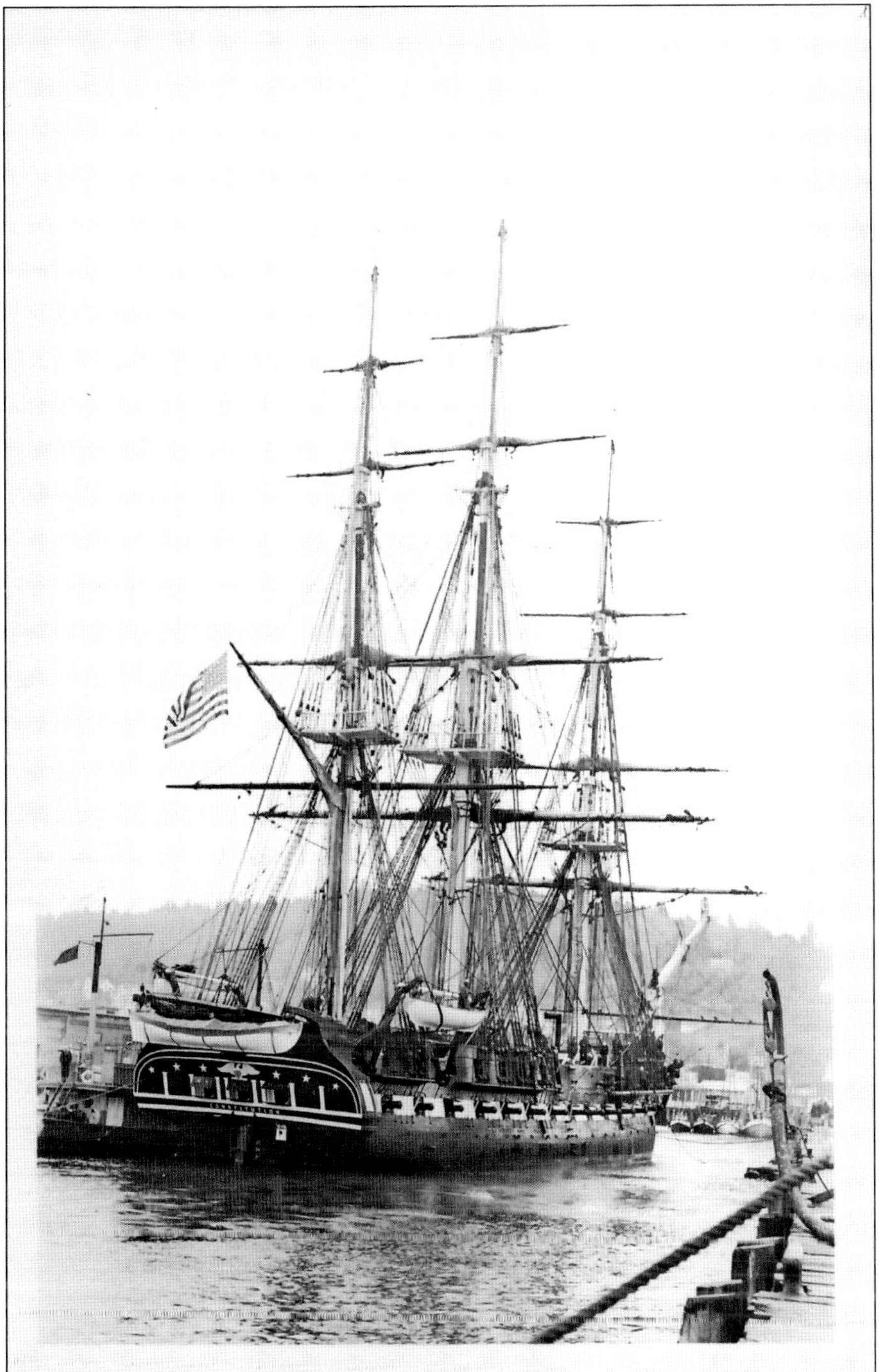

Following an extensive restoration in 1925, the USS *Constitution* or "Old Ironsides" embarked on a three-year tour that took it to 90 port cities along the Atlantic, Gulf, and Pacific coasts. After more than 4.5 million people boarded it on the tour, the ship returned to its home port of Boston in May 1934. The wooden-hulled, three-masted heavy frigate of the US Navy came to Astoria on this tour in May 1933. (Courtesy of Michael Foster.)

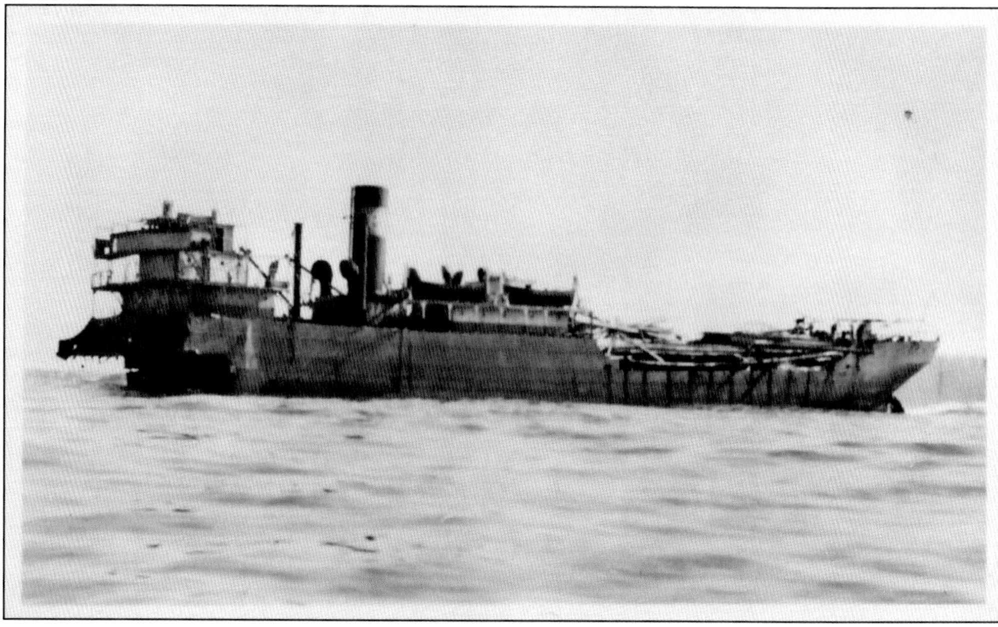

The Columbia River Bar is infamous in seafaring circles and is known as the "Graveyard of the Pacific." Many forces work together, or against each other, to make the river entrance one of the most unpredictable and dangerous in the world. Pictured on this postcard is the SS *Laurel*, wrecked on Peacock Spit (near North Head Lighthouse) in June 1929. It was fully loaded, and gale-force winds and giant waves broke it in two. Cargo and fragments of the ship littered the ocean. Amazingly, only one person died in the disaster. (Courtesy of Michael Foster.)

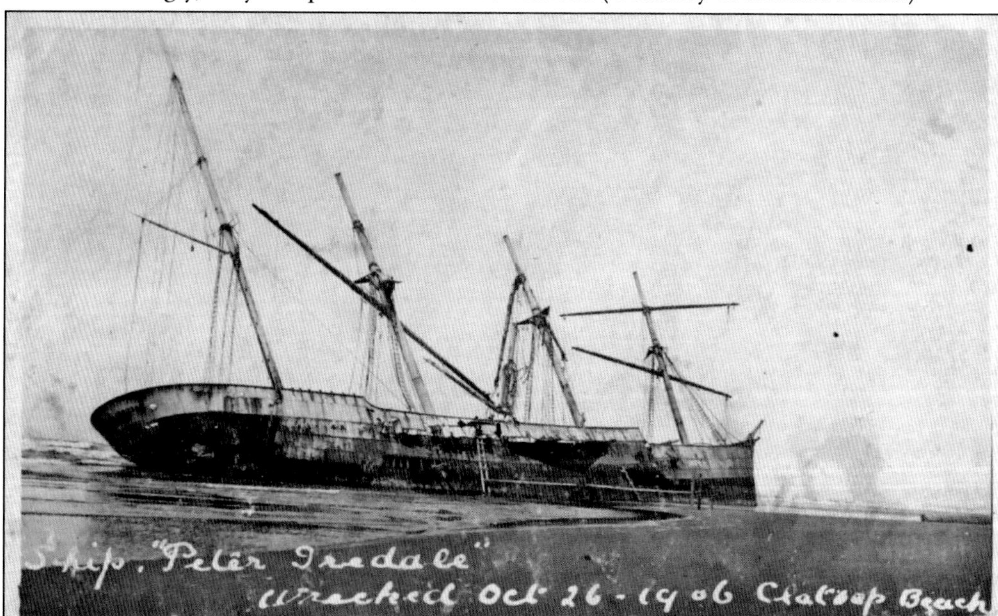

The wreck of the British sailing ship *Peter Iredale* immediately became an attraction on October 25, 1906, when it mistakenly ran aground on Clatsop Beach. It is still an attraction, and the remains of the ship are still visible at the shoreline at Fort Stevens State Park in Warrenton, Oregon. (Courtesy Clatsop County Historical Society 92.035.019.WC.)

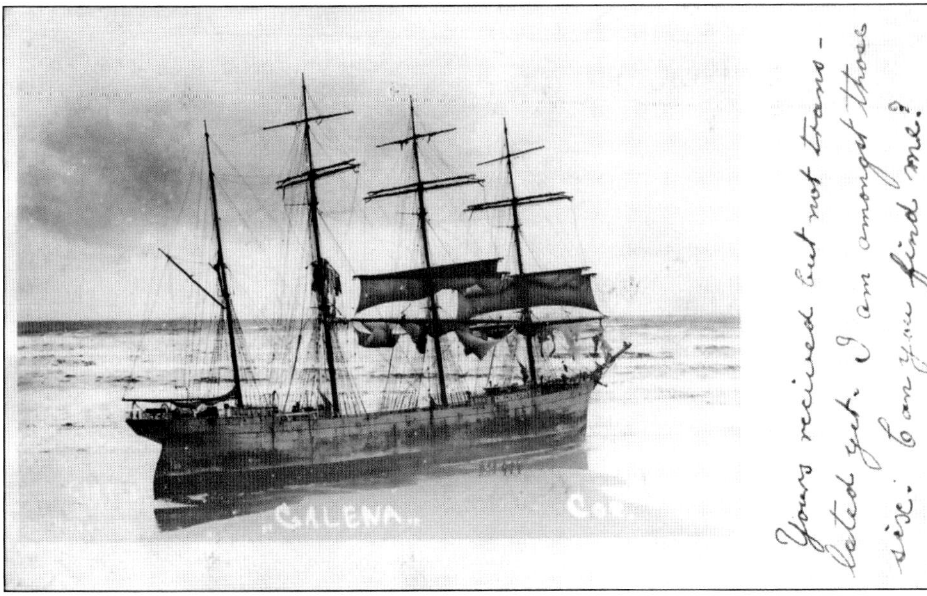

The grounding of the British four-masted barque *Galena* on November 13, 1906, near Gearhart, Oregon, is often overlooked. It happened only three weeks after the wreck of the *Peter Iredale*, a short distance down the coast. It sat during the winter, sank into the sand, and was never salvaged. It is still somewhere under the beach near Seaside. This photo postcard is by Elmer Allen Coe and displays an interesting message from the sender. (Courtesy of Michael Foster.)

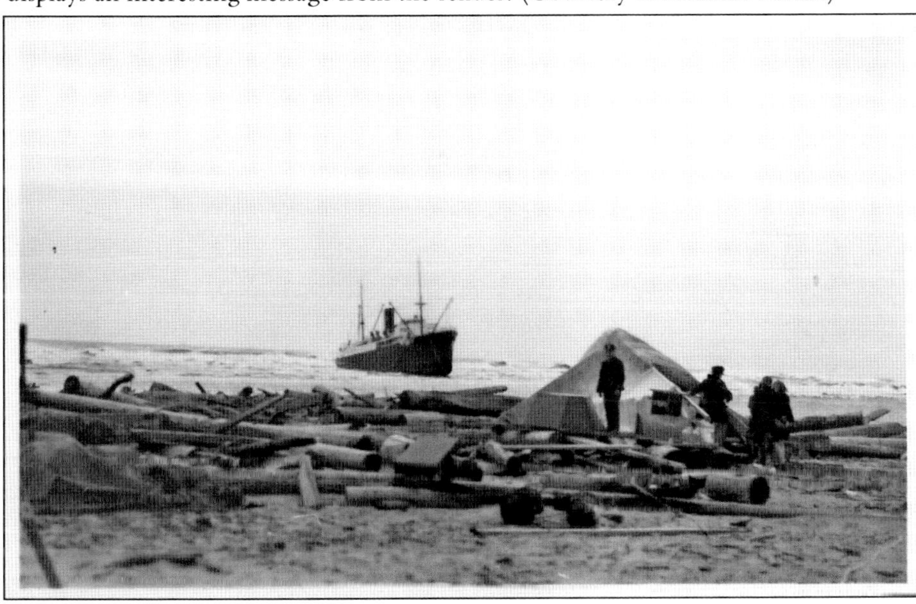

The *Admiral Benson* encountered heavy fog at the mouth of the Columbia on February 15, 1930, and became stuck in the sands of the Columbia River Bar. It was thought it could be refloated, but the situation was complicated by a previous wreck, the *Laurel*. Some passengers and crew used the available lifeboats to get to shore, and the rest were rescued using a cable attached to shore and a canvas sling. No lives were lost. The beach at Fort Canby (on the Washington side of the Columbia river mouth) is named Benson Beach after the wreck. This postcard shows lifeguards camped on the beach, looking after crew and passengers. (Courtesy of Michael Foster.)

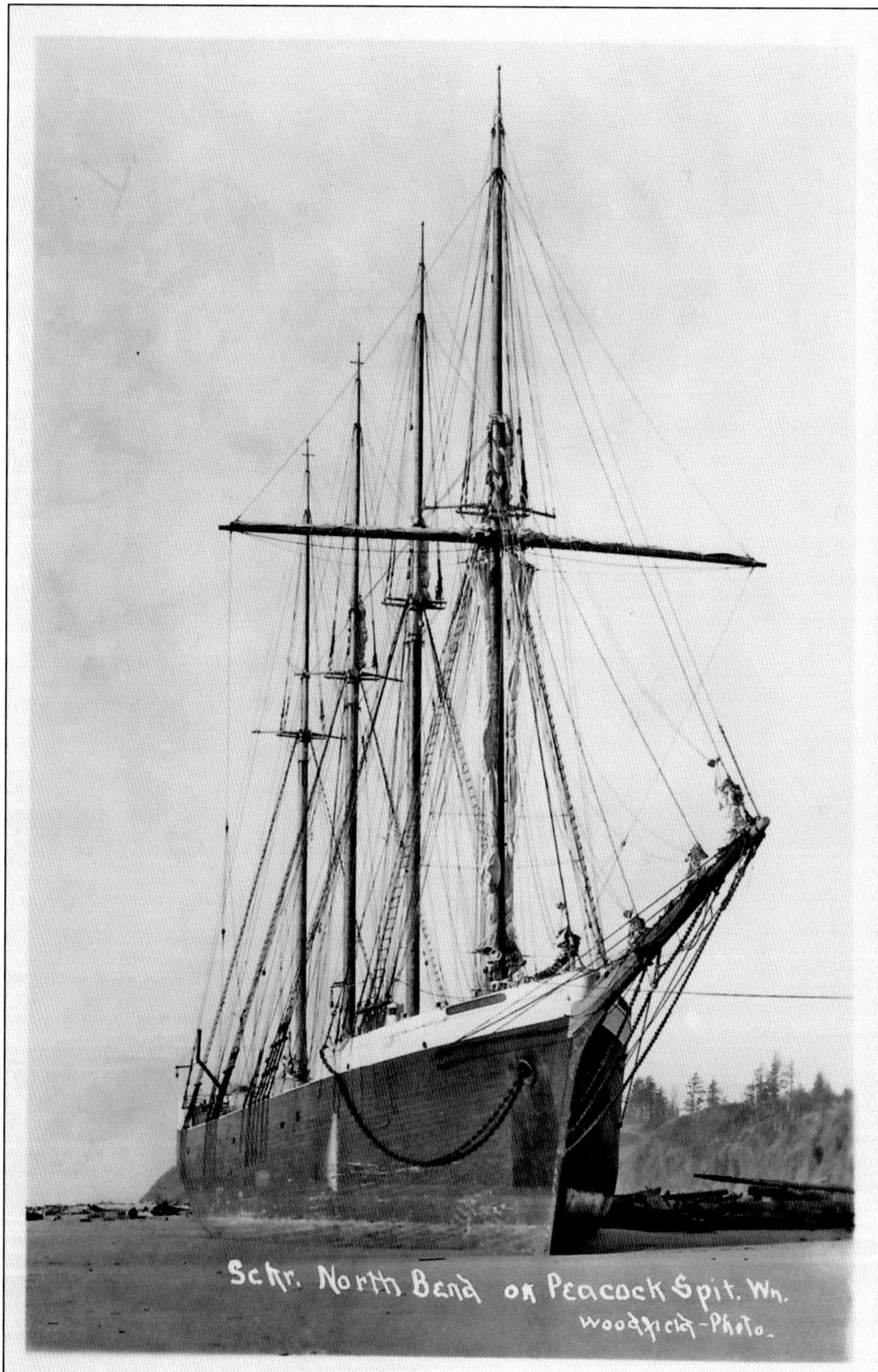

The beautiful schooner ***North Bend*** ran aground on Peacock Spit in February 1928. It was refloated and was saved but was stranded long enough to pose for wonderful photographs, including this one by Frank Woodfield. (Courtesy of Michael Foster.)

Eight

Local Life

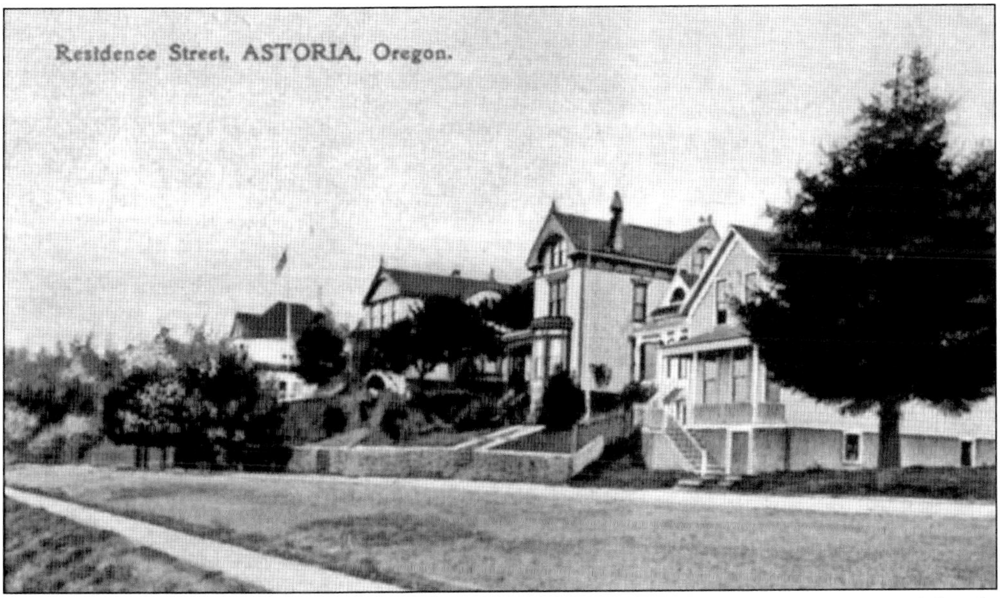

Many homes in Astoria were built before 1900, and most remain fulltime residences and family homes. Over the years, many new residents have sought to restore and preserve the original design and charm of their home's original era. With the limited buildable land in the city of Astoria, the number of homes is finite. The bucolic scene in this postcard highlights the varied architecture and pride of ownership on the block. (Author's collection.)

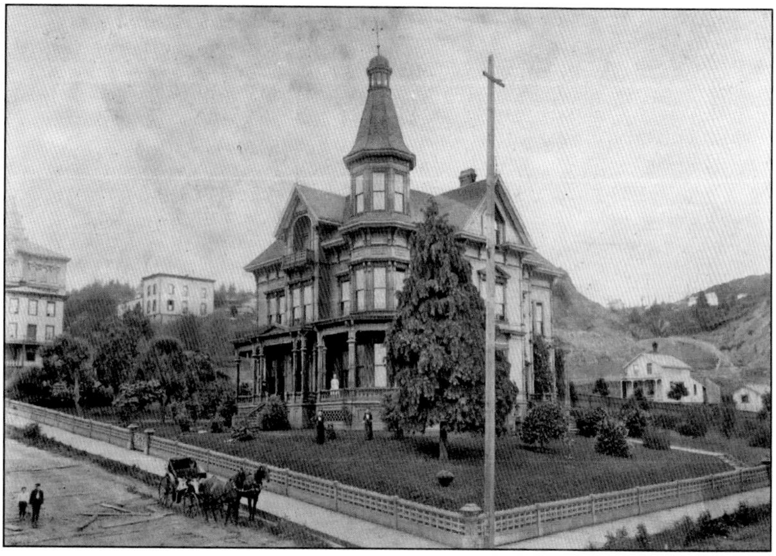

Bar pilot Capt. George Flavel pioneered the pilotage business on the Columbia River. He was a shrewd businessman and community leader. His interests were diverse and usually very profitable. The Flavel House, pictured from the corner of Eighth and Duane Streets (formerly Benson and Jefferson Streets), was designed by Carl Leick. The Queen Anne–style Victorian was completed in 1886. It was intended as Flavel's retirement home, and he lived there until 1893, when he died as Astoria's first millionaire. His wife, Mary, and their daughters, Nellie and Katie, lived there for the rest of their lives. It was saved from demolition and is now a museum of the Clatsop County Historical Society. (Courtesy of Clatsop County Historical Society.)

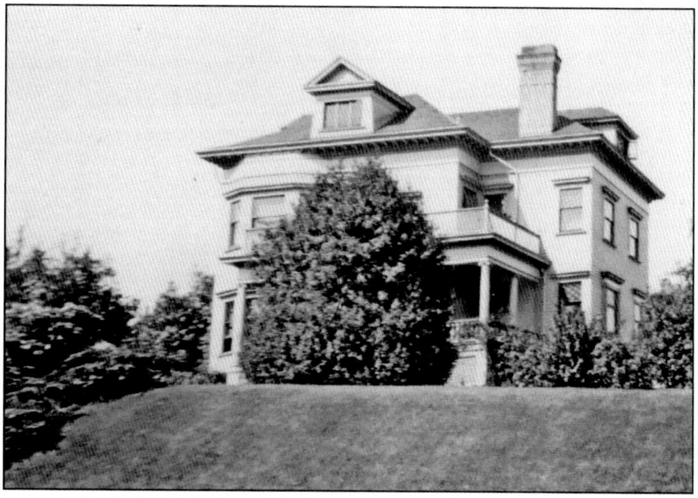

Also a Flavel house, this Colonial Revival–style home was built by Capt. George Conrad Flavel (1855–1923), son of Capt. George Flavel, in 1901 at the corner of Fifteenth Street and Franklin Avenue. Captain Flavel, his second wife, Winona, and their son, Harry, moved from a more modest home in town. They later had a daughter, Mary Louise. This infamous branch of the Flavel family lived in the house until 1990, when they left town and the house in extreme disrepair due to neglect and abuse. Unfortunately, the home has been a blight on the Astoria landscape for 25 years. Recently, however, a local family has purchased the home and begun a much-needed restoration of the property. The entire citizenry applauds the effort. (Courtesy of Clatsop County Historical Society, 11.061.033.)

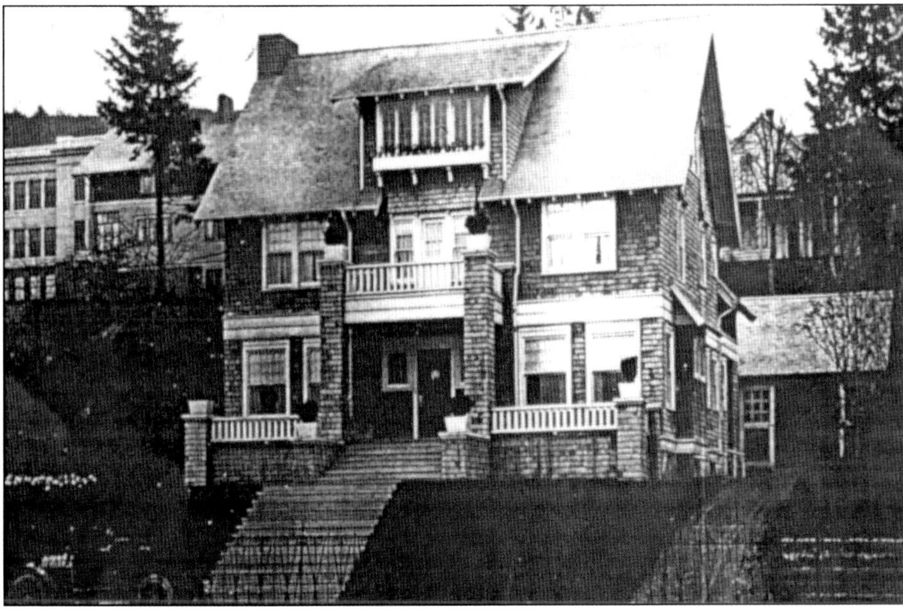

This home was built for Dr. A.A. Finch, the doctor at Fort Stevens. It was built from plans from the September 1908 *Craftsman* magazine and was designed by one of the leaders of the Arts and Crafts movement, Gustav Stickley. The house is plan number 56 and is only the second known version of that plan to be built. Located on Irving Avenue between Fifteenth and Sixteenth Streets, the house was converted to a duplex in the late 1930s when Astoria needed more housing for the war effort. It was converted back to a single-family home in 2003, and is being restored to its original condition. (Courtesy of Beth and Jeff Newenhof.)

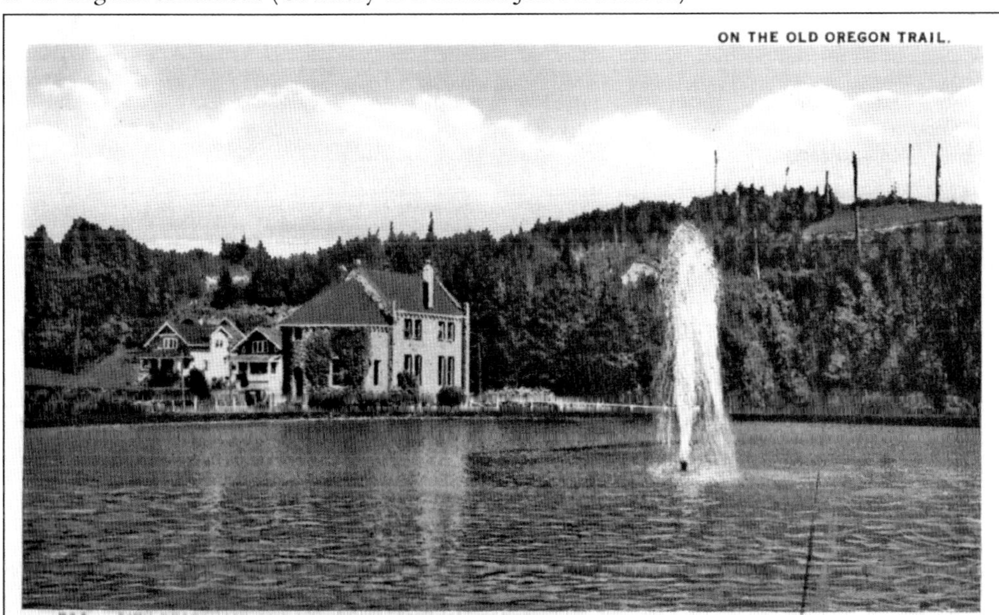

Astoria's City Reservoir was built in 1895 to meet the demand of a burgeoning population that used almost four million gallons of water every 24 hours. The structure appears incredibly similar today and sits just below Shively Park. (Author's collection.)

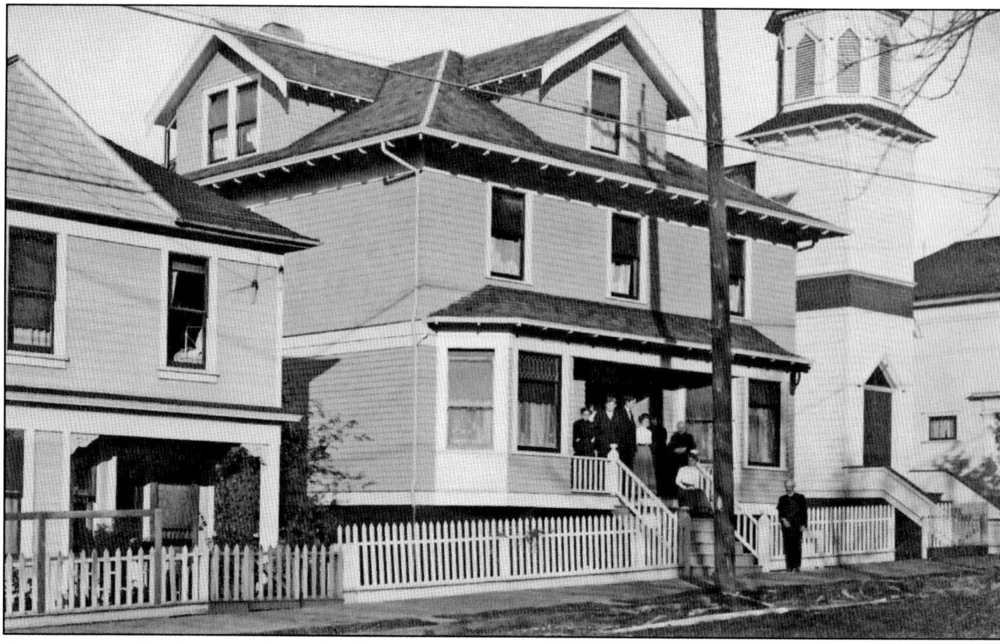

The home of Andrew and Elizabeth Bue from 1904 to 1934 was originally a single-story residence at 1161 Franklin Avenue but was moved and expanded to accommodate Scandinavian immigrant boarders. Its present address is 3418 Franklin Avenue. The Old Bethany Lutheran Church is next door. Family members are pictured on the front porch. (Courtesy of Marian Bue Soderberg.)

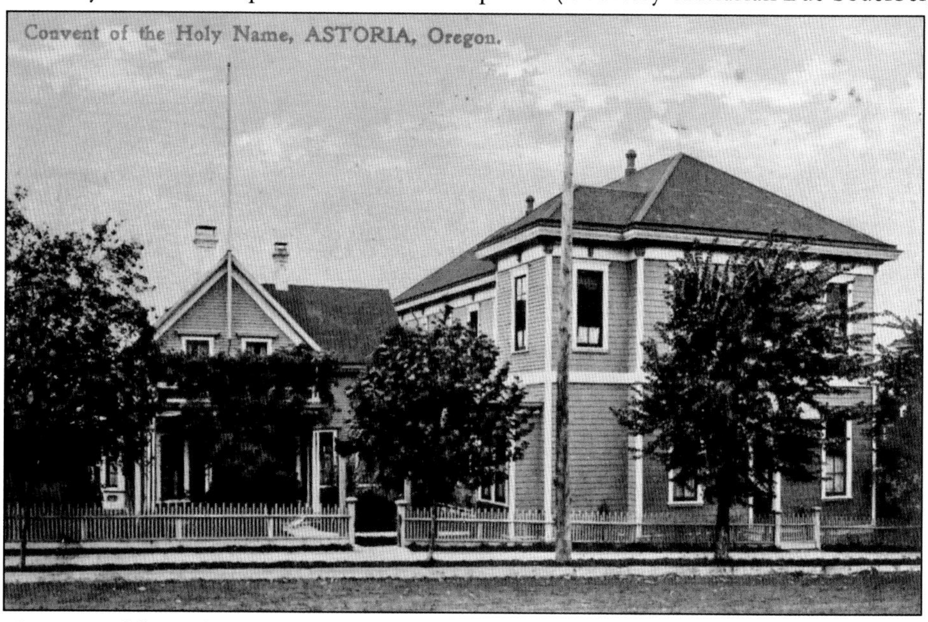

The Convent of the Holy Names was the predecessor of St. Mary, Star of the Sea Catholic School in Astoria. In 1896, the local paper wrote, "The Roman Catholic Church with its usual foresight and alertness has secured a valuable piece of property upon which will be built an institution which will benefit not only the Church but the entire community." This street-view postcard is from around 1909. The school, located at Sixteenth and Franklin Streets, was destroyed by fire in 1923. (Courtesy of Michael Soderberg.)

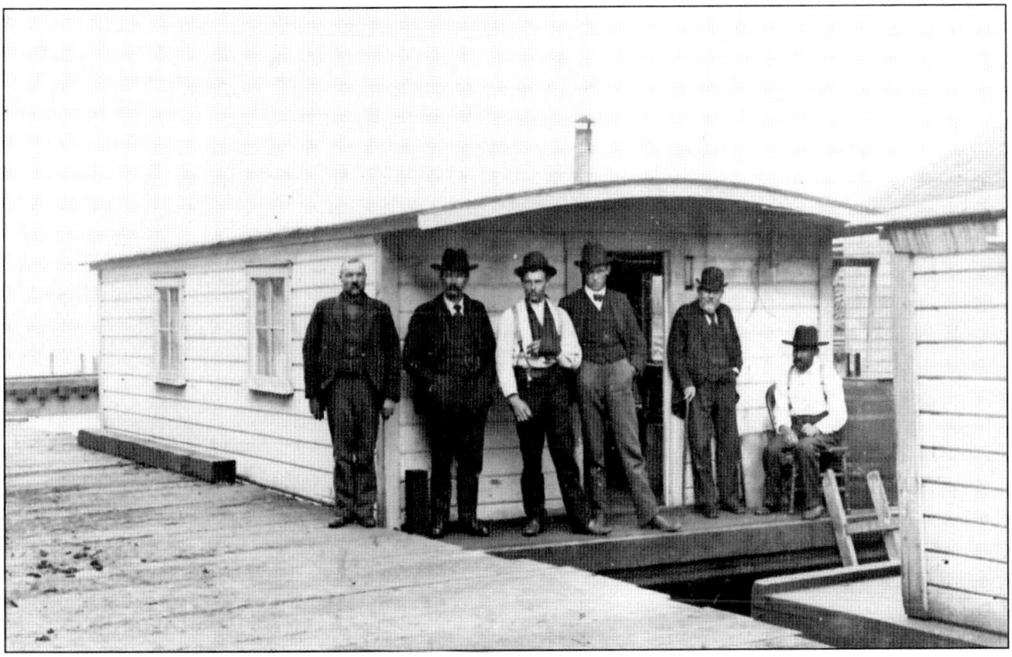

This photo postcard, dated 1903, shows one of many floating scows that served as basic housing for fishermen, cannery workers, and other various laborers on the waterfront. Primarily bachelors used these accommodations, as they were very primitive, without indoor plumbing. This one is at the foot of Second Street, with the railroad tracks visible in the distance where the present-day trolley runs on the Riverwalk. These "homes" were used on the waterfront until the 1950s. (Courtesy of Michael Soderberg.)

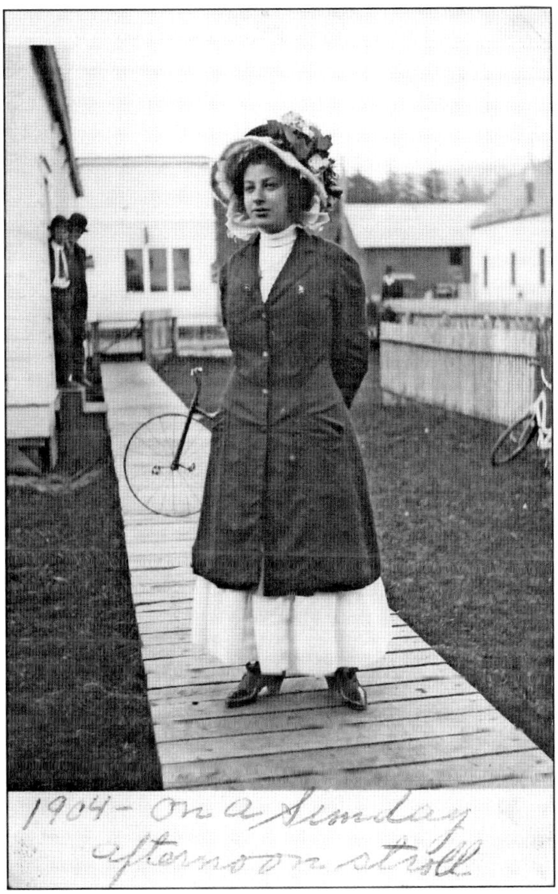

Alma Baker, a friend of the Soderberg family, is out for a Sunday afternoon stroll in her finest. Note the admirers on the left in the background. This c. 1904 photograph was taken somewhere in Astoria. (Courtesy of Michael Soderberg.)

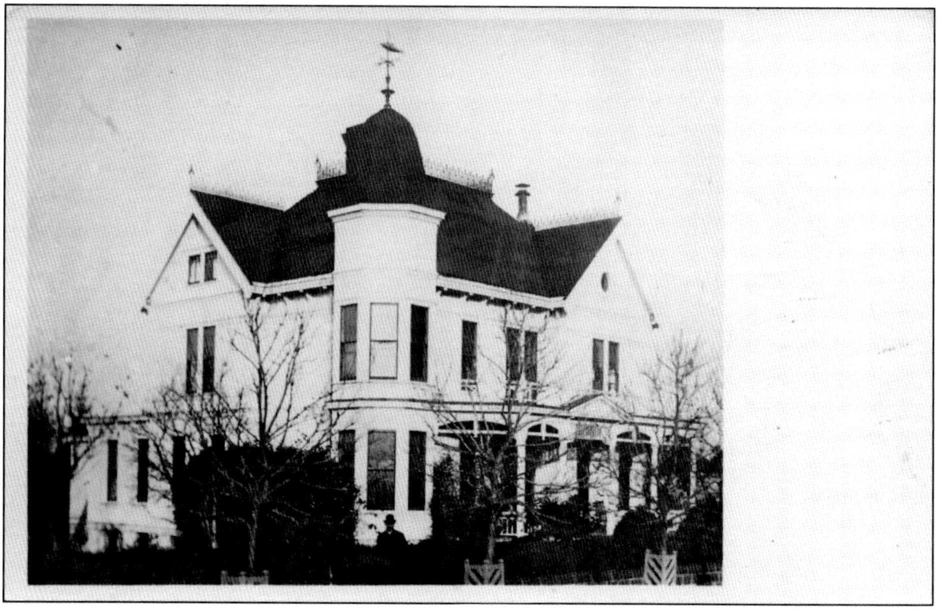

Benjamin Young, pictured in front of his home at Thirty-Sixth and Duane Streets, was a salmon canner, banker, and promoter of Astoria who worked for the British America Packing Company. The Benjamin Young house is one of the most recognizable in the city. Designed and built in 1888 by Benjamin Young in the Queen Anne style, it was listed in the National Register of Historic Places in 1979 and now serves as one of the area's first bed-and-breakfasts. Benjamin's brother, Andrew Young, was in the timber and fishing industries and had a farm in Olney. Family members continue to reside in Astoria. (Courtesy of Bill Young.)

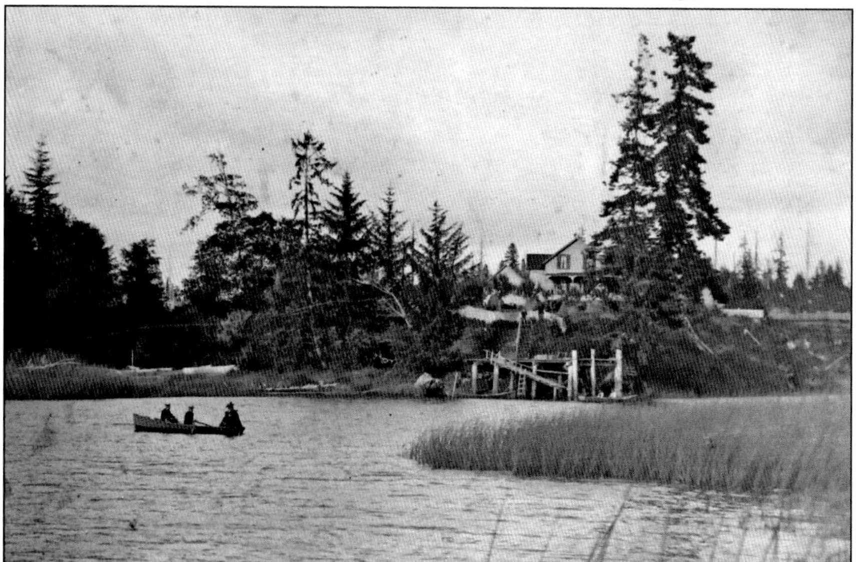

The country home of Andrew Young, brother of Benjamin Young, is pictured around 1885 along Young's River about eight miles south of Astoria. It is easy to assume that the river was named for the family; however, it was actually named upon its discovery in 1792 by William Robert Broughton of the Vancouver Expedition after Adm. Sir George Young of the Royal Navy. (Courtesy of Bill Young.)

In the late 1800s, formal, posed family portraits were very popular. This photograph was taken of Agnes Young, daughter of Andrew Young, about 1890 by the S.B. Crow Studio in Astoria. (Courtesy of Bill Young.)

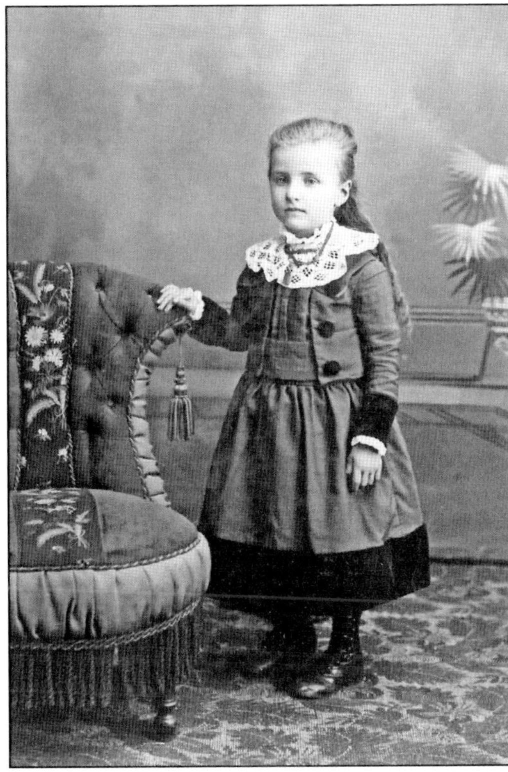

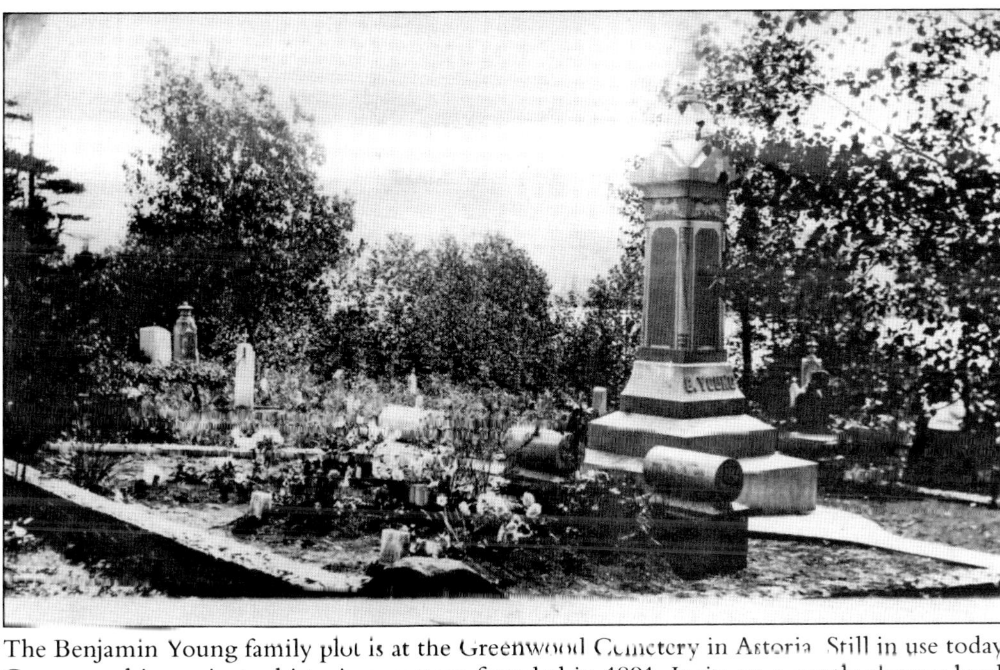

The Benjamin Young family plot is at the Greenwood Cemetery in Astoria. Still in use today, Greenwood is a private, historic cemetery founded in 1891. It sits on a gently sloping knoll overlooking Young's River south of town. Many local pioneers and founding families of Astoria are buried at Greenwood Cemetery. Andrew Young's family plot is also at Greenwood, just up the hill from his brother, Benjamin. (Courtesy of Bill Young.)

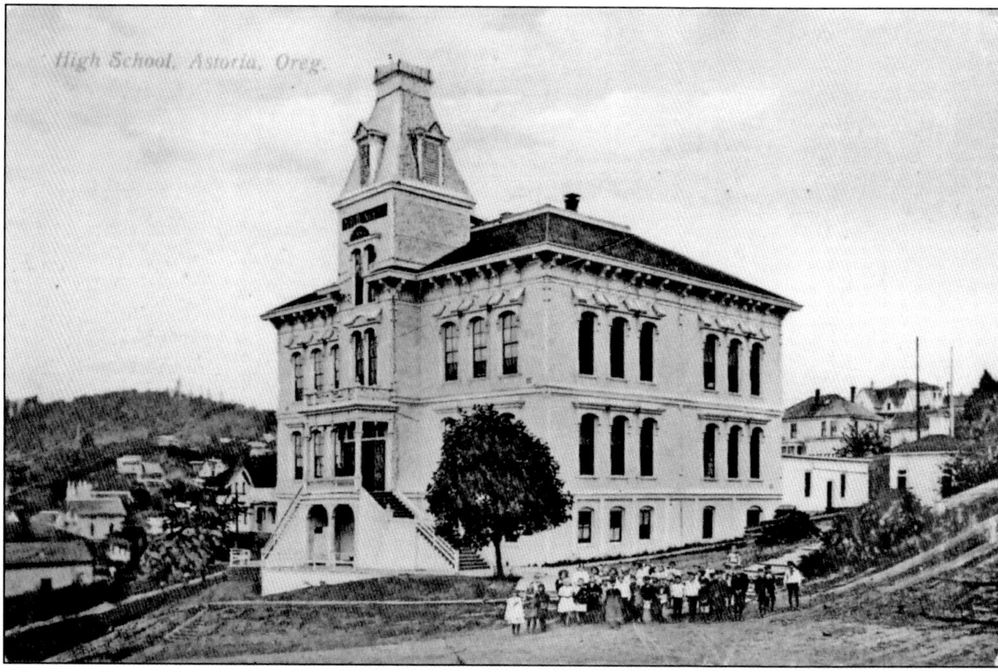

The McClure School stood in the area of Eighth Street and Franklin/Grand Avenue. It was built in 1883 and torn down in 1919. Although the postcard reads "High School," upper-level classes were not added at this school until 1890. It served the upper grades until the new high school was built in 1911. The former location of the school is now McClure Park. The crumbling retaining walls and foundation can be seen from street level. (Courtesy of Michael Foster.)

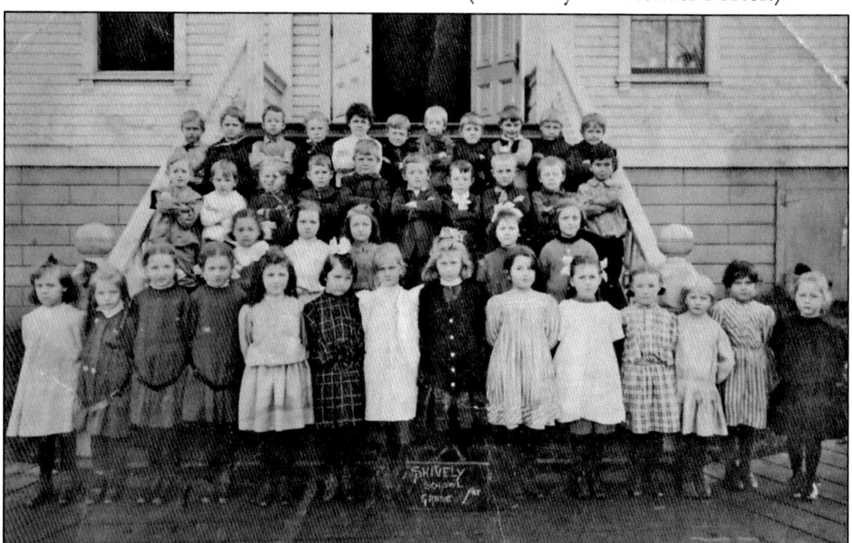

This first-grade class at the Shively School is pictured around 1898. Note the very large class size. Constructed in 1882 at Sixteenth and Exchange Streets, it was demolished in 1938. In the early days, schools were named after original plat holders: Shively, McClure, Taylor, Olney, and Alderbrook. The Astoria School District formed in 1854 and, like many things in Astoria, is one of the oldest west of the Rockies. Its first school was at the corner of Ninth and Exchange Streets, opening in 1859. (Courtesy of Michael Soderberg.)

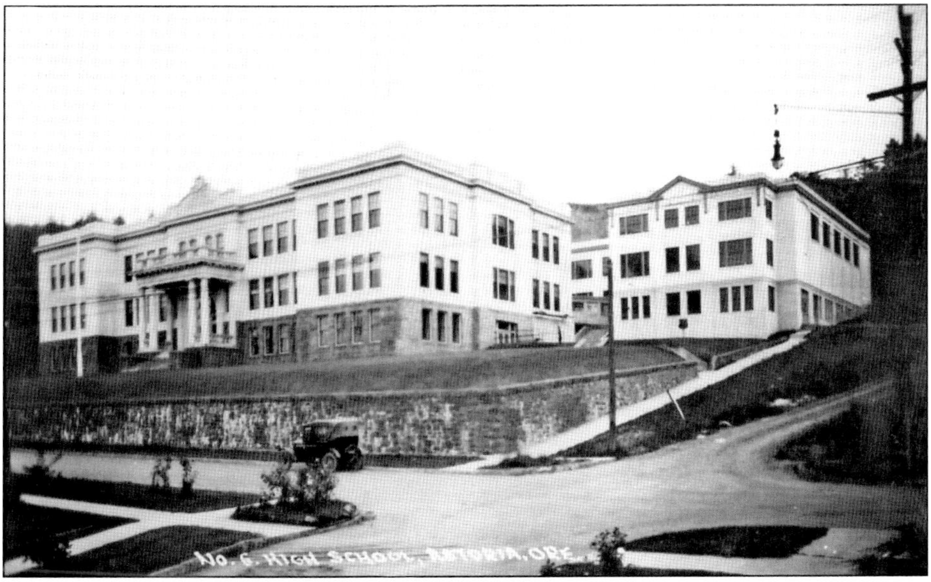

The 1911 *Zephyrus* described the new Astoria High School: "Situated beneath the brow of Coxcomb Hill, it occupies one of the loftiest positions in the City. The grounds cover one block and the building is concrete, about 170 by 80 feet with two stories and a basement. Entrance is through a porch of Doric architecture, constructed of terra cotta. There are 20 rooms that open on to long corridors with walls covered in a subdued salmon colored burlap, cornice and frieze of white glazed plaster." It sounds very grand indeed. This postcard image is from about 1920, after the gymnasium at right was added. (Courtesy of Michael Foster.)

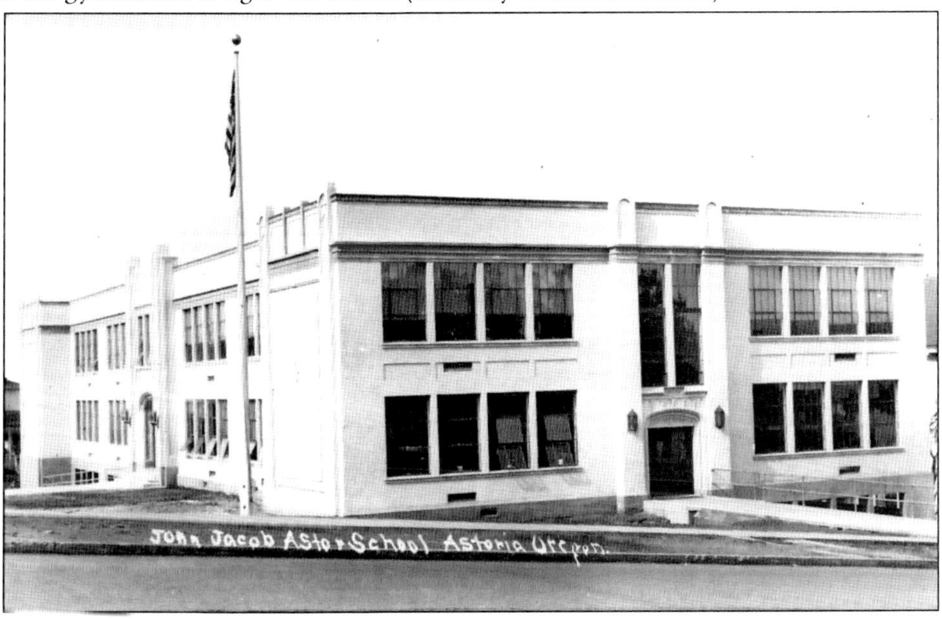

Of course the Astoria School District would have a school named after the town's founder. John Jacob Astor Elementary was designed by "Astoria's Architect," John E. Wicks, and built in 1925. The school might be best known for its key role as a location in the 1990 movie *Kindergarten Cop*. It currently serves students from kindergarten through second grade and is located on the east side of town at 3550 Franklin Avenue. (Courtesy of Michael Foster.)

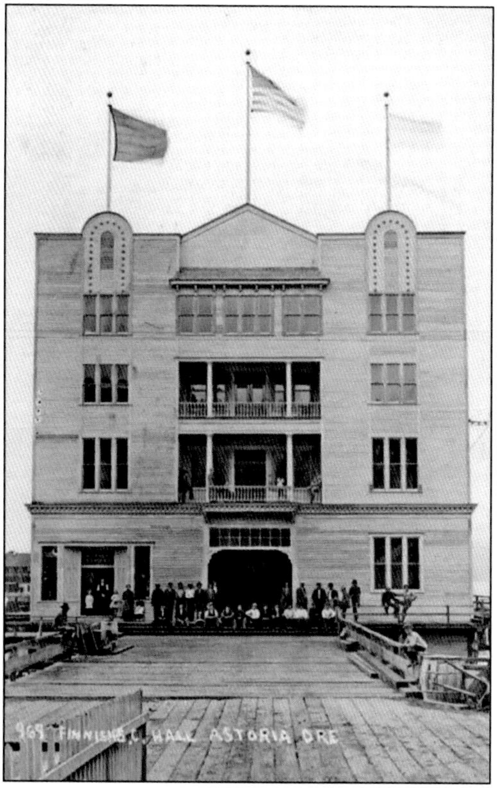

In 1904, the Astoria Finnish Socialist Club was established in the area west of downtown, called Uniontown. The group formally associated with the Socialist Party of America in January 1907. Initially a small group of 27 in 1904, it had grown to 250 by 1911 and comprised nearly 20 percent of all known Socialists in the state of Oregon. The Finns were the largest immigrant group in Astoria for many years. Their ties to Finland were strong, so the interest and enthusiasm for political events in Russia and Finland influenced many who were members at the time. The Finnish Socialist Hall was built in 1911. The structure in the 200 block of Marine Drive included offices, a theater, and gymnasium. It was destroyed by fire in 1923. (Courtesy of Michael Foster.)

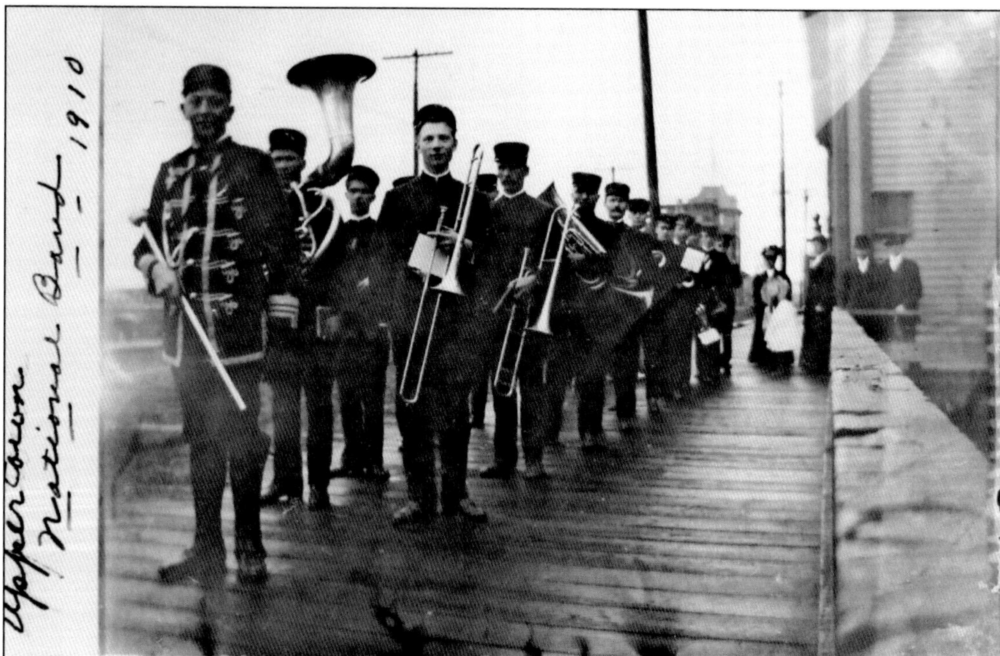

The east end of Astoria, or "Uppertown," had its own National Band in 1910. They must have performed at many events and marched in numerous parades. They even had uniforms. (Courtesy of Michael Foster.)

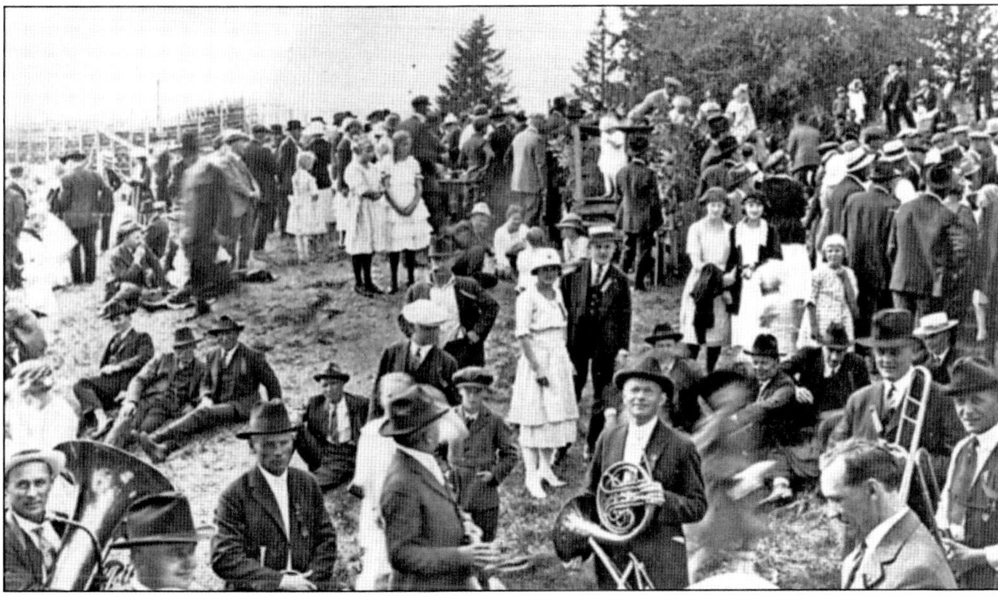

This photograph shows members of the Finnish Socialist Club picnicking in Astoria in 1922. The club was one of Astoria's most prominent ethnic organizations during the first decades of the 20th century. Astoria was home to the largest settlement of Finns west of the Mississippi. By 1905, Astoria's Finnish population numbered 2,027, more than 18 percent of the total population. Most lived in Uniontown, named after the short-lived Union Cannery. (Author's collection.)

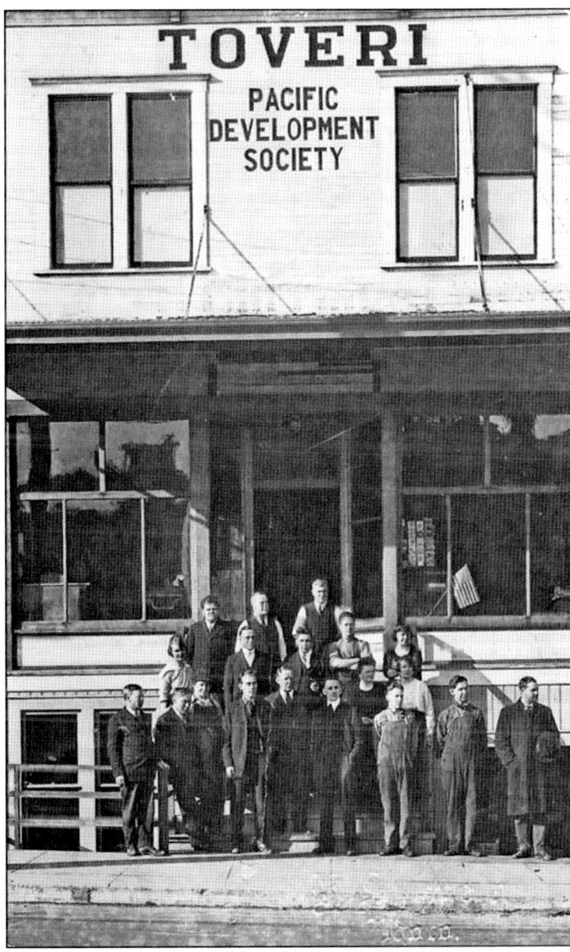

In June 1907, the Finnish Socialists decided to establish a paper in Astoria. The first issue of the *Toveri* ("Comrade") appeared on December 7, 1907, under the editorship of Aku Rissanen, formerly on the editorial staff of *Raivaaja.* Although planned as a biweekly, the paper appeared only sporadically during its first year. It moved to daily status in 1912. Circulation peaked in 1916 at 4,000, larger than any other Astoria newspaper. It ceased publication in 1931. Here, staff pose outside the Taylor Street offices (Seventh Street, between Bond and Commercial Streets). (Author's collection.)

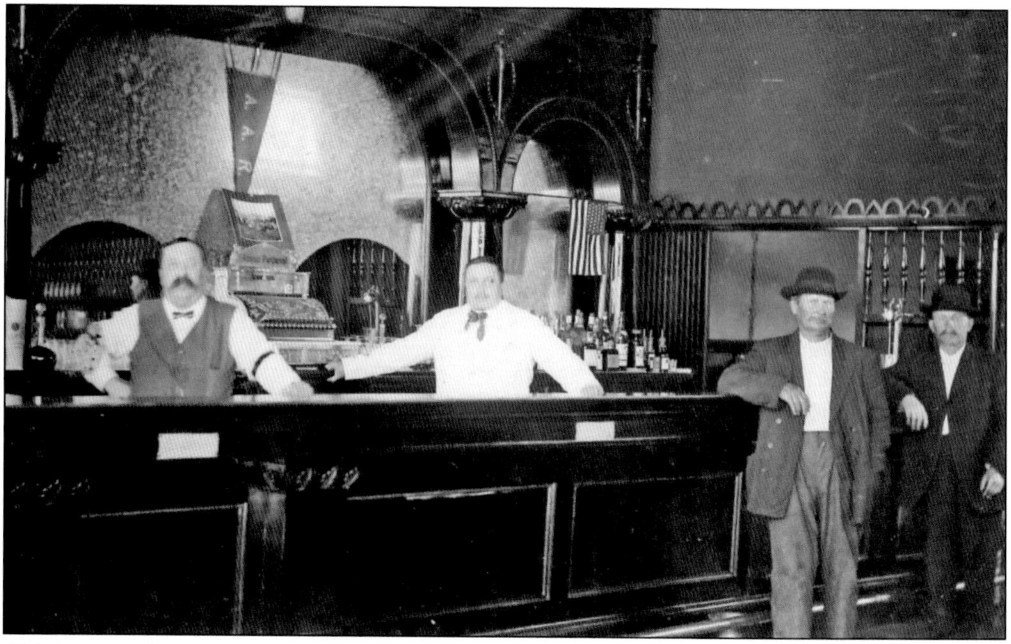

This interior photograph of a saloon in Astoria is undated. Astoria was infamous for its proliferation of drinking establishments, particularly in the Astor Street district. There was said to be a bar on every corner and some along the way, in case you got thirsty. Sometimes, fishermen could pay in fresh salmon if they didn't have any money. (Courtesy of Michael Foster.)

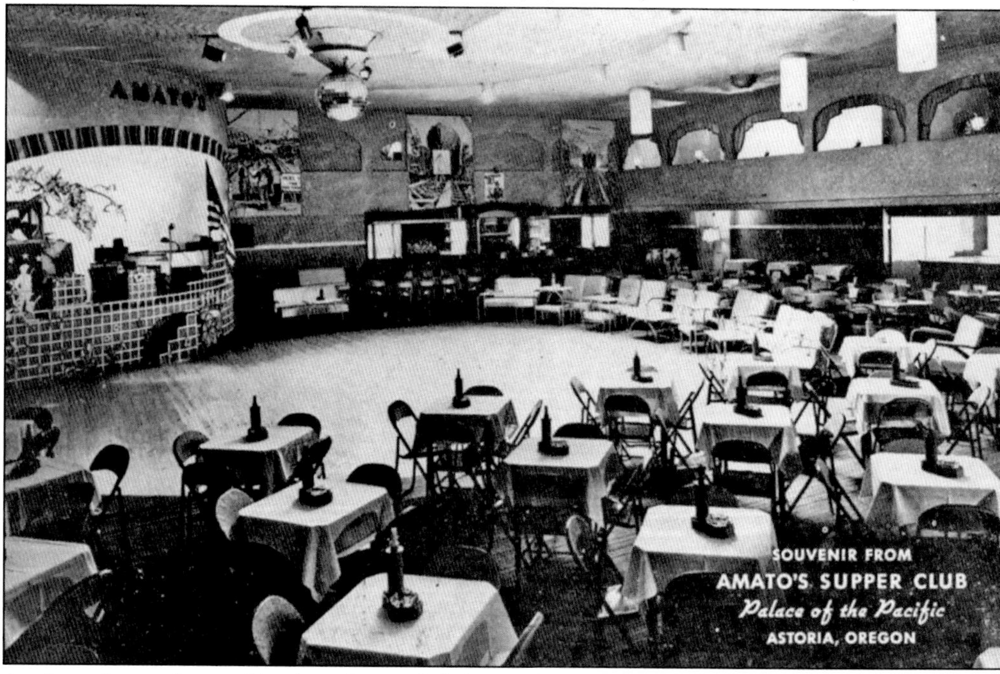

As the culture changed in Astoria, so did the nightclubs. A much more pleasant and popular venue for the mainstream was Amato's Supper Club, seen in this c. 1940s postcard. During World War II, Amato's was a venue for many of the big bands of the era. It was near the foot of Eleventh Street, the current location of JP Plumbing. (Author's collection.)

While he is unidentified by name on this postcard, it is easy to imagine many a character who might earn the title "Mayor of Swilltown" in the Barbary Coast atmosphere that was Astoria at one time. Swilltown was generally described as the area between Fifth and Tenth Streets along Astor Street to the river. (Courtesy of Ray Hakala.)

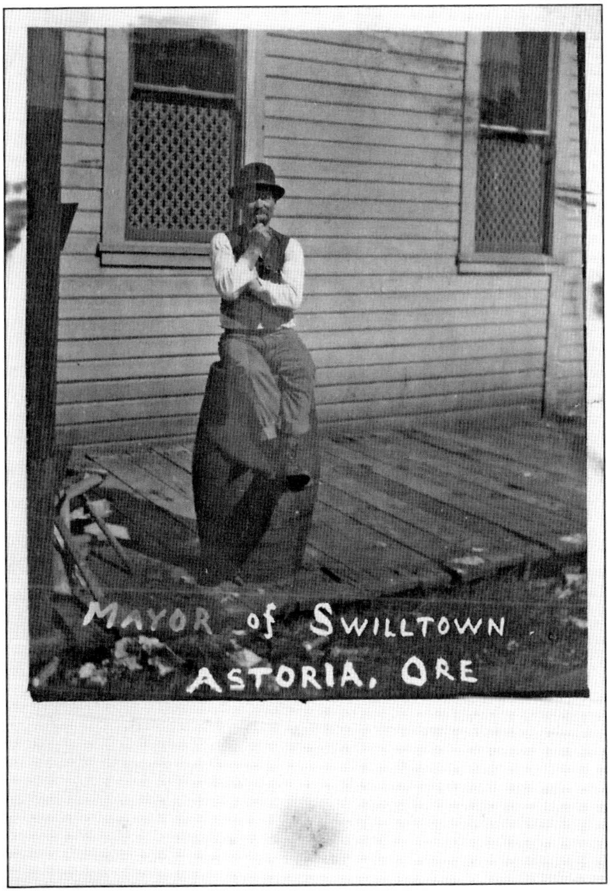

The area where Columbia Memorial Hospital is now (Twenty-First and Exchange Streets) used to be underwater, and was known as Scow Bay. The bay divided Uppertown and downtown Astoria. There was a bridge built in 1878 on what is now Exchange Street from Eighteenth to Twenty-First Street connecting the two sides of Astoria, but before then, one had to row or sail between various areas of town. This well-dressed group in an overcrowded boat demonstrates the practice at an Uppertown dock. (Courtesy of Michael Soderberg.)

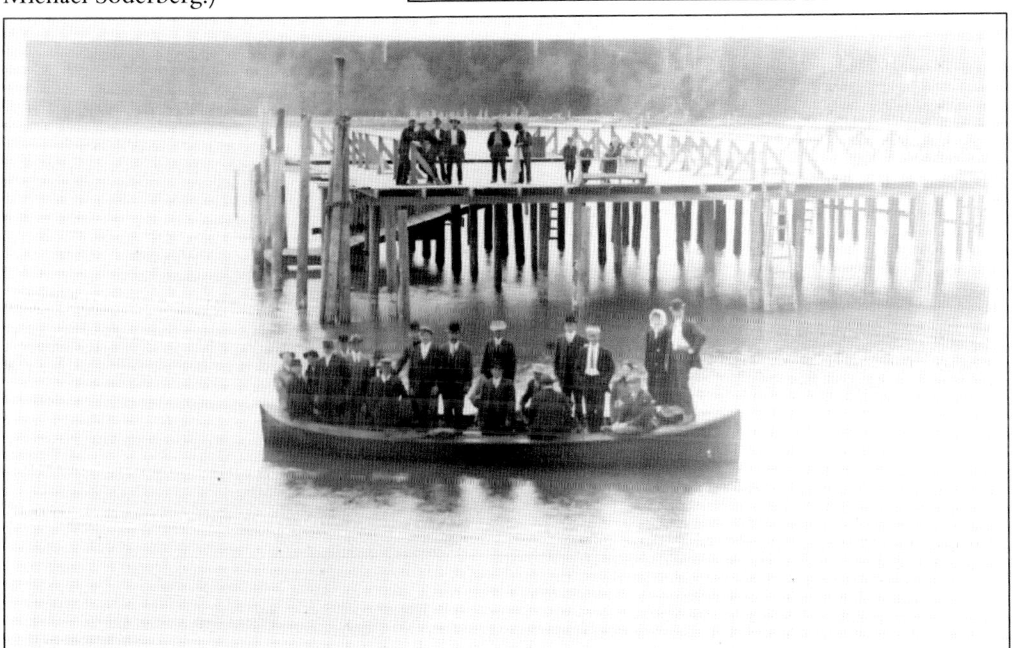

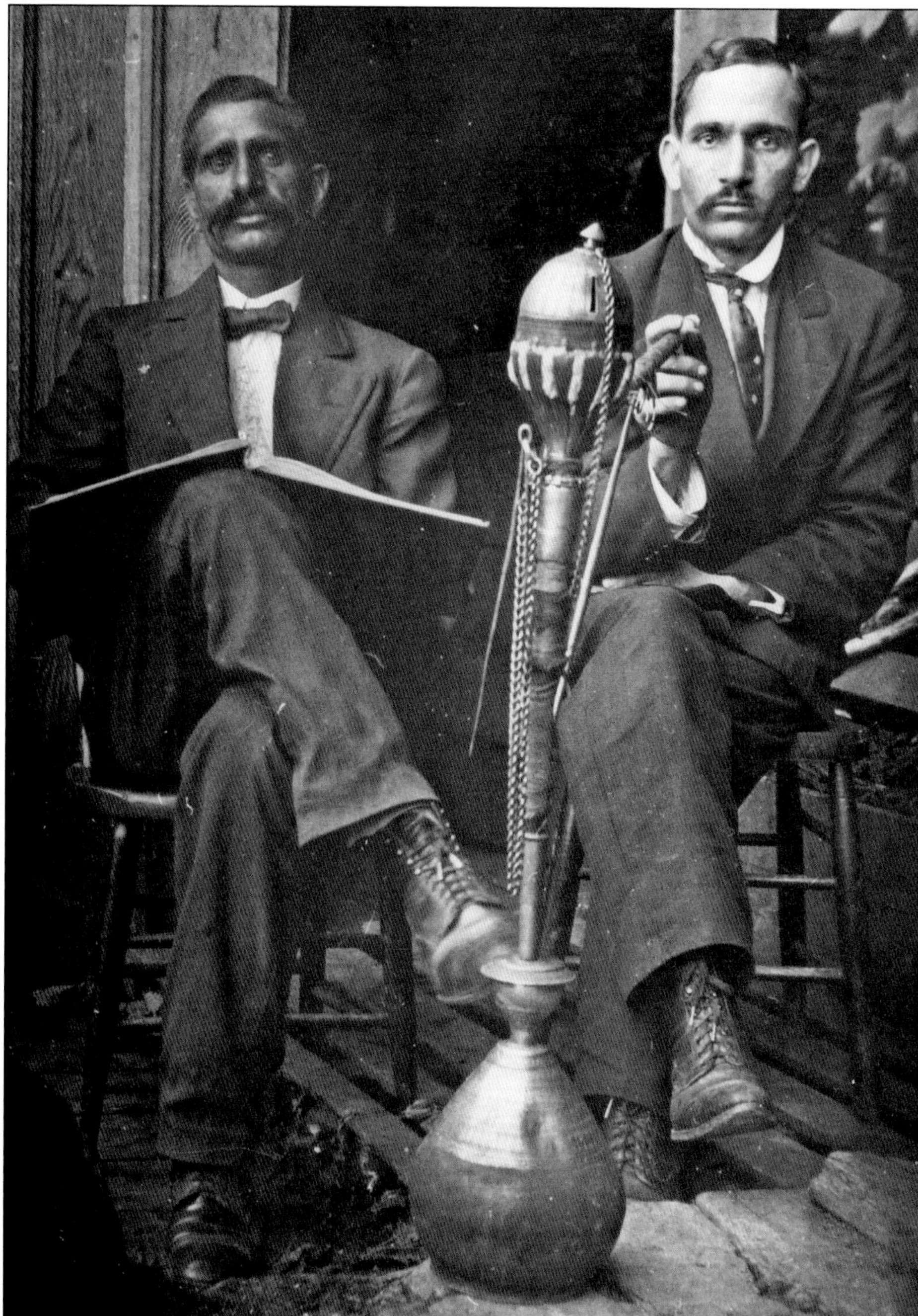

Until recently, little was mentioned about the Sikh population in Astoria in the early 1900s. About 100 Punjabis worked at the Hammond Lumber Mill. Their room and board were provided by the mill. They were politically active on behalf of their homeland, as many had been deported due to their level of education and influence and perceived threat to the ruling government. The first meeting of the Ghadar Party in Astoria was held on April 23, 1913, at the Finnish Socialist Hall. The aim of the Ghadar was "nothing less than the armed overthrown of British rule in India." (Courtesy of Clatsop County Historical Society NA_5887.001.)

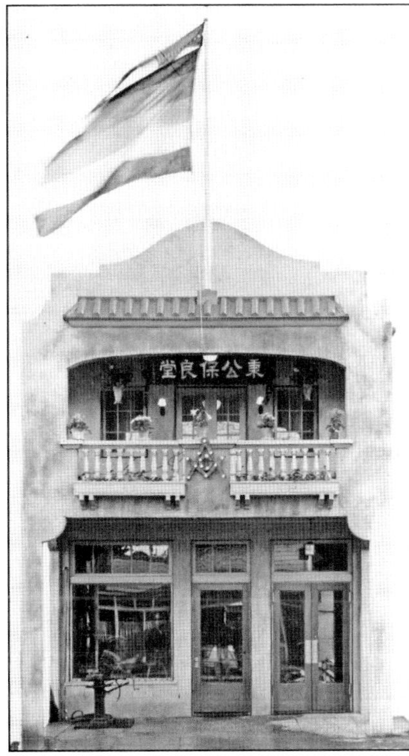

Astoria's China Town was concentrated west of the post office along Bond Street toward Uniontown. Tongs, meaning "hall" or "gathering place," were unique to Chinese immigrant groups and could be a positive or negative force. As benevolent organizations, the tongs were a social hub and a centralized place to access services, and also offered a means to negotiate and import workers from China. Each tong had a meeting hall and Buddhist shrine. They also provided funerary services. At the other end of the spectrum, many tongs in Astoria vied for power and position over gambling, drugs, and prostitution. As Chinese numbers decreased, so did the tongs, and their focus shifted back toward solely beneficial activities. The tong pictured here was on Bond Street near Sixth Street. (Courtesy of Ray Hakala.)

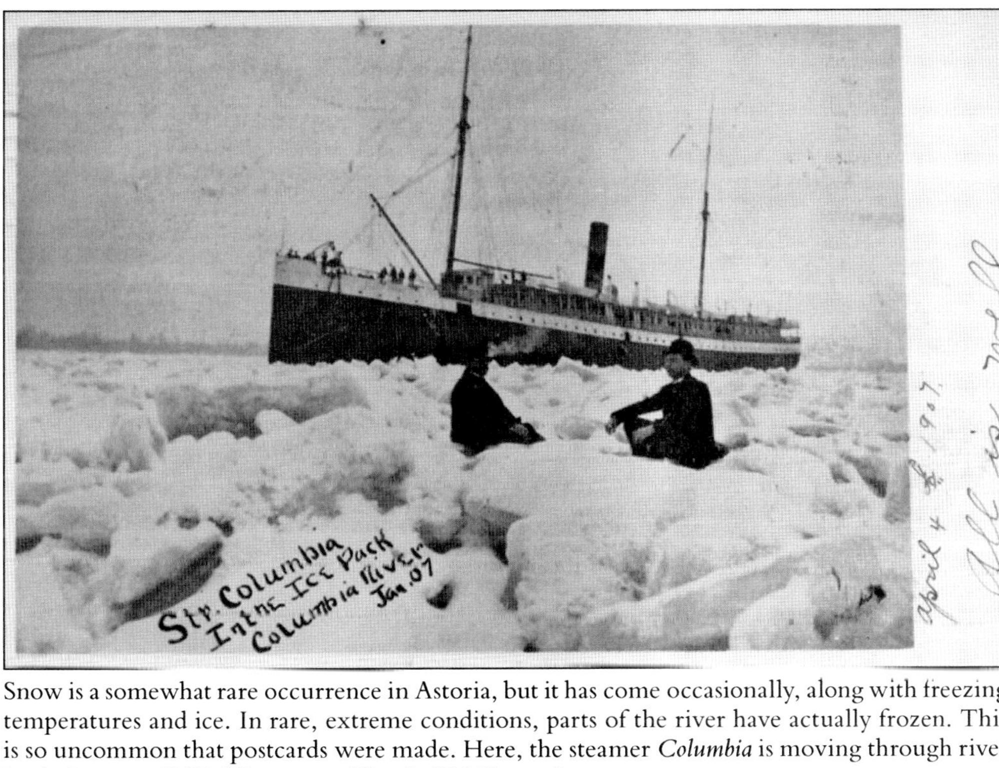

Snow is a somewhat rare occurrence in Astoria, but it has come occasionally, along with freezing temperatures and ice. In rare, extreme conditions, parts of the river have actually frozen. This is so uncommon that postcards were made. Here, the steamer *Columbia* is moving through river ice in January 1907. (Courtesy of Sara's Old Photos.)

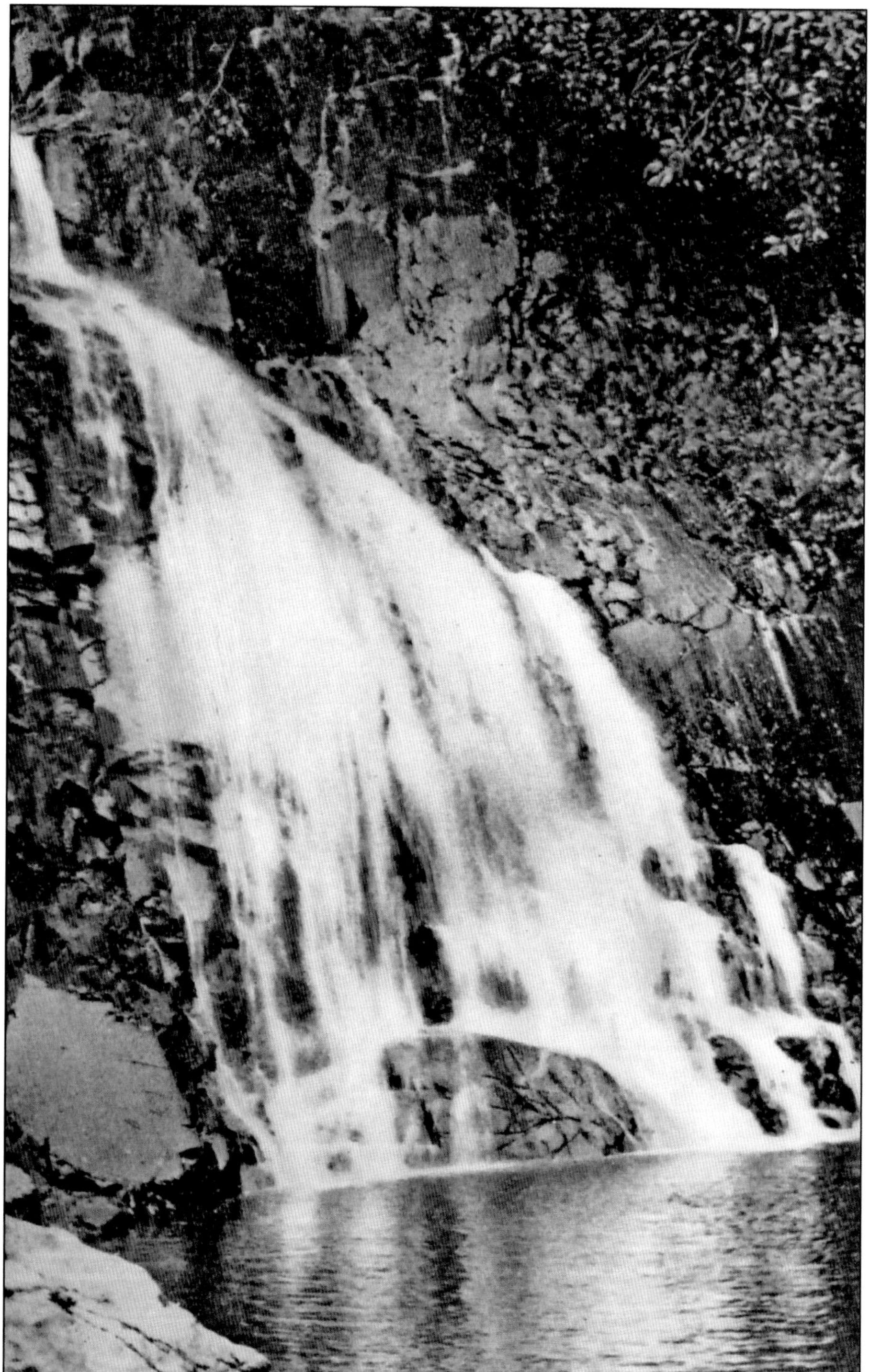

This railroad promotional postcard shows Young's River Falls just outside of Astoria near the little town of Olney, about 10 miles southeast of town off Highway 202. It remains a very popular swimming hole for locals on warm summer days. (Author's collection.)

Nine

Coastal Neighbors

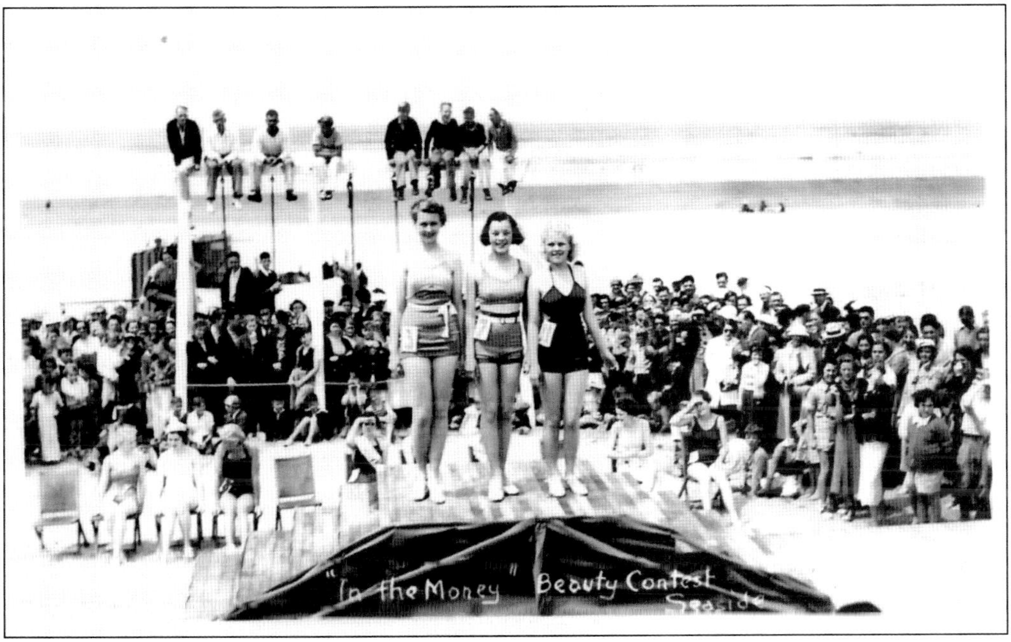

Seaside, Oregon, lies about 20 miles south of Astoria along the coast. Its beachfront, carnival atmosphere was established well over a century ago. This is clear in this real-photo postcard from around 1930. (Courtesy of Michael Foster.)

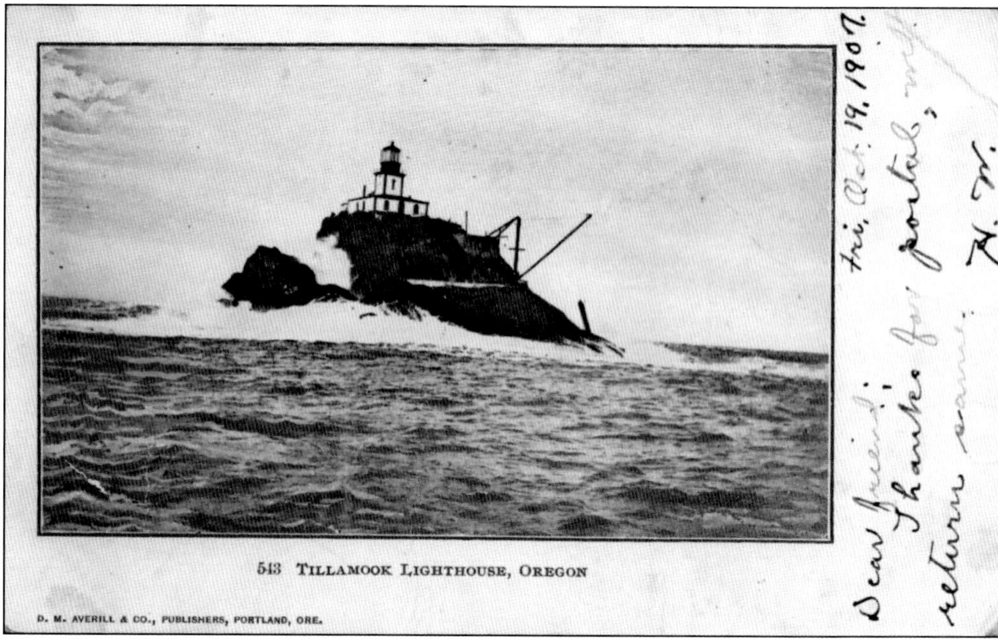

Tillamook Rock Light is just offshore from Tillamook Head, south of Seaside. It was built in 1881 on exposed basalt rock and operated from 1881 until 1957. It is known as "Terrible Tilly" for the stormy conditions of its location. (Courtesy of Michael Foster.)

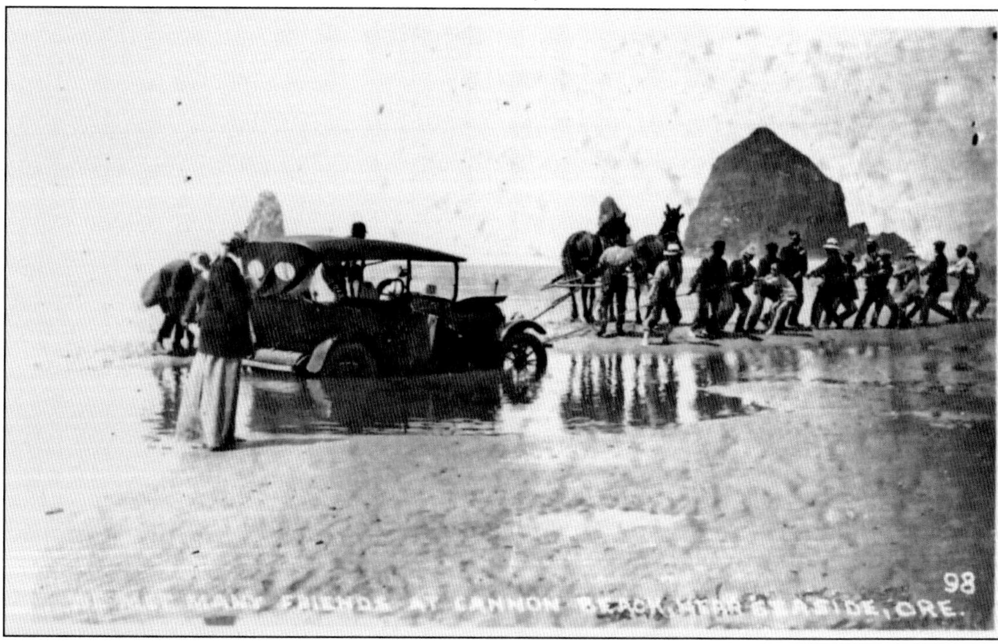

This scene could still be encountered at any moment at a beach on the Oregon coast today. Oregon beaches are state highways and therefore drivable. Many an inexperienced driver gets stuck in the sand or surprised by a "sneaker wave." This photograph was taken at Cannon Beach around 1920. All hands plus two horses are engaged in the rescue. Cannon Beach was named when cannons from the schooner *Shark* surfaced on the shore in 1898. The *Shark* went down at the Columbia River Bar in 1846. (Courtesy of Michael Foster.)

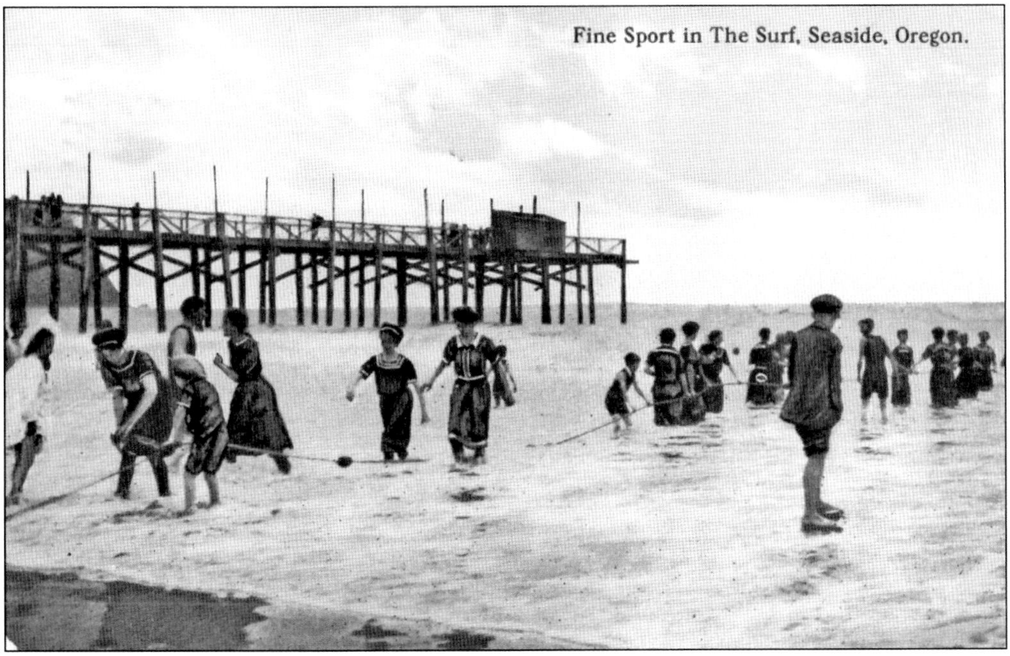

The beach at Seaside has been a family vacation destination for well over a century. At one time, a pier (like the one pictured here around 1910) was built every spring for summer revelers. It was washed away every winter during the storms. The line in the surf was for the safety of swimmers. Wave action, rip tides, and uneven surfaces make wading dangerous on even the sunniest of days. (Courtesy of Michael Foster.)

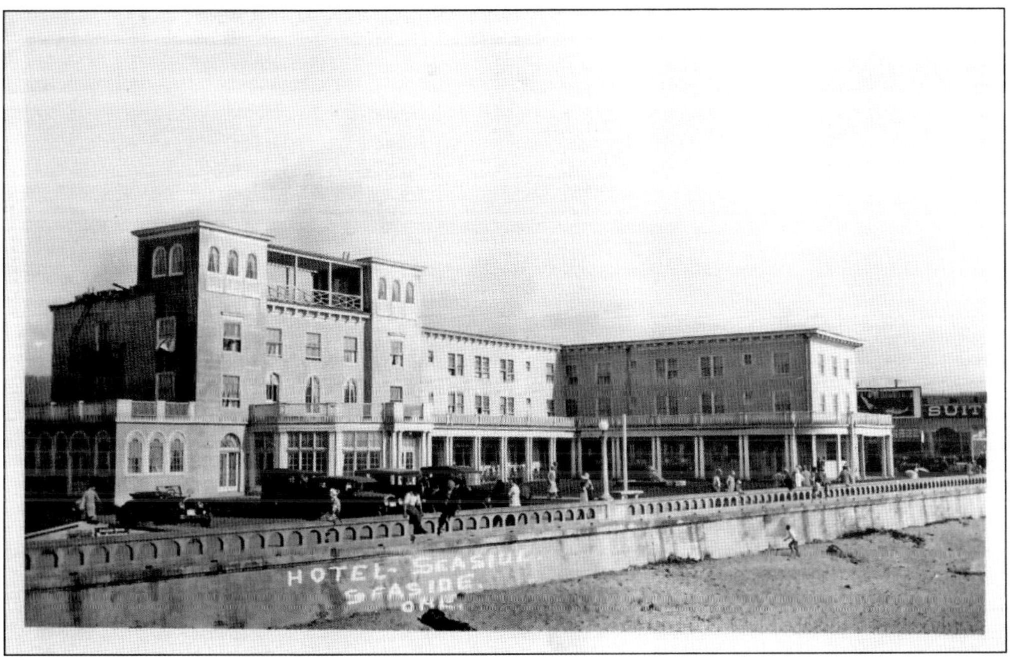

The Hotel Seaside was built about 1925, after the boardwalk and the promenade that was completed in 1921. The hotel was just north of the turnaround. (Courtesy of Michael Foster.)

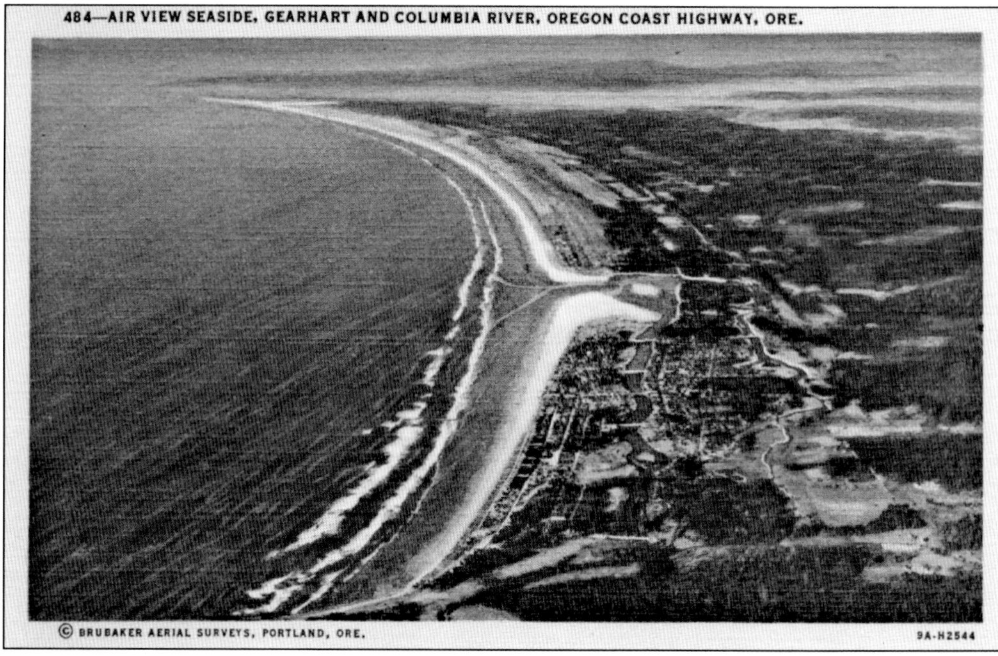

The description on the reverse of this c. 1935 linen postcard reads: "Sheltered by the high promontory of Tillamook Head is the beautiful city of Seaside at the foot of the high timbered mountain which flows the Necanicum River. At Seaside, Lewis and Clark made their camp nearby and the salt cairn they built may still be seen enclosed in an iron fenced memorial." (Courtesy of Michael Foster.)

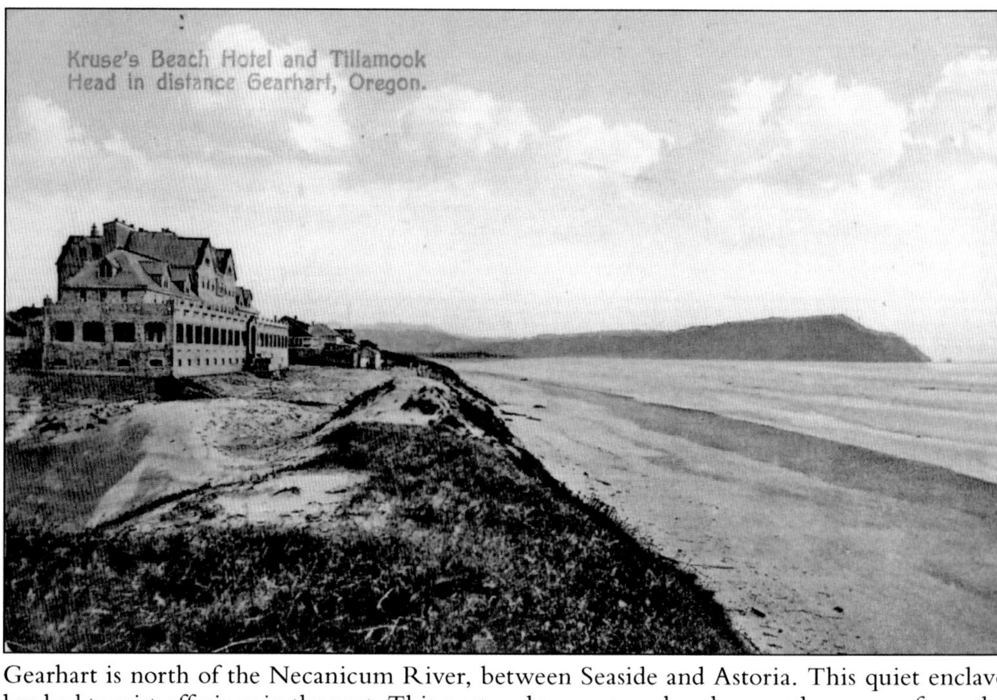

Gearhart is north of the Necanicum River, between Seaside and Astoria. This quiet enclave has had tourist offerings in the past. This postcard promotes a beach resort long gone from the shoreline at Gearhart. (Courtesy of Michael Foster.)

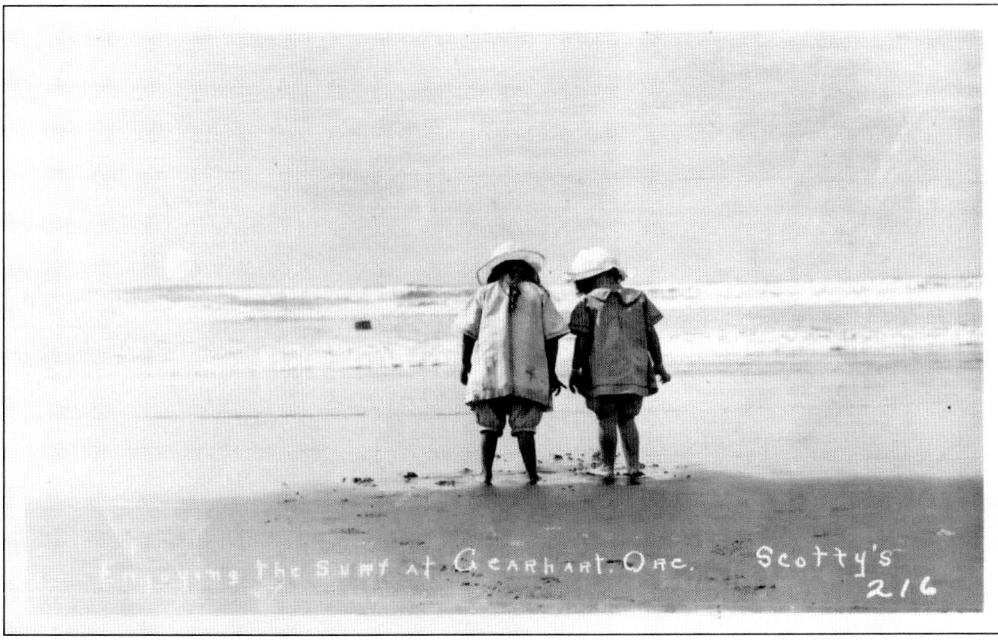

This sweet but undated image shows two little girls at the edge of the surf in Gearhart. (Courtesy of Sean Fitzpatrick and Anne Carpenter.)

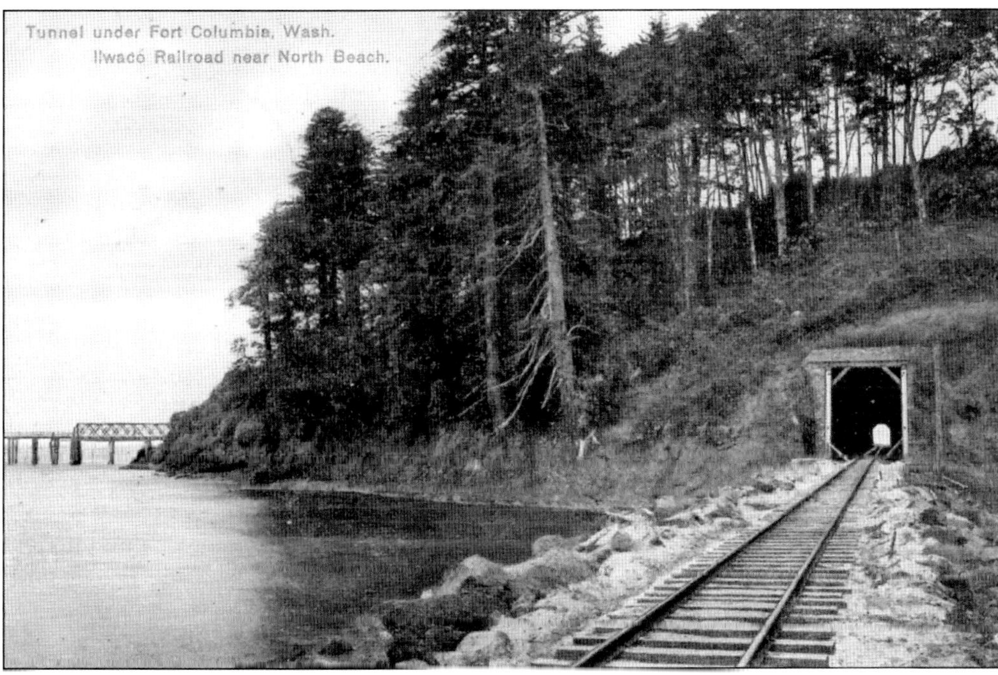

The tunnel under Fort Columbia was built by the railroad company to transport passengers and freight arriving by ferryboats and steamers from Astoria. The Clamshell Railroad ran all the way to Oysterville at the north end of the Long Beach Peninsula. The route has long been paved and is now the road driven by cars. (Courtesy of Sara's Old Photos.)

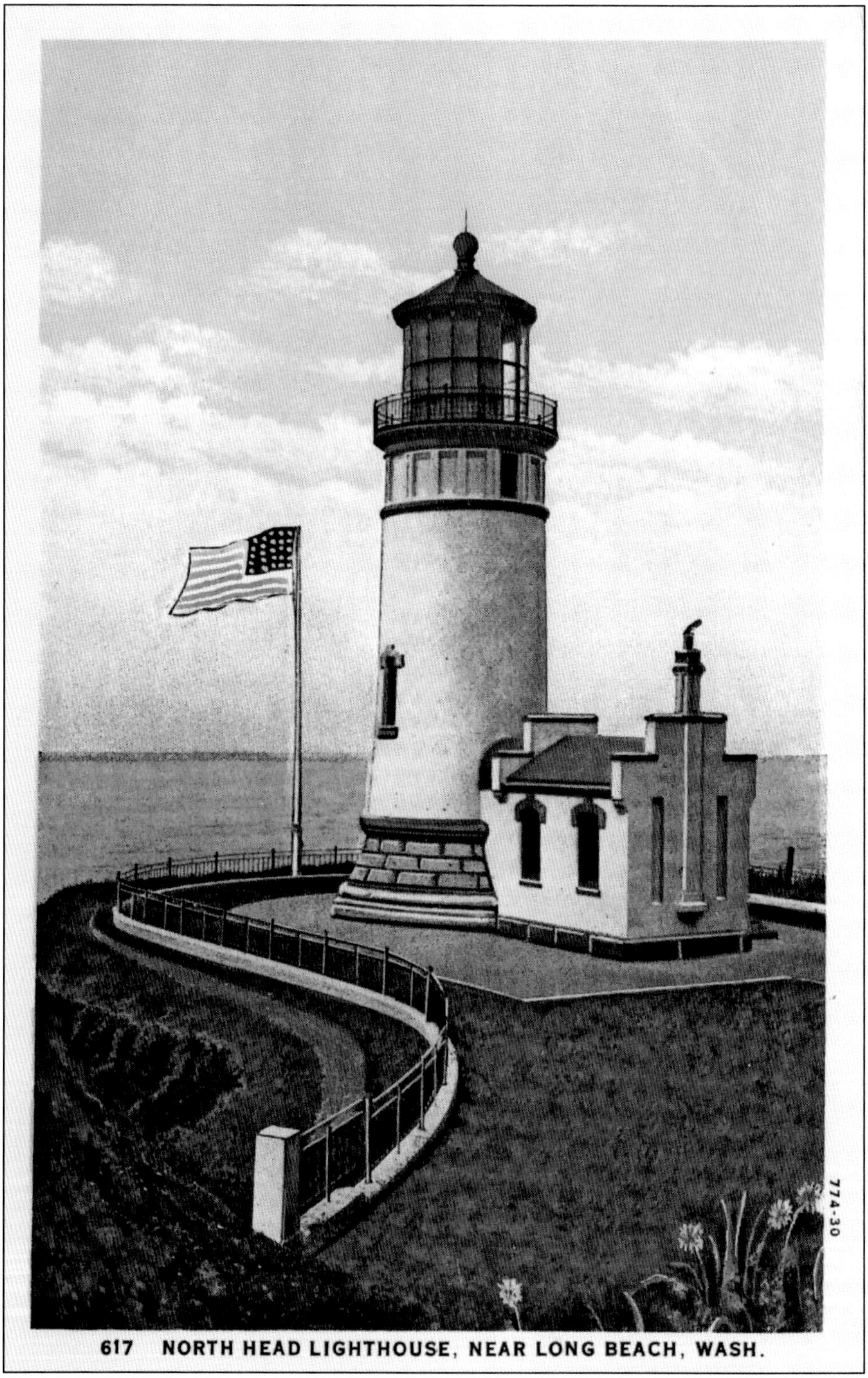

In 1893, Congress authorized the construction of a lighthouse on the North Head with a budget of $50,000. Designed by Carl W. Leick (who also designed the Flavel House in Astoria), the North Head Lighthouse in Ilwaco, Washington, consists of brick masonry built atop a sandstone foundation and finished with cement plaster overlay. The Louis Sauter & Co. Fresnel lens was lit on May 16, 1898. (Courtesy of Sean Fitzpatrick and Anne Carpenter.)

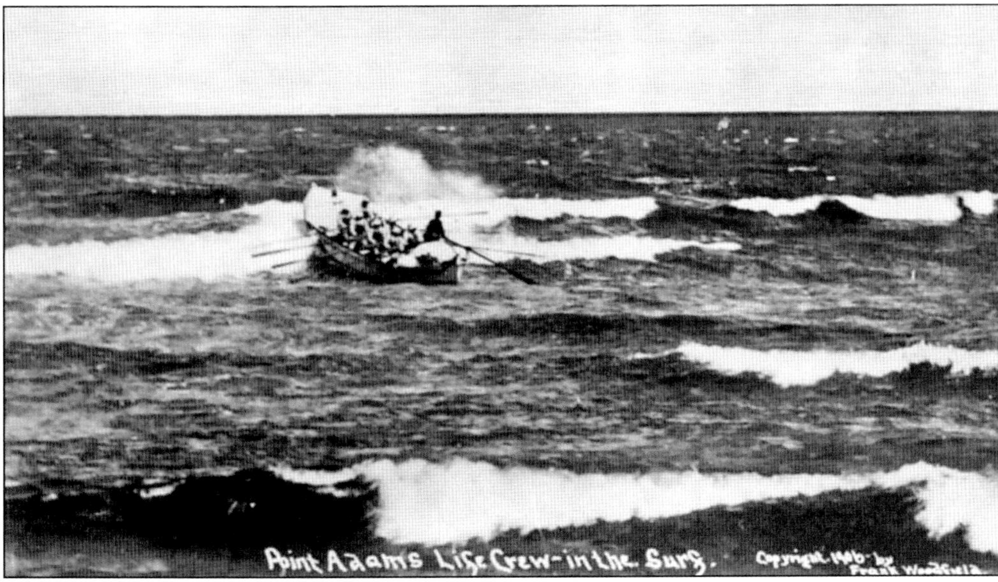

The Coast Guard Motor Lifeboat Service had its humble beginnings at the mouth of the Columbia. In 1865, Cape Disappointment (Washington) Lighthouse keeper Joel Munson grew weary of witnessing death at the hands of the ocean. He started a lifesaving station at Cape Disappointment and was a one man fundraising and promoting machine for his cause. After success and good press, the US government made it an official operation. Another station was added at Point Adams (pictured), and now the Coast Guard trains motor lifeboat crews out of Cape Disappointment. (Courtesy of Michael Foster.)

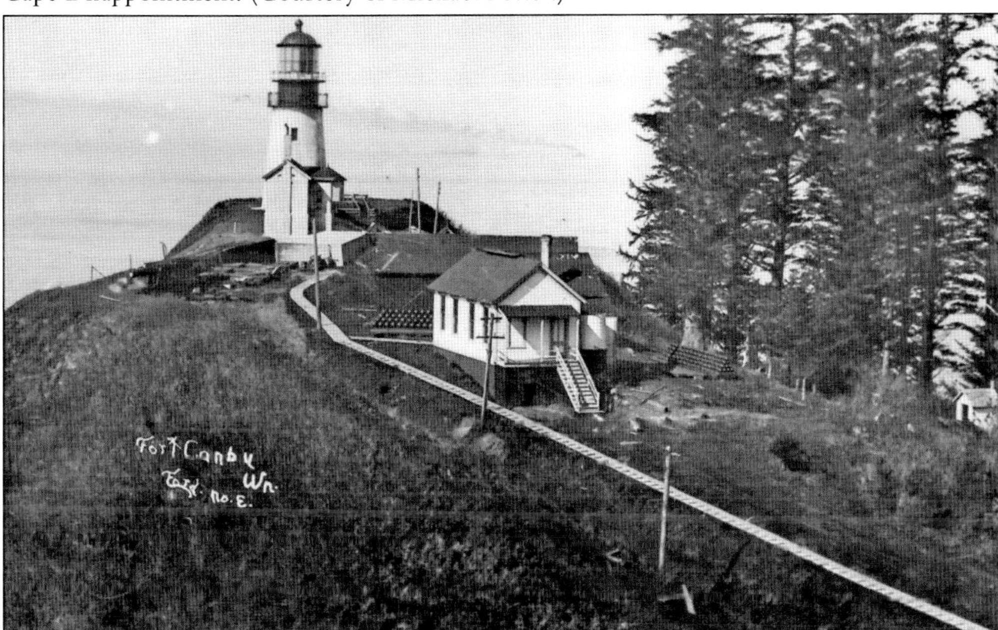

Fort Canby Lighthouse is seen in the early days. It probably looked much like this when lighthouse keeper Joel Munson served at this post. Also located at Ilwaco, Washington, it is now called Cape Disappointment and holds vigil over the Columbia River Bar, the "Graveyard of the Pacific." (Courtesy of Sean Fitzpatrick and Anne Carpenter.)

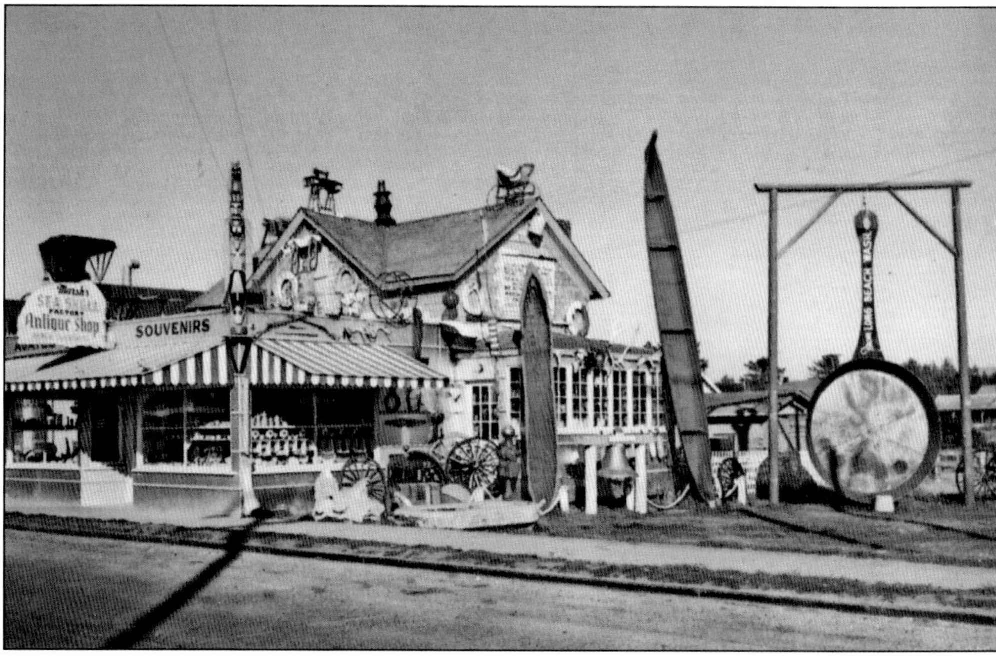

Marsh's Free Museum has entertained visitors to Long Beach, Washington, since 1935. Perhaps best known for tabloid king Jake the Alligator Man, Marsh's is a treasure trove of a curiosity shop and the highlight of many a summer vacation for visitors who arrived via ferry from Astoria. (Courtesy of Michael Foster.)

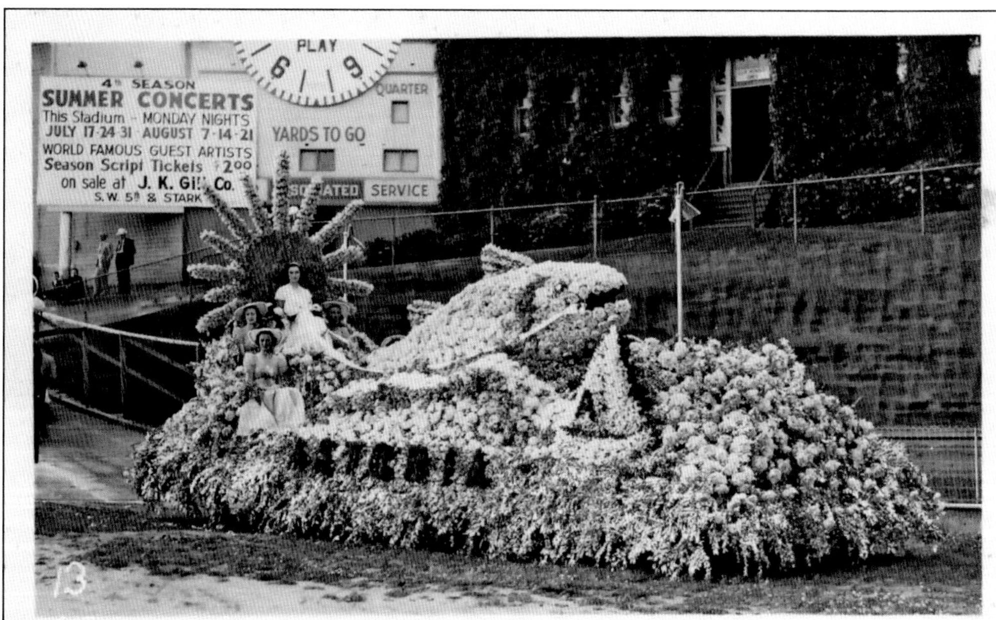

Visitors from all over come to Astoria again and again. Time and effort go into promoting the town's offerings outside of Astoria. This has always been the case. This postcard highlights Astoria's entry in Portland's Rose Festival Parade around 1940. Floats from Astoria regularly appear in regional parades today, often bringing home awards. (Courtesy of Michael Foster.)

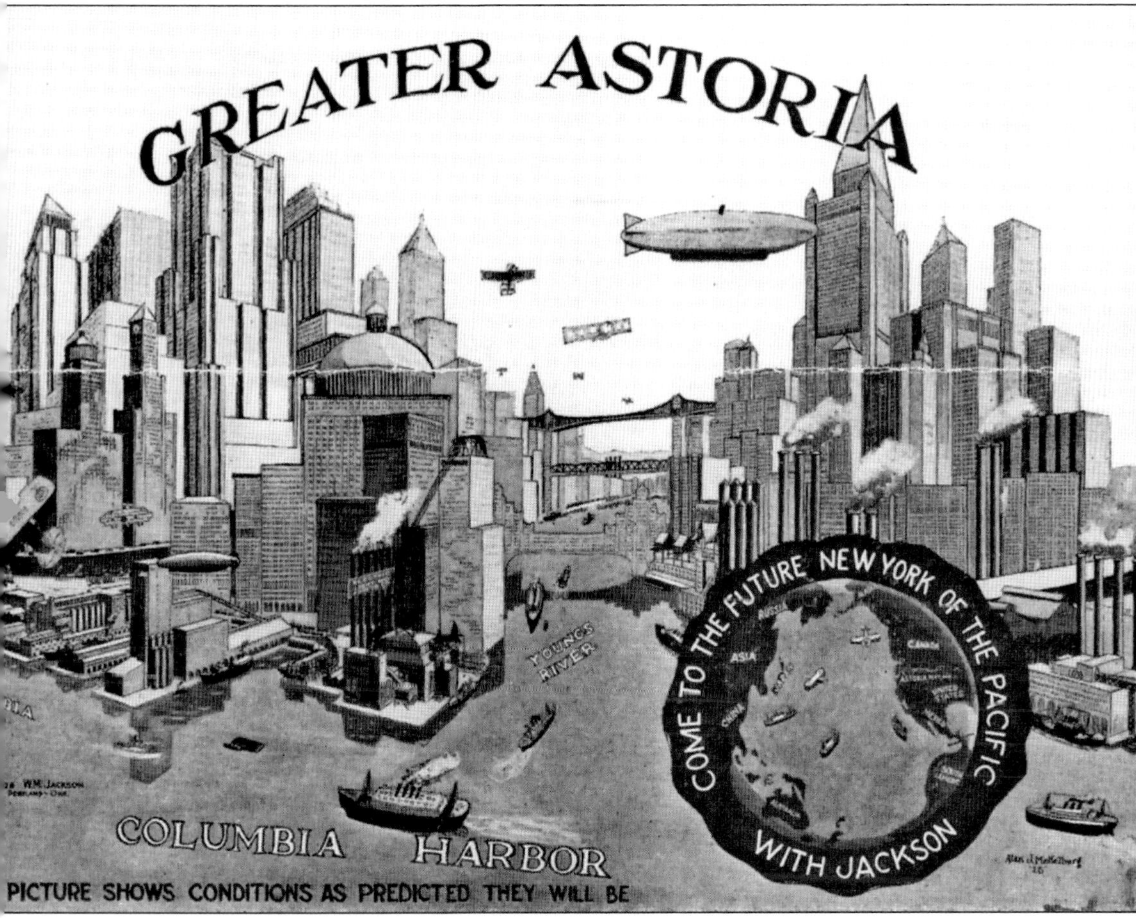

"Come to the Future New York of the Pacific with Jackson." To complete this inspiring journey through Astoria via postcards, this image promotes one c. 1928 vision of what Astoria could become. W.M. Jackson and his Columbia Harbor Development Company from Portland promoted this concept with great enthusiasm until the stock market crash in 1929. (Courtesy of Bill Young.)